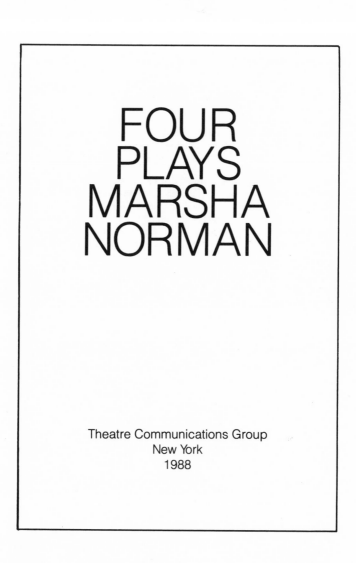

FOUR PLAYS MARSHA NORMAN

Theatre Communications Group
New York
1988

Four Plays is published by Theatre Communications Group, Inc., 355 Lexington Ave., New York, NY 10017.

The publications and programs of Theatre Communications Group, the national organization for the nonprofit professional theatre, are supported by Actors' Equity Foundation, Alcoa Foundation, ARCO Foundation, AT&T Foundation, Center for Arts Criticism, Citicorp/ Citibank, Consolidated Edison Company of New York, Eleanor Naylor Dana Charitable Trust, Dayton Hudson Foundation, Department of Cultural Affairs—City of New York, Exxon Foundation, William and Mary Greve Foundation, Home Box Office, Japan-U.S. Friendship Commission, Joe and Emily Lowe Foundation, Andrew W. Mellon Foundation, Mobil Foundation, National Broadcasting Company, National Endowment for the Arts, New York Community Trust, New York Life Foundation, New York State Council on the Arts, Pew Charitable Trusts, Philip Morris, Rockefeller Foundation, Scherman Foundation, Shell Oil Company Foundation, Shubert Foundation, L. J. Skaggs and Mary C. Skaggs Foundation, Consulate General of Spain and Xerox Foundation.

On the Cover: Photograph of Marsha Norman by Langdon Clay, copyright © 1988.

Library of Congress Cataloging-in-Publication Data

Norman, Marsha.
  Four plays.

  Contents: Getting out—Third and Oak—The holdup—[etc.]
  I. Title.
PS3564.O623A6   1988   812'.54   88-12362
ISBN 0-930452-83-6
ISBN 0-930452-84-4 (pbk.)

Book design by G&H/Soho Ltd.

First Edition, June 1988

For Martha Ellison,
my teacher and friend

Three of my plays are not included in this volume: *'night, Mother,* because it won the Pulitzer Prize and the publisher won't release it; *Circus Valentine,* because its only performance was a total disaster and I won't release it; *Sarah and Abraham,* because I'm still working on it. This is what happens to plays.

What happens to playwrights is that some plays are taken as greater, some as lesser, when in fact all are necessary. The lesser plays are presumed to be pale versions or even failed versions of the greater ones, as though writers were conducting their own Great American Play contests, always struggling to get the big one written. But the way we see it, the lesser plays are only lesser known. Their subjects are as compelling to us as those of our most famous work, and their pages always contain, as we say it, "some of our best writing."

Playwrights are completely mystified by the world's immediate judgments of their plays. We count on history to correct this, to elevate our particular favorite among our works to its proper place in our canon. But since we will be dead by the time history gets around to us, it is a great comfort that there are editors and publishers who care about us, who put together collections through which even our lesser-known work is made available to the audience we trust will be there for it.

My deepest thanks to Terry Nemeth, Jim Leverett and Betty Osborn of Theatre Communications Group for the existence of this book.

—Marsha Norman

Contents

GETTING OUT

ABOUT THE PLAY

Getting Out, Marsha Norman's first play, premiered at Actors Theatre of Louisville on November 3, 1977. A year later it opened at the Phoenix Theatre in New York, and in May of 1979 began its eight-month run at the Theatre de Lys. All of these productions were directed by Jon Jory and featured Susan Kingsley as Arlene. In early 1978 *Getting Out* was given its West Coast premiere by Gordon Davidson at the Mark Taper Forum in Los Angeles.

The co-winner of ATL's Great American Play Contest for 1977, *Getting Out* went on to receive numerous other honors, including the Oppenheimer/ Newsday Award, the John Gassner Playwriting Medallion awarded by the Outer Critics Circle, and the American Theatre Critics Association citation as the outstanding new play produced outside of New York during the 1977– 78 season. The next year *Getting Out* was featured in *The Burns Mantle Theater Yearbook* as one of the best plays of the New York season, chosen as a Fireside Book Club selection, and published by Avon Books.

CHARACTERS

ARLENE, a thin, drawn woman in her late twenties who has just served an eight-year prison term for murder.

ARLIE, Arlene at various times earlier in her life.

BENNIE, an Alabama prison guard in his fifties.

GUARD (EVANS).

GUARD (CALDWELL).

DOCTOR, a psychiatrist in a juvenile institution.

MOTHER, Arlene's mother.

SCHOOL PRINCIPAL, female.

RONNIE, a teenager in a juvenile institution.

CARL, Arlene's former pimp and partner in various crimes, in his late twenties.

WARDEN, superintendent of Pine Ridge Correctional Institute for Women.

RUBY, Arlene's upstairs neighbor, a cook in a diner, also an ex-con, in her late thirties.

PLAYWRIGHT'S NOTES

Arlie is the violent kid Arlene was until her last stretch in prison. Arlie may walk through the apartment quite freely, but no one there will acknowledge her presence. Most of her scenes take place in the prison areas.

Arlie, in a sense, is Arlene's memory of herself, called up by fears, needs and even simple word cues. The memory haunts, attacks and warns. But mainly, the memory will not go away.

Arlie's life should be as vivid as Arlene's, if not as continuous. There must be hints in both physical type and gesture that Arlie and Arlene are the same person, though seen at different times in her life. They both speak with a country twang, but Arlene is suspicious and guarded, withdrawal is always a possibility. Arlie is unpredictable and incorrigible. The change seen in Arlie during the second act represents a movement toward the adult Arlene, but the transition should never be complete. Only in the final scene are they enjoyably aware of each other.

The life in the prison "surround" needs to convince without distracting. The guards do not belong to any specific institution, but rather to all the places where Arlene has done time.

Prologue

Beginning five minutes before the houselights come down, the following announcements are broadcast over the loudspeaker. A woman's voice is preferred, a droning tone is essential.

LOUDSPEAKER VOICE: Kitchen workers, all kitchen workers report immediately to the kitchen. Kitchen workers to the kitchen. The library will not be open today. Those scheduled for book checkout should remain in morning work assignments. Kitchen workers to the kitchen. No library hours today. Library hours resume tomorrow as usual. All kitchen workers to the kitchen.

Frances Mills, you have a visitor at the front gate. All residents and staff, all residents and staff . . . . Do not, repeat, do not, walk on the front lawn today or use the picnic tables on the front lawn during your break after lunch or dinner.

Your attention please. The exercise class for Dorm A residents has been cancelled. Mrs. Fischer should be back at work in another month. She thanks you for your cards and wants all her girls to know she had an eight-pound baby girl.

Doris Creech, see Mrs. Adams at the library before lunch. Frances Mills, you have a visitor at the front gate. The Women's Associates' picnic for the beauty school class has been postponed until Friday. As picnic lunches have already been prepared, any beauty school member who so wishes, may pick up a picnic lunch and eat it at her assigned lunch table during the regular lunch period.

Frances Mills, you have a visitor at the front gate. Doris Creech to see Mrs. Adams at the library before lunch. I'm sorry, that's Frankie Hill, you have a visitor at the front gate. Repeat, Frankie Hill, not Frances Mills, you have a visitor at the front gate.

ACT ONE

The play is set in a dingy one-room apartment in a rundown section of downtown Louisville, Kentucky. There is a twin bed and one chair. There is a sink, an apartment-size combination stove and refrigerator, and a counter with cabinets above. Dirty curtains conceal the bars on the outside of the single window. There is one closet and a door to the bathroom. The door to the apartment opens into a hall.

A catwalk stretches above the apartment and a prison cell, stage right, connects to it by stairways. An area downstage and another stage left complete the enclosure of the apartment by playing areas for the past. The apartment must seem imprisoned.

Following the prologue, lights fade to black and the warden's voice is heard on tape.

WARDEN'S VOICE: The Alabama State Parole Board hereby grants parole to Holsclaw, Arlene, subject having served eight years at Pine Ridge Correctional Institute for the second-degree murder of a cab driver in conjunction with a filling station robbery involving attempted kidnapping of attendant. Crime occurred during escape from Lakewood State Prison where subject Holsclaw was serving three years for forgery and prostitution. Extensive juvenile records from the state of Kentucky appended hereto.

As the warden continues, light comes up on Arlene, walking around the cell, waiting to be picked up for the ride home. Arlie is visible, but just barely, down center.

WARDEN'S VOICE: Subject now considered completely rehabilitated is returned to Kentucky under interstate parole agreement in consideration of family residence and appropriate support personnel in the area. Subject will remain under the supervision of Kentucky parole officers for a period of five years. Prospects for successful integration into community rated good. Psychological evaluation, institutional history and health records attached in Appendix C, this document.

BENNIE'S VOICE: Arlie!

Arlene leaves the cell as light comes up on Arlie, seated down center. She tells this story rather simply. She enjoys it, but its horror is not lost on her. She may be doing some semiabsorbing activity such as painting her toenails.

ARLIE: So, there was this little kid, see, this creepy little fucker next door. Had glasses an somethin' wrong with his foot. I don't know, seven, maybe. Anyhow, ever time his daddy went fishin', he'd bring this kid back some frogs. They built this little fence around 'em in the backyard like they was pets or somethin'. An we'd try to go over an see 'em but he'd start screamin' to his mother to come out an git rid of us. Real snotty like. So we got sick of him bein' such a goody-goody an one night me an June snuck over there an put all his dumb ol' frogs in this sack. You never heared such a fuss. *(Makes croaking sounds)* Slimy bastards, frogs. We was plannin' to let 'em go all over the place, but when they started jumpin' an all, we just figured they was askin' for it. So, we taken 'em out front to the porch an we throwed 'em, one at a time, into the street. *(Laughs)* Some of 'em hit cars goin' by but most of 'em jus' got squashed, you know, runned over? It was great, seein' how far we could throw 'em, over back of our backs an under our legs an God, it was really fun watchin' 'em fly through the air then *splat (Claps hands)* all over somebody's car window or somethin'. Then the next day, we was waitin' and this little kid comes out in his backyard lookin' for his stupid frogs and he don't see any an he gets so crazy, cryin' and everything. So me an June goes over an tells him we seen this big mess out in the street, an he goes out an sees all them frogs' legs and bodies an shit all over the everwhere, an, man, it was so funny. We 'bout killed ourselves laughin'. Then his mother come out and she wouldn't let him go out an pick up all the pieces, so he jus' had to stand there watchin' all the cars go by smush his little babies right into the street. I's gonna run out an git him a frog's head, but June yellin' at me "Arlie, git over here fore some car slips on them frog guts an crashes into you." *(Pause)* I never had so much fun in one day in my whole life.

Arlie remains seated as Arlene enters the apartment. It is late evening. Two sets of footsteps are heard coming up the stairs. Arlene opens the door and walks into the room. She stands still, surveying the littered apartment. Bennie is heard dragging a heavy trunk up the stairs. Bennie is wearing his guard uniform. He is a heavy man, but obviously used to physical work.

BENNIE *(From outside)*: Arlie?
ARLENE: Arlene.
BENNIE: Arlene? *(Bringing the trunk just inside the door)*
ARLENE: Leave it. I'll git it later.
BENNIE: Oh, now, let me bring it in for you. You ain't as strong as you was.
ARLENE: I ain't as mean as I was. I'm strong as ever. You go on now. *(Beginning to walk around the room)*
ARLIE *(Irritated, as though someone is calling her)*: Lay off! *(Gets up and walks past Bennie)*

BENNIE *(Scoots the trunk into the room a little further)*: Go on where, Arlie?

ARLENE: I don't know where. How'd I know where you'd be goin'?

BENNIE: I can't go till I know you're gonna do all right.

ARLENE: Look, I'm gonna do all right. I done all right before Pine Ridge, an I done all right at Pine Ridge. An I'm gonna do all right here.

BENNIE: But you don't know nobody. I mean, nobody nice.

ARLENE: Lay off.

BENNIE: Nobody to take care of you.

ARLENE *(Picking up old newspapers and other trash from the floor)*: I kin take care of myself. I been doin' it long enough.

BENNIE: Sure you have, an you landed yourself in prison doin' it, Arlie girl.

ARLENE *(Wheels around)*: Arlie girl landed herself in prison. Arlene is out, okay?

BENNIE: Hey, now, I know we said we wasn't gonna say nuthin' about that, but I been lookin' after you for a long time. I been watchin' you eat your dinner for eight years now. I got used to it, you know?

ARLENE: Well, you kin jus' git unused to it.

BENNIE: Then why'd you ask me to drive you all the way up here?

ARLENE: I didn't, now. That was all your big ideal.

BENNIE: And what were you gonna do? Ride the bus, pick up some soldier, git yourself in another mess of trouble?

Arlie struts back into the apartment, speaking as if to a soldier in a bar.

ARLIE: Okay, who's gonna buy me a beer?

ARLENE: You oughta go by Fort Knox on your way home.

ARLIE: Fuckin' soldiers, don't care where they get theirself drunk.

ARLENE: You'd like it.

ARLIE: Well, Arlie girl, take your pick.

ARLENE: They got tanks right out on the grass to look at.

ARLIE *(Now appears to lean on a bar rail)*: You git that haircut today, honey?

BENNIE: I just didn't want you given your twenty dollars the warden gave you to the first pusher you come across.

Arlie laughs.

ARLENE: That's what you think I been waitin' for?

A guard appears and motions for Arlie to follow him.

ARLIE: Yeah! I heard ya.

The guard takes Arlie to the cell and slams the door.

BENNIE: But God almighty, I hate to think what you'd done to the first ol' bugger tried to make you in that bus station. You got grit, Arlie girl. I gotta credit you for that.

ARLIE *(From the cell, as she dumps a plate of food on the floor)*: Officer!

BENNIE: The screamin' you'd do. Wake the dead.

ARLENE: Uh-huh.

BENNIE *(Proudly)*: An there ain't nobody can beat you for throwin' plates.

ARLIE: Are you gonna clean up this shit or do I have to sit here and look at it till I vomit?

A guard comes in to clean it up.

BENNIE: Listen, ever prison in Alabama's usin' plastic forks now on account of what you done.

ARLENE: You can quit talkin' just anytime now.

ARLIE: Some life you got, fatso. Bringin' me my dinner then wipin' it off the walls. *(Laughs)*

BENNIE: Some of them officers was pretty leery of you. Even the chaplain.

ARLENE: No he wasn't either.

BENNIE: Not me, though. You was just wild, that's all.

ARLENE: Animals is wild, not people. That's what he said.

ARLIE *(Mocking)*: Good behavior, good behavior. Shit.

BENNIE: Now what could that four-eyes chaplain know about wild? *(Arlene looks up sharply)* Okay. Not wild, then . . .

ARLIE: I kin git outta here anytime I want. *(Leaves the cell)*

BENNIE: But you got grit, Arlie.

ARLENE: I have said for you to call me Arlene.

BENNIE: Okay okay.

ARLENE: Huh?

BENNIE: Don't git riled. You want me to call you Arlene, then Arlene it is. Yes ma'am. Now, *(Slapping the trunk)* where do you want this? *(No response)* Arlene, I said, where do you want this trunk?

ARLENE: I don't care. *(Bennie starts to put it at the foot of the bed)* No! *(Then calmer)* I seen it there too long. *(Bennie is irritated)* Maybe over here. *(Points to a spot near the window)* I could put a cloth on it and sit an look out the . . . *(She pulls the curtains apart, sees the bars on the window)* What's these bars doin' here?

BENNIE *(Stops moving the trunk)*: I think they're to keep out burglars, you know. *(Sits on the trunk)*

ARLENE: Yeah, I know.

Arlie appears on the catwalk, as if stopped during a break-in.

ARLIE: We ain't breakin' in, cop, we're just admirin' this beautiful window.

ARLENE: I don't want them there. Pull them out.

BENNIE: You can't go tearin' up the place, Arlene. Landlord wouldn't like it.

ARLIE *(To the unseen policeman)*: Maybe I got a brick in my hand and maybe I don't.

BENNIE: Not one bit.

ARLIE: An I'm standin' on this garbage can because I like to, all right?

ARLENE *(Walking back toward Bennie)*: I ain't gonna let no landlord tell me what to do.

BENNIE: The landlord owns the building. You gotta do what he says or he'll throw you out right on your pretty little behind. *(Gives her a familiar pat)*

ARLENE *(Slaps his hand away)*: You watch your mouth. I won't have no dirty talk.

ARLIE: Just shut the fuck up, cop! Go bust a wino or somethin'. *(Returns to the cell)*

ARLENE *(Points down right)*: Here, put the trunk over here.

BENNIE *(Carrying the trunk over to the spot she has picked)*: What you got in here, anyhow? Rocks? Rocks from the rock pile?

ARLENE: That ain't funny.

BENNIE: Oh sweetie, I didn't mean nuthin' by that.

ARLENE: And I ain't your sweetie.

BENNIE: We really did have us a rock pile, you know, at the old men's prison, yes we did. And those boys, time they did nine or ten years carryin' rocks around, they was pret-ty mean, I'm here to tell you. And strong? God.

ARLENE: Well, what did you expect? *(Beginning to unpack the trunk)*

BENNIE: You're tellin' me. It was dumb, I kept tellin' the warden that. They coulda killed us all, easy, anytime, that outfit. Except, we did have the guns.

ARLENE: Uh-huh.

BENNIE: One old bastard sailed a throwin' rock at me one day, woulda took my eye out if I hadn't turned around just then. Still got the scar, see? *(Reaches up to the back of his head)*

ARLENE: You shoot him?

BENNIE: Nope. Somebody else did. I forget who. Hey! *(Walking over to the window)* These bars won't be so bad. Maybe you could get you some plants so's you don't even see them. Yeah, plants'd do it up just fine. Just fine.

ARLENE *(Pulls a cheaply framed picture of Jesus out of the trunk)*: Chaplain give me this.

BENNIE: He got it for free, I bet.

ARLENE: Now, look here. That chaplain was good to me, so you can shut up about him.

BENNIE *(Backing down)*: Fine. Fine.

ARLENE: Here. *(Handing him the picture)* You might as well be useful fore you go.

BENNIE: Where you want it?

ARLENE: Don't matter.

BENNIE: Course it matters. Wouldn't want me puttin' it inside the closet, would you? You gotta make decisions now, Arlene. Gotta decide things.

ARLENE: I don't care.

BENNIE *(Insisting)*: Arlene.

ARLENE *(Pointing to a prominent position on the apartment wall, center)*: There.

BENNIE: Yeah. Good place. See it first thing when you get up.

Arlene lights a cigarette, as Arlie retrieves a hidden lighter from the toilet in the cell.

ARLIE: There's ways . . . gettin' outta bars . . . *(Lights a fire in the cell, catching her blouse on fire too)*

BENNIE *(As Arlie is lighting the fire)*: This ol' nail's pretty loose. I'll find something better to hang it with . . . somewhere or other . . .

Arlie screams and the doctor runs toward her, getting the attention of a guard who has been goofing off on the catwalk.

ARLIE: Let me outta here! There's a fuckin' fire in here!

The doctor arrives at the cell, pats his pockets as if looking for the keys.

ARLIE: Officer!

DOCTOR: Guard!

Guard begins his run to the cell.

ARLIE: It's burnin' me!

DOCTOR: Hurry!

GUARD (EVANS): I'm comin'! I'm comin'!

DOCTOR: What the hell were you—

GUARD (EVANS) *(Fumbling for the right key)*: Come on, come on.

DOCTOR *(Urgent)*: For Chrissake!

The guard gets the door open, they rush in. The doctor, wrestling Arlie to the ground, opens his bag.

DOCTOR: Lay still, dammit.

Arlie collapses. The doctor gives an injection.

DOCTOR: *(Grabbing his hand)*: Ow!

GUARD (EVANS) *(Lifting Arlie up to the bed)*: Get bit, Doc?

DOCTOR: You going to let her burn this place down before you start payin' attention up there?

GUARD (EVANS) *(Walks to the toilet, feels under the rim)*: Uh-huh.

BENNIE: There, that what you had in mind?

ARLENE: Yeah, thanks.

GUARD (EVANS): She musta had them matches hid right here.

BENNIE *(Staring at the picture he's hung)*: How you think he kept his beard trimmed all nice?

ARLENE *(Preoccupied with unloading the trunk)*: Who?

BENNIE *(Pointing to the picture)*: Jesus.

DOCTOR: I'll have to report you for this, Evans.

ARLENE: I don't know.

DOCTOR: That injection should hold her. I'll check back later. *(Leaves)*

GUARD (EVANS) *(Walking over to the bed)*: Report me, my ass. We got cells don't have potties, Holsclaw. *(Begins to search her and the bed, handling her very roughly)* So where is it now? Got it up your pookie, I bet. Oh, that'd be good. Doc comin' back an me with my fingers up your . . . roll over . . . don't weigh hardly nuthin', do you, dollie?

BENNIE: Never seen him without a moustache either.

ARLENE: Huh?

BENNIE: The picture.

GUARD (EVANS): Aw now . . . *(Finding the lighter under the mattress)* That wasn't hard at all. Don't you know 'bout hide an seek, Arlie, girl? Gonna hide somethin', hide it where it's fun to find it. *(Standing up, going to the door)* Crazy fuckin' someday-we-ain't-gonna-come-save-you bitch!

Guard slams cell door and leaves.

BENNIE: Well, Arlie girl, that ol' trunk's 'bout as empty as my belly.

ARLENE: You have been talkin' 'bout your belly ever since we left this mornin'.

BENNIE: You hungry? Them hotdogs we had give out around Nashville.

ARLENE: No. Not really.

BENNIE: You gotta eat, Arlene.

ARLENE: Says who?

BENNIE *(Laughs)*: How 'bout I pick us up some chicken, give you time to clean yourself up. We'll have a nice little dinner, just the two of us.

ARLENE: I git sick if I eat this late. Besides, I'm tired.

BENNIE: You'll feel better soon's you git somethin' on your stomach. Like I always said, "Can't plow less'n you feed the mule."

ARLENE: I ain't never heard you say that.

BENNIE: There's lots you don't know about me, Arlene. You been seein' me ever day, but you ain't been payin' attention. You'll get to like me now we're out.

ARLENE: You . . . was always out.

BENNIE: Yes sir, I'm gonna like bein' retired. I kin tell already. An I can take care of you, like I been, only now—

ARLENE: You tol' me you was jus' takin' a vacation.

BENNIE: I was gonna tell you.

ARLENE: You had some time off an nothin' to do . . .

BENNIE: Figured you knew already.

ARLENE: You said you ain't never seen Kentucky like you always wanted to. Now you tell me you done quit at the prison?

BENNIE: They wouldn't let me drive you up here if I was still on the payroll, you know. Rules, against the rules. Coulda got me in big trouble doin' that.

ARLENE: You ain't goin' back to Pine Ridge?

BENNIE: Nope.

ARLENE: An you drove me all the way up here plannin' to stay here?

BENNIE: I was thinkin' on it.

ARLENE: Well what are you gonna do?

BENNIE *(Not positive, just a possibility)*: Hardware.

ARLENE: Sell guns?

BENNIE *(Laughs)*: Nails. Always wanted to. Some little store with bins and barrels full of nails and screws. Count 'em out. Put 'em in little sacks.

ARLENE: I don't need nobody hangin' around remindin' me where I been.

BENNIE: We had us a good time drivin' up here, didn't we? You throwin' that tomato outta the car . . . hit that no litterin' sign square in the middle. *(Grabs her arm as if to feel the muscle)* Good arm you got.

ARLENE *(Pulling away sharply)*: Don't you go grabbin' me.

BENNIE: Listen, you take off them clothes and have yourself a nice hot bath. *(Heading for the bathroom)* See, I'll start the water. And me, I'll go get us some chicken. *(Coming out of the bathroom)* You like slaw or potato salad?

ARLENE: Don't matter.

BENNIE *(Asking her to decide)*: Arlene . . .

ARLENE: Slaw.

BENNIE: One big bucket of slaw comin' right up. An extra rolls. You have a nice bath, now, you hear? I'll take my time so's you don't have to hurry fixin' yourself up.

ARLENE: I ain't gonna do no fixin'.

BENNIE *(A knowing smile)*: I know how you gals are when you get in the tub. You got any bubbles?

ARLENE: What?

BENNIE: Bubbles. You know, stuff to make bubbles with. Bubble bath.

ARLENE: I thought you was goin'.

BENNIE: Right. Right. Goin' right now.

Bennie leaves, locking the door behind him. He has left his hat on the bed. Arlene checks the stove and refrigerator.

GUARD (CALDWELL) *(Opening the cell door, carrying a plastic dinner carton)*: Got your grub, girlie.

ARLIE: Get out!

GUARD (CALDWELL): Can't. Doc says you gotta take the sun today.

ARLIE: You take it! I ain't hungry.

The guard and Arlie begin to walk to the downstage table area.

GUARD (CALDWELL): You gotta eat, Arlie.

ARLIE: Says who?

GUARD (CALDWELL): Says me. Says the warden. Says the Department of Corrections. Brung you two rolls.

ARLIE: And you know what you can do with your—

GUARD (CALDWELL): Stuff 'em in your bra, why don't you?

ARLIE: Ain't you got somebody to go beat up somewhere?

GUARD (CALDWELL): Gotta see you get fattened up.

ARLIE: What do you care?

Arlene goes into the bathroom.

GUARD (CALDWELL): Oh, we care all right. *(Setting the food down on the table)* Got us a two-way mirror in the shower room. *(She looks up, hostile)* And you don't know which one it is, do you? *(He forces her onto the seat)* Yes ma'am. Eat. *(Pointing to the food)* We sure do care if you go gittin' too skinny. *(Walks away but continues to watch her)* Yes ma'am. We care a hog-lickin' lot.

ARLIE *(Throws the whole carton at him)*: Sons-a-bitches!

Mother's knock is heard on the apartment door.

MOTHER'S VOICE: Arlie? Arlie girl you in there?

Arlene walks out of the bathroom. She stands still, looking at the door. Arlie hears the knock at the same time and slips into the apartment and over to the bed, putting the pillow between her legs and holding the yellow teddy bear Arlene has unpacked. The knocking gets louder.

MOTHER'S VOICE: Arlie?

ARLIE *(Pulling herself up weakly on one elbow, speaking with the voice of a very young child)*: Mama? Mama?

Arlene walks slowly toward the door.

MOTHER'S VOICE *(Now pulling the doorknob from the outside, angry that the door is locked)*: Arlie? I know you're in there.

ARLIE: I can't git up, Mama. *(Hands between her legs)* My legs is hurt.

MOTHER'S VOICE: What's takin' you so long?

ARLENE *(Smoothing out her dress)*: Yeah, I'm comin'. *(Puts Bennie's hat out of sight under the bed)* Hold on.

MOTHER'S VOICE: I brung you some stuff but I ain't gonna stand here all night.

Arlene opens the door and stands back. Mother looks strong but badly worn. She is wearing her cab driver's uniform and is carrying a plastic laundry basket stuffed with cleaning fluids, towels, bug spray, etc.

ARLENE: I didn't know if you'd come.

MOTHER: Ain't I always?

ARLENE: How are you?

Arlene moves as if to hug her. Mother stands still, Arlene backs off.

MOTHER: 'Bout the same. *(Walking into the room)*

ARLENE: I'm glad to see you.

MOTHER *(Not looking at Arlene)*: You look tired.

ARLENE: It was a long drive.

MOTHER *(Putting the laundry basket on the trunk)*: Didn't fatten you up none, I see. *(Walks around the room, looking the place over)* You always was too skinny. *(Arlene straightens her clothes again)* Shoulda beat you like your daddy said. Make you eat.

ARLIE: Nobody done this to me, Mama. *(Protesting, in pain)* No! No!

MOTHER: He weren't a mean man, though, your daddy.

ARLIE: Was . . . *(Quickly)* my bike. My bike hurt me. The seat bumped me.

MOTHER: You remember that black chewing gum he got you when you was sick?

ARLENE: I remember he beat up on you.

MOTHER: Yeah, *(Proudly)* and he was real sorry a coupla times. *(Looking in the closet)* Filthy dirty. Hey! *(Slamming the closet door. Arlene jumps at the noise)* I brung you all kinda stuff. Just like Candy not leavin' you nuthin'. *(Walking back to the basket)* Some kids I got.

ARLIE *(Curling up into a ball)*: No, Mama, don't touch it. It'll git well. It git well before.

ARLENE: Where is Candy?

MOTHER: You got her place so what do you care? I got her outta my house so whatta I care? This'll be a good place for you.

ARLENE *(Going to the window)*: Wish there was a yard, here.

MOTHER *(Beginning to empty the basket)*: Nice things, see? Bet you ain't had no colored towels where you been.

ARLENE: No.

MOTHER *(Putting some things away in cabinets)*: No place like home. Got that up on the kitchen wall now.

ARLIE: I don't want no tea, Mama.

ARLENE: Yeah?

MOTHER *(Repeating Arlene's answers)*: No . . . yeah? . . . You forgit how to talk? I ain't gonna be here all that long. Least you can talk to me while I'm here.

ARLENE: You ever git that swing you wanted?

MOTHER: Dish towels, an see here? June sent along this teapot. You drink tea, Arlie?

ARLENE: No.

MOTHER: June's havin' another baby. Don't know when to quit, that girl. Course, I ain't one to talk. *(Starting to pick up trash on the floor)*

ARLENE: Have you seen Joey?

ARLIE: I'm tellin' you the truth.

MOTHER: An Ray . . .

ARLIE *(Pleading)*: Daddy didn't do nuthin' to me.

MOTHER: Ray ain't had a day of luck in his life.

ARLIE: Ask him. He saw me fall on my bike.

MOTHER: Least bein' locked up now, he'll keep off June till the baby gits here.

ARLENE: Have you seen Joey?

MOTHER: Your daddy ain't doin' too good right now. Man's been dyin' for ten years, to hear him tell it. You'd think he'd git tired of it an jus' go ahead . . . pass on.

ARLENE *(Wanting an answer)*: Mother . . .

MOTHER: Yeah, I seen 'im. 'Bout two years ago. Got your stringy hair.

ARLENE: You got a picture?

MOTHER: You was right to give him up. Foster homes is good for some kids.

ARLIE: Where's my Joey-bear? Yellow Joey-bear? Mama?

ARLENE: How'd you see him?

MOTHER: I was down at Detention Center pickin' up Pete. *(Beginning her serious cleaning now)*

ARLENE *(Less than interested)*: How is he?

MOTHER: I could be workin' at the Detention Center I been there so much. All I gotta do's have somethin' big goin' on an I git a call to come after one of you. Can't jus' have kids, no, gotta be pickin' 'em up all· over town.

ARLENE: You was just tellin' me—

MOTHER: Pete is taller, that's all.

ARLENE: You was just tellin' me how you saw Joey.

MOTHER: I'm comin' back in the cab an I seen him waitin' for the bus.

ARLENE: What'd he say?

MOTHER: Oh, I didn't stop. *(Arlene looks up quickly, hurt and angry)* If the kid don't even know you, Arlie, he sure ain't gonna know who I am.

ARLENE: How come he couldn't stay at Shirley's?

MOTHER: 'Cause Shirley never was crazy about washin' more diapers. She's the only smart kid I got. Anyway, social worker only put him there till she could find him a foster home.

ARLENE: But I coulda seen him.

MOTHER: Thatta been trouble, him bein' in the family. Kid wouldn't have known who to listen to, Shirley or you.

ARLENE: But I'm his mother.

MOTHER: See, now you don't have to be worryin' about him. No kids, no worryin'.

ARLENE: He just had his birthday, you know.

ARLIE: Don't let Daddy come in here, Mama. Just you an me. Mama?

ARLENE: When I git workin', I'll git a nice rug for this place. He could come live here with me.

MOTHER: Fat chance.

ARLENE: I done my time.

MOTHER: You never really got attached to him anyway.

ARLENE: How do you know that?

MOTHER: Now don't you go gettin' het up. I'm telling you . . .

ARLENE: But . . .

MOTHER: Kids need rules to go by an he'll get 'em over there.

ARLIE *(Screaming)*: No Daddy! I didn't tell her nuthin'. I didn't! I didn't! *(Gets up from the bed, terrified)*

MOTHER: Here, help me with these sheets. *(Hands Arlene the sheets from the laundry basket)* Even got you a spread. Kinda goes with them curtains. *(Arlene is silent)* You ain't thanked me, Arlie girl.

ARLENE *(Going to the other side of the bed)*: They don't call me Arlie no more. It's Arlene now.

Arlene and Mother make up the bed. Arlie jumps up, looks around and goes over to Mother's purse. She looks through it hurriedly and pulls out the wallet. She takes some money and runs down left, where she is caught by a school principal.

PRINCIPAL: Arlie? You're in an awfully big hurry for such a little girl. *(Brushes at Arlie's hair)* That is you under all that hair, isn't it? *(Arlie resists this gesture)* Now, you can watch where you're going.

ARLIE: Gotta git home.

PRINCIPAL: But school isn't over for another three hours. And there's peanut butter and chili today.

ARLIE: Ain't hungry. *(Struggling free)*

The principal now sees Arlie's hands clenched behind her back.

PRINCIPAL: What do we have in our hands, Arlie?

ARLIE: Nuthin'.

PRINCIPAL: Let me see your hands, Arlie. Open up your hands.

Arlie brings her hands around in front, opening them, showing crumpled dollars.

ARLIE: It's my money. I earned it.

PRINCIPAL *(Taking the money)*: And how did we earn this money?

ARLIE: Doin' things.

PRINCIPAL: What kind of things?

ARLIE: For my daddy.

PRINCIPAL: Well, we'll see about that. You'll have to come with me.

Arlie resists as the principal pulls her.

ARLIE: No.

PRINCIPAL: Your mother was right after all. She said put you in a special school. *(Quickly)* No, what she said was put you away somewhere and I said, no, she's too young, well I was wrong. I have four hundred other children to take care of here and what have I been doing? Breaking up your fights, talking to your truant officer and washing your writing off the bathroom wall. Well, I've had enough. You've made your choice. You *want* out of regular school and you're going to *get* out of regular school.

ARLIE *(Becoming more violent)*: You can't make me go nowhere, bitch!

PRINCIPAL *(Backing off in cold anger)*: I'm not making you go. You've earned it. You've worked hard for this, well, they're used to your type over there. They'll know exactly what to do with you. *(She stalks off, leaving Arlie alone)*

MOTHER *(Smoothing out the spread)*: Spread ain't new, but it don't look so bad. Think we got it right after we got you. No, I remember now. I was pregnant with you an been real sick the whole time.

Arlene lights a cigarette, Mother takes one, Arlene retrieves the pack quickly.

MOTHER: Your daddy brung me home this big bowl of chili an some jelly doughnuts. Some fare from the airport give him a big tip. Anyway, I'd been eatin' peanut brittle all day, only thing that tasted any good. Then in he come with this chili an no sooner'n I got in bed I thrown up all over everwhere. Lucky I didn't throw you up, Arlie girl. Anyhow, that's how come us to get a new spread. This one here. *(Sits on the bed)*

ARLENE: You drivin' the cab any?

MOTHER: Any? Your daddy ain't drove it at all a long time now. Six years, seven maybe.

ARLENE: You meet anybody nice?

MOTHER: Not anymore. Mostly drivin' old ladies to get their shoes. Guess it got around the nursin' homes I was reliable. *(Sounds funny to her)* You remember that time I took you drivin' with me that night after you been in a fight an that soldier bought us a beer? Shitty place, hole in the wall?

ARLENE: You made me wait in the car.

MOTHER *(Standing up)*: Think I'd take a child of mine into a dump like that?

ARLENE: You went in.

MOTHER: Weren't no harm in it. *(Walking over for the bug spray)* I didn't always look so bad, you know.

ARLENE: You was pretty.

MOTHER *(Beginning to spray the floor)*: You could look better'n you do. Do somethin' with your hair. I always thought if you'd looked better you wouldn't have got in so much trouble.

ARLENE *(Pleased and curious)*: Joey got my hair?

MOTHER: And skinny.

ARLENE: I took some beauty school at Pine Ridge.

MOTHER: Yeah, a beautician?

ARLENE: I don't guess so.

MOTHER: Said you was gonna work.

ARLENE: They got a law here. Ex-cons can't get no license.

MOTHER: Shoulda stayed in Alabama, then. Worked there.

ARLENE: They got a law there, too.

MOTHER: Then why'd they give you the trainin'?

ARLENE: I don't know.

MOTHER: Maybe they thought it'd straighten you out.

ARLENE: Yeah.

MOTHER: But you are gonna work, right?

ARLENE: Yeah. Cookin' maybe. Somethin' that pays good.

MOTHER: You? Cook? *(Laughs)*

ARLENE: I could learn it.

MOTHER: Your daddy ain't never forgive you for that bologna sandwich. *(Arlene laughs a little, finally enjoying a memory)* Oh, I wish I'd seen you spreadin' that Colgate on that bread. He'd have smelled that toothpaste if he hadn't been so sloshed. Little snotty-nosed kid tryin' to kill her daddy with a bologna sandwich. An him bein' so pleased when you brung it to him . . . *(Laughing)*

ARLENE: He beat me good.

MOTHER: Well, now, Arlie, you gotta admit you had it comin' to you. *(Wiping tears from laughing)*

ARLENE: I guess.

MOTHER: You got a broom?

ARLENE: No.

MOTHER: Well, I got one in the cab I brung just in case. I can't leave it here, but I'll sweep up fore I go. *(Walking toward the door)* You jus' rest till I git back. Won't find no work lookin' the way you do.

Mother leaves. Arlene finds some lipstick and a mirror in her purse, makes an attempt to look better while Mother is gone.

ARLIE *(Jumps up, as if talking to another kid)*: She is not skinny!

ARLENE *(Looking at herself in the mirror)*: I guess I could . . .

ARLIE: And she don't have to git them stinky permanents. Her hair just comes outta her head curly.

ARLENE: Some lipstick.

ARLIE *(Serious)*: She drives the cab to buy us stuff, 'cause we don't take no charity from nobody, 'cause we got money 'cause she earned it.

ARLENE *(Closing the mirror, dejected, afraid Mother might be right)*: But you're too skinny and you got stringy hair. *(Sitting on the floor)*

ARLIE *(More angry)*: She drives at night 'cause people needs rides at night.

People goin' to see their friends that are sick, or people's cars broken down an they gotta get to work at the . . . nobody calls my mama a whore!

MOTHER *(Coming back in with the broom)*: If I'd known you were gonna sweep up with your butt, I wouldn't have got this broom. Get up! *(Sweeps at Arlene to get her to move)*

ARLIE: You're gonna take that back or I'm gonna rip out all your ugly hair and stuff it down your ugly throat.

ARLENE *(Tugging at her own hair)*: You still cut hair?

MOTHER *(Noticing some spot on the floor)*: Gonna take a razor blade to get out this paint.

ARLENE: Nail polish.

ARLIE: Wanna know what I know about your mama? She's dyin'. Somethin's eatin' up her insides piece by piece, only she don't want you to know it.

MOTHER *(Continuing to sweep)*: So, you're callin' yourself Arlene, now?

ARLENE: Yes.

MOTHER: Don't want your girlie name no more?

ARLENE: Somethin' like that.

MOTHER: They call you Arlene in prison?

ARLENE: Not at first when I was bein' hateful. Just my number then.

MOTHER: You always been hateful.

ARLENE: There was this chaplain, he called me Arlene from the first day he come to talk to me. Here, let me help you. *(She reaches for the broom)*

MOTHER: I'll do it.

ARLENE: You kin rest.

MOTHER: Since when? *(Arlene backs off)* I ain't hateful, how come I got so many hateful kids? *(Sweeping harder now)* Poor dumb-as-hell Pat, stealin' them wigs, Candy screwin' since day one, Pete cuttin' up ol' Mac down at the grocery, June sellin' dope like it was Girl Scout cookies, and you . . . thank God I can't remember it all.

ARLENE *(A very serious request)*: Maybe I could come out on Sunday for . . . you still make that pot roast?

MOTHER *(Now sweeping over by the picture of Jesus)*: That your picture?

ARLENE: That chaplain give it to me.

MOTHER: The one give you your "new name."

ARLENE: Yes.

MOTHER: It's crooked. *(Doesn't straighten it)*

ARLENE: I liked those potatoes with no skins. An that ketchup squirter we had, jus' like in a real restaurant.

MOTHER: People that run them institutions now, they jus' don't know how to teach kids right. Let 'em run around an get in more trouble. They should get you up at the crack of dawn an set you to scrubbin' the floor. That's what kids need. Trainin'. Hard work.

ARLENE *(A clear request)*: I'll probably git my Sundays off.

MOTHER: Sunday . . . is my day to clean house now.

Arlene gets the message, finally walks over to straighten the picture. Mother now feels a little bad about this rejection, stops sweeping for a moment.

MOTHER: I woulda wrote you but I didn't have nuthin' to say. An no money to send, so what's the use?

ARLENE: I made out.

MOTHER: They pay you for workin'?

ARLENE: 'Bout three dollars a month.

MOTHER: How'd you make it on three dollars a month? *(Answers her own question)* You do some favors?

ARLENE *(Sitting down in the chair under the picture, a somewhat smug look)*: You jus' can't make it by yourself.

MOTHER *(Pauses, suspicious, then contemptuous)*: You play, Arlie?

ARLENE: You don't know nuthin' about that.

MOTHER: I hear things. Girls callin' each other "mommy" an bringin' things back from the canteen for their "husbands." Makes me sick. You got family, Arlie, what you want with that playin'? Don't want nobody like that in my house.

ARLENE: You don't know what you're talkin' about.

MOTHER: I still got two kids at home. Don't want no bad example. *(Not finishing the sweeping. Has all the dirt in one place, but doesn't get it up off the floor yet)*

ARLENE: I could tell them some things.

MOTHER *(Vicious)*: Like about that cab driver.

ARLENE: Look, that was a long time ago. I wanna work, now, make somethin' of myself. I learned to knit. People'll buy nice sweaters. Make some extra money.

MOTHER: We sure could use it.

ARLENE: An then if I have money, maybe they'd let me take Joey to the fair, buy him hotdogs an talk to him. Make sure he ain't foolin' around.

MOTHER: What makes you think he'd listen to you? Alice, across the street? Her sister took care her kids while she was at Lexington. You think they pay any attention to her now? Ashamed, that's what. One of 'em told me his mother done died. Gone to see a friend and died there.

ARLENE: Be different with me and Joey.

MOTHER: He don't even know who you are, Arlie.

ARLENE *(Wearily)*: Arlene.

MOTHER: You forgot already what you was like as a kid. At Waverly, tellin' them lies about that campin' trip we took, sayin' your daddy made you watch while he an me . . . you know. I'd have killed you then if them social workers hadn't been watchin'.

ARLENE: Yeah.

MOTHER: Didn't want them thinkin' I weren't fit. Well, what do they know?

Each time you'd get out of one of them places, you'd be actin' worse than ever. Go right back to that junkie, pimp, Carl, sellin' the stuff he steals, savin' his ass from the police. He follow you home this time, too?

ARLENE: He's got four more years at Bricktown.

MOTHER: Glad to hear it. Here . . . *(Handing her a bucket)* Water.

Arlene fills up the bucket and Mother washes several dirty spots on the walls, floor and furniture. Arlene knows better than to try to help. The doctor walks downstage to find Arlie for their counseling session.

DOCTOR: So you refuse to go to camp?

ARLIE: Now why'd I want to go to your fuckin' camp? Camp's for babies. You can go shit in the woods if you want to, but I ain't goin'.

DOCTOR: Oh, you're goin'.

ARLIE: Wanna bet?

MOTHER: Arlie, I'm waitin'. *(For the water)*

ARLIE: 'Sides, I'm waitin'.

DOCTOR: Waiting for what?

ARLIE: For Carl to come git me.

DOCTOR: And who is Carl?

ARLIE: Jus' some guy. We're goin' to Alabama.

DOCTOR: You don't go till we say you can go.

ARLIE: Carl's got a car.

DOCTOR: Does he have a driver's license to go with it?

ARLIE *(Enraged, impatient)*: I'm goin' now.

Arlie stalks away, then backs up toward the doctor again. He has information she wants.

DOCTOR: Hey!

ARLENE: June picked out a name for the baby?

MOTHER: Clara . . . or Clarence. Got it from this fancy shampoo she bought.

ARLIE: I don't feel good. I'm pregnant, you know.

DOCTOR: The test was negative.

ARLIE: Well, I should know, shouldn't I?

DOCTOR: No. You want to be pregnant, is that it?

ARLIE: I wouldn't mind. Kids need somebody to bring 'em up right.

DOCTOR: Raising children is a big responsibility, you know.

ARLIE: Yeah, I know it. I ain't dumb. Everybody always thinks I'm so dumb.

DOCTOR: You could learn if you wanted to. That's what the teachers are here for.

ARLIE: Shit.

DOCTOR: Or so they say.

ARLIE: All they teach us is about geography. Why'd I need to know about Africa. Jungles and shit.

DOCTOR: They want you to know about other parts of the world.

ARLIE: Well, I ain't goin' there so whatta I care?

DOCTOR: What's this about Cindy?

ARLIE *(Hostile)*: She told Mr. Dawson some lies about me.

DOCTOR: I bet.

ARLIE: She said I fuck my daddy for money.

DOCTOR: And what did you do when she said that?

ARLIE: What do you think I did? I beat the shit out of her.

DOCTOR: And that's a good way to work out your problem?

ARLIE *(Proudly)*: She ain't done it since.

DOCTOR: She's been in traction, since.

ARLIE: So, whatta I care? She say it again, I'll do it again. Bitch!

ARLENE *(Looking down at the dirt Mother is gathering on the floor)*: I ain't got a can. Just leave it.

MOTHER: And have you sweep it under the bed after I go? *(Wraps the dirt in a piece of newspaper and puts it in her laundry basket)*

DOCTOR *(Looking at his clipboard)*: You're on unit cleanup this week.

ARLIE: I done it last week!

DOCTOR: Then you should remember what to do. The session is over. *(Getting up, walking away)* And stand up straight! And take off that hat!

Doctor and Arlie go offstage as Mother finds Bennie's hat.

MOTHER: This your hat?

ARLENE: No.

MOTHER: Guess Candy left it here.

ARLENE: Candy didn't leave nuthin'.

MOTHER: Then whose is it? *(Arlene doesn't answer)* Do you know whose hat this is? *(Arlene knows she made a mistake)* I'm askin' you a question and I want an answer. *(Arlene turns her back)* Whose hat is this? You tell me right now, whose hat is this?

ARLENE: It's Bennie's.

MOTHER: And who's Bennie?

ARLENE: Guy drove me home from Pine Ridge. A guard.

MOTHER *(Upset)*: I knew it. You been screwin' a goddamn guard. *(Throws the hat on the bed)*

ARLENE: He jus' drove me up here, that's all.

MOTHER: Sure.

ARLENE: I git sick on the bus.

MOTHER: You expect me to believe that?

ARLENE: I'm tellin' you, he jus'—

MOTHER: No man alive gonna drive a girl five hundred miles for nuthin'.

ARLENE: He ain't never seen Kentucky.

MOTHER: It ain't Kentucky he wants to see.

ARLENE: He ain't gettin' nuthin' from me.

MOTHER: That's what you think.

ARLENE: He done some nice things for me at Pine Ridge. Gum, funny stories.

MOTHER: He'd be tellin' stories all right, tellin' his buddies where to find you.

ARLENE: He's gettin' us some dinner right now.

MOTHER: And how're you gonna pay him? Huh? Tell me that.

ARLENE: I ain't like that no more.

MOTHER: Oh you ain't. I'm your mother. I know what you'll do.

ARLENE: I tell you I ain't.

MOTHER: I knew it. Well, when you got another bastard in you, don't come cryin' to me, 'cause I done told you.

ARLENE: Don't worry.

MOTHER: An I'm gettin' myself outta here fore your boyfriend comes back.

ARLENE *(Increasing anger)*: He ain't my boyfriend.

MOTHER: I been a lotta things, but I ain't dumb, Arlene. *("Arlene" is mocking.)*

ARLENE: I didn't say you was. *(Beginning to know how this is going to turn out)*

MOTHER: Oh no? You lied to me!

ARLENE: How?

MOTHER: You took my spread without even sayin' thank you. You're hintin' at comin' to my house for pot roast just like nuthin' ever happened, an all the time you're hidin' a goddamn guard under your bed. *(Furious)* Uh-huh.

ARLENE *(Quietly)*: Mama?

MOTHER *(Cold, fierce)*: What?

ARLENE: What kind of meat makes a pot roast?

MOTHER: A roast makes a pot roast. Buy a roast. Shoulder, chuck . . .

ARLENE: Are you comin' back?

MOTHER: You ain't got no need for me.

ARLENE: I gotta ask you to come see me?

MOTHER: I come tonight, didn't I, an nobody asked me?

ARLENE: Just forget it.

MOTHER *(Getting her things together)*: An if I hadn't told them about this apartment, you wouldn't be out at all, how 'bout that!

ARLENE: Forget it!

MOTHER: Don't you go talkin' to me that way. You remember who I am. I'm the one took you back after all you done all them years. I brung you that teapot. I scrubbed your place. You remember that when you talk to me.

ARLENE: Sure.

MOTHER: Uh-huh. *(Now goes to the bed, rips off the spread and stuffs it in her basket)* I knowed I shouldn't have come. You ain't changed a bit.

ARLENE: Same hateful brat, right?

MOTHER *(Arms full, heading for the door)*: Same hateful brat. Right.
ARLENE *(Rushing toward her)*: Mama . . .
MOTHER: Don't you touch me.

Mother leaves. Arlene stares out the door, stunned and hurt. Finally, she slams the door and turns back into the room.

ARLENE: No! Don't you touch Mama, Arlie.

Ronnie, a fellow juvenile offender, runs across the catwalk, waving a necklace and being chased by Arlie.

RONNIE: Arlie got a boyfriend, Arlie got a boyfriend. *(Throws the necklace downstage)* Whoo!
ARLIE *(Chasing him)*: Ronnie, you ugly mother, I'll smash your fuckin'—
ARLENE *(Getting more angry)*: You might steal all—
RONNIE *(Running down the stairs)*: Arlie got a boyfriend . . .
ARLIE: Gimme that necklace or I'll—
ARLENE: —or eat all Mama's precious pot roast.
RONNIE *(As they wrestle downstage)*: You'll tell the doctor on me? And get your private room back? *(Laughing)*
ARLENE *(Cold and hostile)*: No, don't touch Mama, Arlie. 'Cause you might slit Mama's throat. *(Goes into the bathroom)*
ARLIE: You wanna swallow all them dirty teeth?
RONNIE: Tell me who give it to you.
ARLIE: No, you tell me where it's at.

Ronnie breaks away, pushing Arlie in the opposite direction, and runs for the necklace.

RONNIE: It's right here. *(Drops it down his pants)* Come an git it.
ARLIE: Oh now, that was really ignorant, you stupid pig.
RONNIE *(Backing away, daring her)*: Jus' reach right in. First come, first served.
ARLIE: Now, how you gonna pee after I throw your weenie over the fence?
RONNIE: You ain't gonna do that, girl. You gonna fall in love.

Arlie turns vicious, pins Ronnie down, attacking. This is no longer play. He screams. The doctor appears on the catwalk.

DOCTOR: Arlie! *(Heads down the stairs to stop this)*
CARL'S VOICE *(From outside the apartment door)*: Arlie!
DOCTOR: Arlie!
ARLIE: Stupid, ugly—
RONNIE: Help!

Arlie runs away and hides down left.

DOCTOR: That's three more weeks of isolation, Arlie. *(Bending down to Ronnie)* You all right? Can you walk?

RONNIE *(Looking back to Arlie as he gets up in great pain)*: She was tryin' to kill me.

DOCTOR: Yeah. Easy now. You should've known, Ronnie.

ARLIE *(Yelling at Ronnie)*: You'll get yours, crybaby.

CARL'S VOICE: Arlie . . .

ARLIE: Yeah, I'm comin'!

CARL'S VOICE: Bad-lookin' dude says move your ass an open up this here door, girl.

Arlene does not come out of the bathroom. Carl twists the door knob violently, then kicks in the door and walks in. Carl is thin and cheaply dressed. Carl's walk and manner are imitative of black pimps, but he can't quite carry it off.

CARL: Where you at, mama?

ARLENE: Carl?

CARL: Who else? You 'spectin' Leroy Brown?

ARLENE: I'm takin' a bath!

CARL *(Walking toward the bathroom)*: I like my ladies clean. Matter of professional pride.

ARLENE: Don't come in here.

CARL *(Mocking her tone)*: Don't come in here. I seen it all before, girl.

ARLENE: I'm gittin' out. Sit down or somethin'.

CARL *(Talking loud enough for her to hear him through the door)*: Ain't got the time. *(Opens her purse, then searches the trunk)* Jus' come by to tell you it's tomorrow. We be takin' our feet to the New York street. *(As though she will be pleased)* No more fuckin' around with these jiveass southern turkeys. We're goin' to the big city, baby. Get you some red shades and some red shorts an' the johns be linin' up fore we hit town. Four tricks a night. How's that sound? No use wearin' out that cute ass you got. Way I hear it, only way to git busted up there's be stupid, an I ain't lived this long bein' stupid.

ARLENE *(Coming out of the bathroom wearing a towel)*: That's exactly how you lived your whole life—bein' stupid.

CARL: Arlie . . . *(Moving in on her)* be sweet, sugar.

ARLENE: Still got your curls.

CARL *(Trying to bug her)*: You're looking okay yourself.

ARLENE: Oh, Carl. *(Noticing the damage to the door, breaking away from any closeness he might try to force)*

CARL *(Amused)*: Bent up your door, some.

ARLENE: How come you're out?

CARL: Sweetheart, you done broke out once, been nabbed and sent to Pine Ridge and got yourself paroled since I been in. I got a right to a little free time too, ain't that right?

ARLENE: You escape?

CARL: Am I standin' here or am I standin' here? They been fuckin' with you, I can tell.

ARLENE: They gonna catch you.

CARL *(Going to the window)*: Not where we're going. Not a chance.

ARLENE: Where you goin' they won't git you?

CARL: Remember that green hat you picked out for me down in Birmingham? Well, I ain't ever wore it yet, but I kin wear it in New York 'cause New York's where you wear whatever you feel like. One guy tol' me he saw this dude wearin' a whole ring of feathers roun' his leg, right here *(Grabs his leg above the knee)* an he weren't in no circus nor no Indian neither.

ARLENE: I ain't seen you since Birmingham. How come you think I wanna see you now?

Arlie appears suddenly, confronts Carl.

ARLIE *(Pointing as if there is a trick waiting)*: Carl, I ain't goin' with that dude, he's weird.

CARL: 'Cause we gotta go collect the johns' money, that's "how come."

ARLIE: I don't need you pimpin' for me.

ARLENE *(Very strong)*: I'm gonna work.

CARL: Work?

ARLENE: Yeah.

CARL: What's this "work"?

ARLIE: You always sendin' me to them ol' droolers . . .

CARL: You kin do two things, girl—

ARLIE: They slobberin' all over me . . .

CARL: Breakin' out an hookin'.

ARLIE: They tyin' me to the bed!

ARLENE: I mean real work.

ARLIE *(Now screaming, gets further away from him)*: I could git killed working for you. Some sicko, some crazy drunk . . .

Arlie goes offstage. A guard puts her in the cell sometime before Bennie's entrance.

CARL: You forget, we seen it all on TV in the day room, you bustin' outta Lakewood like that. Fakin' that palsy fit, then beatin' that guard half to death with his own key ring. Whoo-ee! Then that spree you went on . . . stoppin' at that fillin' station for some cash, then kidnappin' the old dude pumpin' the gas.

ARLENE: Yeah.

CARL: Then that cab driver comes outta the bathroom an tries to mess with you and you shoots him with his own piece. *(Fires an imaginary pistol)*

That there's nice work, mama. *(Going over to her, putting his arms around her)*

ARLENE: That gun . . . it went off, Carl.

CARL *(Getting more determined with his affection)*: That's what guns do, doll. They go off.

BENNIE'S VOICE *(From outside)*: Arlene? Arlene?

CARL: Arlene? *(Jumping up)* Well, la-de-da.

Bennie opens the door, carrying the chicken dinners. He is confused, seeing Arlene wearing a towel and talking to Carl.

ARLENE: Bennie, this here's Carl.

CARL: You're interruptin', Jack. Me an Arlie got business.

BENNIE: She's callin' herself Arlene.

CARL: I call my ladies what I feel like, chicken man, an you call yourself "gone."

BENNIE: I don't take orders from you.

CARL: Well, you been takin' orders from somebody, or did you git that outfit at the army surplus store?

ARLENE: Bennie brung me home from Pine Ridge.

CARL *(Walking toward him)*: Oh, it's a guard now, is it? That chicken break out or what? *(Grabs the chicken)*

BENNIE: I don't know what you're doin' here, but—

CARL: What you gonna do about it, huh? Lock me up in the toilet? You an who else, Batman?

BENNIE *(Taking the chicken back, walking calmly to the counter)*: Watch your mouth, punk.

CARL *(Kicks a chair toward Bennie)*: Punk!

ARLENE *(Trying to stop this)*: I'm hungry.

BENNIE: You heard her, she's hungry.

CARL *(Vicious)*: Shut up! *(Mocking)* Ossifer.

BENNIE: Arlene, tell this guy if he knows what's good for him . . .

CARL *(Walking to the counter where Bennie has left the chicken)*: Why don't you write me a parkin' ticket? *(Shoves the chicken on the floor)* Don't fuck with me, dad. It ain't healthy.

Bennie pauses. A real standoff. Finally, Bennie bends down and picks up the chicken.

BENNIE: You ain't worth dirtyin' my hands.

Carl walks by him, laughing.

CARL: Hey, Arlie. I got some dude to see. *(For Bennie's benefit as he struts to the door)* What I need with another beat-up guard? All that blood, jus' ugly up my threads. *(Very sarcastic)* Bye y'all.

ARLENE: Bye, Carl.

Carl turns back quickly at the door, stopping Bennie, who was following him.

CARL: You really oughta shine them shoes, man. *(Vindictive laugh, slams the door in Bennie's face)*
BENNIE *(Relieved, trying to change the atmosphere)*: Well, how 'bout if we eat? You'll catch your death dressed like that.
ARLENE: Turn around then.

Arlene gets a shabby housecoat from the closet. She puts it on over her towel, buttons it up, then pulls the towel out from under it. This has the look of a prison ritual.

BENNIE *(As she is dressing)*: Your parole officer's gonna tell you to keep away from guys like that . . . for your own good, you know. Those types, just like the suckers on my tomatoes back home. Take everything right outta you. Gotta pull 'em off, Arlie, uh, Arlene.
ARLENE: Now, I'm decent now.
BENNIE: You hear what I said?
ARLENE *(Going to the bathroom for her hairbrush)*: I told him that. That's exactly what I did tell him.
BENNIE: Who was that anyhow? *(Sits down on the bed, opens up the chicken)*
ARLENE *(From the bathroom)*: Long time ago, me an Carl took a trip together.
BENNIE: When you was a kid, you mean?
ARLENE: I was at this place for kids.
BENNIE: And Carl was there?
ARLENE: No, he picked me up an we went to Alabama. There was this wreck an all. I ended up at Lakewood for forgery. It was him that done it. Got me pregnant too.
BENNIE: That was Joey's father?
ARLENE: Yeah, but he don't know that. *(Sits down)*
BENNIE: Just as well. Guy like that, don't know what they'd do.
ARLENE: Mother was here while ago. Says she's seen Joey. *(Taking a napkin from Bennie)*
BENNIE: Wish I had a kid. Life ain't, well, complete, without no kids to play ball with an take fishin'. Dorrie, though, she had them backaches an that neuralgia, day I married her to the day she died. Good woman though. No drinkin', no card playin', real sweet voice . . . what was that song she used to sing? . . . Oh, yeah . . .
ARLENE: She says Joey's a real good-lookin' kid.
BENNIE: Well, his mom ain't bad.
ARLENE: At Lakewood, they tried to git me to have an abortion.
BENNIE: They was just thinkin' of you, Arlene.

ARLENE *(Matter-of-fact, no self-pity)*: I told 'em I'd kill myself if they done that. I would have too.

BENNIE: But they took him away after he was born.

ARLENE: Yeah. *(Bennie waits, knowing she is about to say more)* An I guess I went crazy after that. Thought if I could jus' git out an find him . . .

BENNIE: I don't remember any of that on the TV.

ARLENE: No.

BENNIE: Just remember you smilin' at the cameras, yellin' how you tol' that cab driver not to touch you.

ARLENE: I never seen his cab. *(Forces herself to eat)*

ARLIE *(In the cell, holding a pillow and singing)*: Rock-a-bye baby, in the tree top, when the wind blows, the cradle will . . . *(Not remembering)* cradle will . . . *(Now talking)* What you gonna be when you grow up, pretty boy baby? You gonna be a doctor? You gonna give people medicine an take out they . . . no, don't be no doctor . . . be . . . be a preacher . . . sayin' Our Father who is in heaven . . . heaven, that's where people go when they dies, when doctors can't save 'em or somebody kills 'em fore they even git a chance to . . . no, don't be no preacher neither . . . be . . . go to school an learn good *(Tone begins to change)* so you kin . . . make everbody else feel so stupid all the time. Best thing you to be is stay a baby 'cause nobody beats up on babies or puts them . . . *(Much more quiet)* that ain't true, baby. People is mean to babies, so you stay right here with me so nobody kin git you an make you cry an they lay one finger on you *(Hostile)* an I'll beat the screamin' shit right out of 'em. They even blow on you an I'll kill 'em.

Bennie and Arlene have finished their dinner. Bennie puts one carton of slaw in the refrigerator, then picks up all the paper, making a garbage bag out of one of the sacks.

BENNIE: Ain't got a can, I guess. Jus' use this ol' sack for now.

ARLENE: I ain't never emptyin' another garbage can.

BENNIE: Yeah, I reckon you know how by now. *(Yawns)* You 'bout ready for bed?

ARLENE *(Stands up)*: I s'pose.

BENNIE *(Stretches)*: Little tired myself.

ARLENE *(Dusting the crumbs off the bed)*: Thanks for the chicken.

BENNIE: You're right welcome. You look beat. How 'bout I rub your back. *(Grabs her shoulders)*

ARLENE *(Pulling away)*: No. *(Walking to the sink)* You go on now.

BENNIE: Oh come on. *(Wiping his hands on his pants)* I ain't all that tired.

ARLENE: *I'm* tired.

BENNIE: Well, see then, a back rub is just what the doctor ordered.

ARLENE: No. I don't . . . *(Pulling away)*

Bennie grabs her shoulders and turns her around, sits her down hard on the trunk, starts rubbing her back and neck.

BENNIE: Muscles git real tightlike, right in here.

ARLENE: You hurtin' me.

BENNIE: Has to hurt a little or it won't do no good.

ARLENE *(Jumps, he has hurt her)*: Oh, stop it! *(She slips away from him and out into the room. She is frightened)*

BENNIE *(Smiling, coming after her, toward the bed)*: Be lot nicer if you was layin' down. Wouldn't hurt as much.

ARLENE: Now, I ain't gonna start yellin'. I'm jus' tellin' you to go.

BENNIE *(Straightens up as though he's going to cooperate)*: Okay then. I'll jus' git my hat.

He reaches for the hat, then turns quickly, grabs her and throws her down on the bed. He starts rubbing again.

BENNIE: Now, you just relax. Don't you go bein' scared of me.

ARLENE: You ain't gettin' nuthin' from me.

BENNIE: I don't want nuthin', honey. Jus' tryin' to help you sleep.

ARLENE *(Struggling)*: Don't you call me honey.

Bennie stops rubbing, but keeps one hand on her back. He rubs her hair with his free hand.

BENNIE: See? Don't that feel better?

ARLENE: Let me up.

BENNIE: Why, I ain't holdin' you down.

ARLENE: Then let me up.

BENNIE *(Takes hands off)*: Okay. Git up.

Arlene turns over slowly, begins to lift herself up on her elbows. Bennie puts one hand on her leg.

ARLENE: Move your hand. *(She gets up, moves across the room)*

BENNIE: I'd be happy to stay here with you tonight. Make sure you'll be all right. You ain't spent a night by yourself for a long time.

ARLENE: I remember how.

BENNIE: Well how you gonna git up? You got a alarm?

ARLENE: It ain't all that hard.

BENNIE *(Puts one hand in his pocket, leers a little)*: Oh yeah it is. *(Walks toward her again)* Gimme a kiss. Then I'll go.

ARLENE *(Edging along the counter, seeing she's trapped)*: You stay away from me.

Bennie reaches for her, clamping her hands behind her, pressing up against her.

BENNIE: Now what's it going to hurt you to give me a little ol' kiss?

ARLENE *(Struggling)*: Git out! I said git out!

BENNIE: You don't want me to go. You're jus' beginning to git interested. Your ol' girlie temper's flarin' up. I like that in a woman.

ARLENE: Yeah, you'd love it if I'd swat you one. *(Getting away from him)*

BENNIE: I been hit by you before. I kin take anything you got.

ARLENE: I could mess you up good.

BENNIE: Now, Arlie. You ain't had a man in a long time. And the ones you had been no-count.

ARLENE: Git out!

She slaps him. He returns the slap.

BENNIE *(Moving in)*: Ain't natural goin' without it too long. Young thing like you. Git all shriveled up.

ARLENE: All right, you sunuvabitch, you asked for it!

She goes into a violent rage, hitting and kicking him. Bennie overpowers her capably, prison-guard style.

BENNIE *(Amused)*: Little outta practice, ain't you?

ARLENE *(Screaming)*: I'll kill you, you creep!

The struggle continues, Bennie pinning her arms under his legs as he kneels over her on the bed. Arlene is terrified and in pain.

BENNIE: You will? You'll kill ol' Bennie . . . kill ol' Bennie like you done that cab driver?

A cruel reminder he employs to stun and mock her. Arlene looks as though she has been hit. Bennie, still fired up, unzips his pants.

ARLENE *(Passive, cold and bitter)*: This how you got your Dorrie, rapin'?

BENNIE *(Unbuttoning his shirt)*: That what you think this is, rape?

ARLENE: I oughta know.

BENNIE: Uh-huh.

ARLENE: First they unzip their pants.

Bennie pulls his shirttail out.

ARLENE: Sometimes they take off their shirt.

BENNIE: They do huh?

ARLENE: But mostly, they just pull it out and stick it in.

Bennie stops, finally hearing what she has been saying. He straightens up, obviously shocked. He puts his arms back in his shirt.

BENNIE: Don't you call me no rapist. *(Pause, then insistent)* No, I ain't no rapist, Arlie. *(Gets up, begins to tuck his shirt back in and zip up his pants)*

ARLENE: And I ain't Arlie.

Arlene remains on the bed as he continues dressing.

BENNIE: No I guess you ain't.
ARLENE *(Quietly and painfully)*: Arlie coulda killed you.

End of Act One

Prologue

These announcements are heard during the last five minutes of the intermission.

LOUDSPEAKER VOICE: Garden workers will, repeat, will, report for work this afternoon. Bring a hat and raincoat and wear boots. All raincoats will be checked at the front gate at the end of work period and returned to you after supper.

Your attention please. A checkerboard was not returned to the recreation area after dinner last night. Anyone with information regarding the black and red checkerboard missing from the recreation area will please contact Mrs. Duvall after lunch. No checkerboards or checkers will be distributed until this board is returned.

Betty Rickey and Mary Alice Wolf report to the laundry. Doris Creech and Arlie Holsclaw report immediately to the superintendent's office. The movie this evening will be *Dirty Harry* starring Clint Eastwood. Doris Creech and Arlie Holsclaw report to the superintendent's office immediately.

The bus from St. Mary's this Sunday will arrive at 1:00 P.M. as usual. Those residents expecting visitors on that bus will gather on the front steps promptly at 1:20 and proceed with the duty officer to the visiting area after it has been confirmed that you have a visitor on the bus.

Attention all residents. Attention all residents. *(Pause)* Mrs. Helen Carson has taught needlework classes here at Pine Ridge for thirty years. She will be retiring at the end of this month and moving to Florida where her husband has bought a trailer park. The resident council and the superintendent's staff has decided on a suitable retirement present. We want every resident to participate in this project—which is—a quilt, made from scraps of material collected from the residents and sewn together by residents and staff alike. The procedure will be as follows. A quilting room has been set up in an empty storage area just off the infirmary. Scraps of fabric will be collected as officers do evening count. Those residents who would enjoy cutting up old uniforms and bedding no longer in use should sign up for this detail with your dorm officer. If you would like to sign your name or send Mrs. Carson some special message on your square of fabric, the officers will have tubes of embroidery paint for that purpose. The backing for the quilt has been donated by the Women's Associates as well as the refreshments for the retirement party to be held after lunch on the thirtieth. Thank you very much for your attention and participation in this worthwhile tribute to someone we are all very fond of here. You may resume work at this time. Doris Creech and Arlie Holsclaw report to the superintendent's office immediately.

ACT
TWO

Lights fade. When they come up, it is the next morning. Arlene is asleep on the bed. Arlie is locked in a maximum-security cell. We do not see the officer to whom she speaks.

ARLIE: No, I don't have to shut up, neither. You already got me in seg-re-ga-tion, what else you gonna do? I got all day to sleep, while everybody else is out bustin' ass in the laundry. *(Laughs)* Hey! I know . . . you ain't gotta go do no dorm count, I'll just tell you an you jus' sit. Huh? You 'preciate that? Ease them corns you been moanin' about . . . yeah . . . okay. Write this down. *(Pride, mixed with alternating contempt and amusement)* Startin' down by the john on the back side, we got Mary Alice. Sleeps with her pillow stuffed in her mouth. Says her mom says it'd keep her from grindin' down her teeth or somethin'. She be suckin' that pillow like she gettin' paid for it. *(Laughs)* Next, it's Betty the Frog. Got her legs all opened out like some fuckin' . . . *(Makes croaking noises)* Then it's Doris eatin' pork rinds. Thinks somebody gonna grab 'em outta her mouth if she eats 'em during the day. Doris ain't dumb. She fat, but she ain't dumb. Hey! You notice how many girls is fat here? Then it be Rhonda, snorin', Marvene, wheezin', and Suzanne, coughin'. Then Clara an Ellie be still whisperin'. Family shit, who's gettin' outta line, which girls is gittin' a new work 'signment, an who kin git extra desserts an for how much. Them's the two really run this place. My bed right next to Ellie, for sure it's got some of her shit hid in it by now. Crackers or some crap gonna leak out all over my sheets. Last time I found a fuckin' grilled cheese in my pillow. Even had two of them little warty pickles. Christ! Okay. Linda and Lucille. They be real quiet, but they ain't sleepin'. Prayin', that's them. Linda be sayin' them Hell Marys till you kin just about scream. An Lucille, she tol' me once she didn't believe in no God, jus' some stupid spirits whooshin' aroun' everwhere makin' people do stuff. Weird. Now, I'm goin' back down the other side, there's . . . *(Screams)* I'd like to see you try it! I been listenin' at you for the last three hours. Your husband's gettin' laid off an your lettuce is gettin' eat by rabbits. Crap City. *You* shut up! Whadda I care if I wake everybody up? I want the nurse . . . I'm gittin' sick in here . . . an there's bugs in here!

The light comes up in the apartment. Faint morning traffic sounds are heard. Arlene does not wake up. The warden walks across the catwalk. A guard catches up with him near Arlie's cell. Bennie is stationed at the far end of the walk.

LOUDSPEAKER VOICE: Dorm A may now eat lunch.

GUARD (EVANS): Warden, I thought 456 . . . *(Nodding in Arlie's direction)* was leavin' here.

WARDEN: Is there some problem?

GUARD (EVANS): Oh, we can take care of her all right. We're just tired of takin' her shit, if you'll pardon the expression.

ARLIE: You ain't seen nuthin' yet, you mother.

WARDEN: Washington will decide on her transfer. Till then, you do your job.

GUARD (EVANS): She don't belong here. Rest of—

LOUDSPEAKER VOICE: Betty Rickey and Mary Alice Wolf report to the laundry.

GUARD (EVANS): Most of these girls are mostly nice people, go along with things. She needs a cage.

ARLIE *(Vicious)*: I need a knife.

WARDEN *(Very curt)*: Had it occurred to you that we could send the rest of them home and just keep her? *(Walks away)*

LOUDSPEAKER VOICE: Dorm A may now eat lunch. A Dorm to lunch.

GUARD (EVANS) *(Turning around, muttering to himself)*: Oh, that's a swell idea. Let everybody out except bitches like Holsclaw. *(She makes an obscene gesture at him, he turns back toward the catwalk)* Smartass warden, thinks he's runnin' a hotel.

BENNIE: Give you some trouble, did she?

GUARD (EVANS): I can wait.

BENNIE: For what?

GUARD (EVANS): For the day she tries gettin' out an I'm here by myself. I'll show that screechin' slut a thing or two.

BENNIE: That ain't the way, Evans.

GUARD (EVANS): The hell it ain't. Beat the livin'—

BENNIE: Outta a little thing like her? Gotta do her like all the rest. You got your shorts washed by givin' Betty Rickey Milky Ways. You git your chairs fixed givin' Frankie Hill extra time in the shower with Lucille Smith. An you git ol' Arlie girl to behave herself with a stick of gum. Gotta have her brand, though.

GUARD (EVANS): You screwin' that wildcat?

BENNIE *(Starts walk to Arlie's cell)*: Watch. *(Arlie is silent as he approaches, but is watching intently)* Now, *(To nobody in particular)* where was that piece of Juicy Fruit I had in this pocket. Gotta be here somewhere. *(Takes a piece of gum out of his pocket and drops it within Arlie's reach)* Well, *(Feigning disappointment)* I guess I already chewed it. *(Arlie reaches for the gum and gets it)* Oh, *(Looking down at her now)* how's it goin', kid?

ARLIE: Okay.

Arlie says nothing more, but unwraps the gum and chews it. Bennie leaves the cell area, motioning to the other guard as if to say, "See, that's how it's done." A loud siren goes by in the street below the apartment. Arlene bolts up out of bed, then turns back to it quickly, making it up in a frenzied, ritual manner. As she tucks the spread up under the pillow, the siren stops and so does she. For the first time, now, she realizes where she is and the inappropriateness of the habit she has just played out. A jackhammer noise gets louder. She walks over to the window and looks out. There is a wolf-whistle from a worker below. She shuts the window in a fury. She looks around the room as if trying to remember what she is doing there. She looks at her watch, now aware that it is late and that she has slept in her clothes.

ARLENE: People don't sleep in their clothes, Arlene. An people git up fore noon.

Arlene makes a still-disoriented attempt to pull herself together—changing shoes, combing her hair, washing her face—as prison life continues on the catwalk. The warden walks toward Arlie, stopping some distance from her but talking directly to her, as he checks files or papers.

WARDEN: Good afternoon, Arlie.

ARLIE: Fuck you. *(Warden walks away)* Wait! I wanna talk to you.

WARDEN: I'm listening.

ARLIE: When am I gittin' outta here?

WARDEN: That's up to you.

ARLIE: The hell it is.

WARDEN: When you can show that you can be with the other girls, you can get out.

ARLIE: How'm I supposed to prove that bein' in here?

WARDEN: And then you can have mail again and visitors.

ARLIE: You're just fuckin' with me. You ain't ever gonna let me out. I been in this ad-just-ment room four months, I think.

WARDEN: Arlie, you see the other girls in the dorm walking around, free to do whatever they want? If we felt the way you seem to think we do, everyone would be in lockup. When you get out of segregation, you can go to the records office and have your time explained to you.

ARLIE: It won't make no sense.

WARDEN: They'll go through it all very slowly . . . when you're eligible for parole, how many days of good time you have, how many industrial days you've earned, what constitutes meritorious good time . . . and how many days you're set back for your write-ups and all your time in segregation.

ARLIE: I don't even remember what I done to git this lockup.

WARDEN: Well, I do. And if you ever do it again, or anything like it again, you'll be right back in lockup where you will stay until you forget *how* to do it.

ARLIE: What was it?

WARDEN: You just remember what I said.

ARLENE: Now then . . . *(Sounds as if she has something in mind to do. Looks as though she doesn't)*

ARLIE: What was it?

WARDEN: Oh, and Arlie, the prison chaplain will be coming by to visit you today.

ARLIE: I don't want to see no chaplain!

WARDEN: Did I ask you if you wanted to see the chaplain? No, I did not. I said, the chaplain will be coming by to visit you today. *(To an unseen guard)* Mrs. Roberts, why hasn't this light bulb been replaced?

ARLIE *(Screaming)*: Get out of my hall!

The warden walks away. Arlene walks to the refrigerator and opens it. She picks out the carton of slaw Bennie put there last night. She walks away from the door, then turns around, remembering to close it. She looks at the slaw, as a guard comes up to Arlie's cell with a plate.

ARLENE: I ain't never eatin' no more scrambled eggs.

GUARD (CALDWELL): Chow time, cutie pie.

ARLIE: These eggs ain't scrambled, they's throwed up! And I want a fork!

Arlene realizes she has no fork, then fishes one out of the garbage sack from last night. She returns to the bed, takes a bite of slaw and gets her wallet out of her purse. She lays the bills out on the bed one at a time.

ARLENE: That's for coffee . . . and that's for milk and bread . . . an that's cookies . . . an cheese and crackers . . . and shampoo an soap . . . and bacon an livercheese. No, pickle loaf . . . an ketchup and some onions . . . an peanut butter an jelly . . . and shoe polish. Well, ain't no need gettin' everything all at once. Coffee, milk, ketchup, cookies, cheese, onions, jelly. Coffee, milk . . . oh, shampoo . . .

There is a banging on the door.

RUBY'S VOICE *(Yelling)*: Candy, I gotta have my five dollars back.

ARLENE *(Quickly stuffing her money back in her wallet)*: Candy ain't here!

RUBY'S VOICE: It's Ruby, upstairs. She's got five dollars I loaned her . . . Arlie? That Arlie? Candy told me her sister be . . .

Arlene opens the door hesitantly.

RUBY: It is Arlie, right?

ARLENE: It's Arlene. *(Does not extend her hand)*

RUBY: See, I got these shoes in layaway . . . *(Puts her hand back in her pocket)* she said you been . . . you just got . . . you seen my money?

ARLENE: No.

RUBY: I don't get 'em out today they go back on the shelf.

ARLENE *(Doesn't understand)*: They sell your shoes?

RUBY: Yeah. Welcome back.

ARLENE: Thank you.

RUBY: She coulda put it in my mailbox.

Ruby starts to leave. Arlene is closing the door when Ruby turns around.

RUBY: Uh . . . listen . . . if you need a phone, I got one most of the time.

ARLENE: I do have to make this call.

RUBY: Ain't got a book though . . . well, I got one but it's holdin' up my bed. *(Laughs)*

ARLENE: I got the number.

RUBY: Well, then . . .

ARLENE: Would you . . . wanna come in?

RUBY: You sure I'm not interruptin' anything?

ARLENE: I'm s'posed to call my parole officer.

RUBY: Good girl. Most of them can't talk but you call 'em anyway. *(Arlene does not laugh)* Candy go back to that creep?

ARLENE: I guess.

RUBY: I's afraid of that. *(Looking around)* Maybe an envelope with my name on it? Really cleaned out the place, didn't she?

ARLENE: Yeah. Took everything.

They laugh a little.

RUBY: Didn't have much. Didn't do nuthin' here 'cept . . . sleep.

ARLENE: Least the rent's paid till the end of the month. I'll be workin' by then.

RUBY: You ain't seen Candy in a while.

ARLENE: No. Think she was in the seventh grade when—

RUBY: She's growed up now, you know.

ARLENE: Yeah. I was thinkin' she might come by.

RUBY: Honey, she won't be comin' by. He keeps all his . . . *(Starting over)* his place is pretty far from here. But . . . *(Stops, trying to decide what to say)*

ARLENE: But what?

RUBY: But she had a lot of friends, you know. *They* might be comin' by.

ARLENE: Men, you mean.

RUBY: Yeah. *(Quietly, waiting for Arlene's reaction)*

ARLENE *(Realizing the truth)*: Mother said he was her boyfriend.

RUBY: I shouldn't have said nuthin'. I jus' didn't want you to be surprised if some john showed up, his tongue hangin' out an all. *(Sits down on the bed)*

ARLENE: It's okay. I shoulda known anyway. *(Now suddenly angry)* No, it ain't okay. Guys got their dirty fingernails all over her. Some pimp's out buyin' green pants while she . . . . Goddamn her.

RUBY: Hey now, that ain't your problem. *(Moves toward her, Arlene backs away)*

ARLIE *(Pointing)*: You stick your hand in here again Doris an I'll bite it off.

RUBY: She'll figure it out soon enough.

ARLIE *(Pointing to another person)*: An you, you ain't my mama, so you can cut the mama crap.

ARLENE: I wasn't gonna cuss no more.

RUBY: Nuthin' in the parole rules says you can't get pissed. My first day outta Gilbertsville I done the damn craziest . . . *(Arlene looks around, surprised to hear she has done time)* Oh yeah, a long time ago, but . . . hell, I heaved a whole gallon of milk right out the window my first day.

ARLENE *(Somewhat cheered)*: It hit anybody?

RUBY: It bounced! Made me feel a helluva lot better. I said, "Ruby, if a gallon of milk can bounce back, so kin you."

ARLENE: That's really what you thought?

RUBY: Well, not exactly. I had to keep sayin' it for 'bout a year fore I finally believed it. I's moppin' this lady's floor once an she come in an heard me sayin' "gallon a milk, gallon a milk," fired me. She did. Thought I was too crazy to mop her floors.

Ruby laughs, but is still bitter. Arlene wasn't listening. Ruby wants to change the subject now.

RUBY: Hey! You have a good trip? Candy said you was in Arkansas.

ARLENE: Alabama. It was okay. This guard, well he used to be a guard, he just quit. He ain't never seen Kentucky, so he drove me. *(Watching for Ruby's response)*

RUBY: Pine Ridge?

ARLENE: Yeah.

RUBY: It's coed now, ain't it?

ARLENE: Yeah. That's dumb, you know. They put you with men so's they can git you if you're seen with 'em.

RUBY: S'posed to be more natural, I guess.

ARLENE: I guess.

RUBY: Well, I say it sucks. Still a prison. No matter how many pictures they stick up on the walls or how many dirty movies they show, you still gotta be counted five times a day. *(Now beginning to worry about Arlene's silence)* You don't seem like Candy said.

ARLENE: She tell you I was a killer?

RUBY: More like the meanest bitch that ever walked. I seen lots worse than you.

ARLENE: I been lots worse.

RUBY: Got to you, didn't it?

Arlene doesn't respond, but Ruby knows she's right.

RUBY: Well, you jus' gotta git over it. Bein' out, you gotta—

ARLENE: Don't you start in on me.

RUBY *(Realizing her tone)*: Right, sorry.

ARLENE: It's okay.

RUBY: Ex-cons is the worst. I'm sorry.

ARLENE: It's okay.

RUBY: Done that about a year ago. New waitress we had. Gave my little goin'-straight speech, "No booze, no men, no buyin' on credit," shit like that, she quit that very night. Stole my fuckin' raincoat on her way out. Some speech, huh? *(Laughs, no longer resenting this theft)*

ARLENE: You a waitress?

RUBY: I am the Queen of Grease. Make the finest french fries you ever did see.

ARLENE: You make a lot of money?

RUBY: I sure know how to. But I ain't about to go back inside for doin' it. Cookin' out's better'n eatin' in, I say.

ARLENE: You think up all these things you say?

RUBY: Know what I hate? Makin' salads—cuttin' up all that stuff 'n floppin' it in a bowl. Some day . . . some day . . . I'm gonna hear "tossed salad" an I'm gonna do jus' that. Toss out a tomato, toss out a head a lettuce, toss out a big ol' carrot. *(Miming the throwing and enjoying herself immensely)*

ARLENE *(Laughing)*: Be funny seein' all that stuff flyin' outta the kitchen.

RUBY: Hey Arlene! *(Gives her a friendly pat)* You had your lunch yet?

ARLENE *(Pulling away immediately)*: I ain't hungry.

RUBY *(Carefully)*: I got raisin toast.

ARLENE: No. *(Goes over to the sink, twists knobs as if to stop a leak)*

ARLIE: Whaddaya mean, what did she do to me? You got eyes or is they broke? You only seein' what you feel like seein'. I git ready to protect myself from a bunch of weirdos an then you look.

ARLENE: Sink's stopped up. *(Begins to work on it)*

ARLIE: You ain't seein' when they's leavin' packs of cigarettes on my bed an then thinking I owe 'em or somethin'.

RUBY: Stopped up, huh? *(Squashing a bug on the floor)*

ARLIE: You ain't lookin' when them kitchen workers lets up their mommies in line nights they know they only baked half enough brownies.

RUBY: Let me try.

ARLIE: You ain't seein' all the letters comin' in an goin' out with visitors. I'll tell you somethin'. One of them workmen buries dope for Betty Rickey in little plastic bottles under them sticker bushes at the water tower. You see that? No, you only seein' me. Well, you don't see shit.

RUBY *(A quiet attempt)*: Gotta git you some Drano if you're gonna stay here.

ARLIE: I'll tell you what she done. Doris brung me some rollers from the beauty-school class. Three fuckin' pink rollers. Them plastic ones with the little holes. I didn't ask her. She jus' done it.

RUBY: Let me give her a try.

ARLENE: I can fix my own sink.

ARLIE: I's stupid. I's thinkin' maybe she were different from all them others. Then that night everbody disappears from the john and she's wantin' to brush my hair. Sure, brush my hair. How'd I know she was gonna crack her head open on the sink. I jus' barely even touched her.

RUBY *(Walking to the bed now, digging through her purse)*: Want a Chiclet?

ARLIE: You ain't asked what she was gonna do to me. Huh? When you gonna ask that? You don't give a shit about that 'cause Doris such a good girl.

ARLENE *(Giving up)*: Don't work.

RUBY: We got a dishwasher quittin' this week if you're interested.

ARLENE: I need somethin' that pays good.

RUBY: You type?

ARLENE: No.

RUBY: Do any clerk work?

ARLENE: No.

RUBY: Any keypunch?

ARLENE: No.

RUBY: Well, then I hate to tell you, but all us old-timers already got all the good cookin' and cleanin' jobs. *(Smashes another bug, goes to the cabinet to look for the bug spray)* She even took the can of Raid! Just as well, empty anyway. *(Arlene doesn't respond)* She hit the bugs with it. *(Still no response)* Now, there's that phone call you was talkin' about.

ARLENE: Yeah.

RUBY *(Walking toward the door)*: An I'll git you that number for the dishwashin' job, just in case. *(Arlene backs off)* How 'bout cards? You play any cards? Course you do. I get sick of beatin' myself all the time at solitaire. Damn borin' bein' so good at it.

ARLENE *(Goes for her purse)*: Maybe I'll jus' walk to the corner an make my call from there.

RUBY: It's always broke.

ARLENE: What?

RUBY: The phone . . . at the corner. Only it ain't at the corner. It's inside the A & P.

ARLENE: Maybe it'll be fixed.

RUBY: Look, I ain't gonna force you to play cards with me. It's time for my programs anyway.

ARLENE: I gotta git some pickle loaf an . . . things.

RUBY: Suit yourself. I'll be there if you change your mind.

ARLENE: I have some things I gotta do here first.

RUBY (*Trying to leave on a friendly basis*): Look, I'll charge you a dime if it'll make you feel better.

ARLENE (*Takes her seriously*): Okay.

RUBY (*Laughs, then realizes Arlene is serious*): Mine's the one with the little picture of Johnny Cash on the door.

Ruby leaves. Singing to the tune of "I'll Toe the Line," Bennie walks across the catwalk carrying a tray with cups and a pitcher of water. Arlene walks toward the closet. She is delaying going to the store, but is determined to go. She checks little things in the room, remembers to get a scarf, changes shoes, checks her wallet. Finally, as she is walking out, she stops and looks at the picture of Jesus, then moves closer, having noticed a dirty spot. She goes back into the bathroom for a tissue, wets it in her mouth, then dabs at the offending spot. She puts the tissue in her purse, then leaves the room when noted.

BENNIE: I keep my pants up with a piece of twine. I keep my eyes wide open all the time. Da da da da-da da da da da da. If you'll be mine, please pull the twine.

ARLIE: You can't sing for shit.

BENNIE (*Starts down the stairs toward Arlie's cell*): You know what elephants got between their toes?

ARLIE: I don't care.

BENNIE: Slow natives. (*Laughs*)

ARLIE: That ain't funny.

GUARD (EVANS) (*As Bennie opens Arlie's door*): Hey, Davis.

BENNIE: Conversation is rehabilitatin', Evans. Want some water?

ARLIE: Okay.

BENNIE: How about some Kool-Aid to go in it? (*Gives her a glass of water*)

ARLIE: When does the chaplain come?

BENNIE: Want some gum?

ARLIE: Is it today?

BENNIE: Kool-Aid's gone up, you know. Fifteen cents and tax. You get out, you'll learn all about that.

ARLIE: Does the chaplain come today?

BENNIE (*Going back up the catwalk*): Income tax, sales tax, property tax, gas and electric, water, rent—

ARLIE: Hey!

BENNIE: Yeah, he's comin', so don't mess up.

ARLIE: I ain't.

BENNIE: What's he tell you anyway, get you so starry-eyed?

ARLIE: He jus' talks to me.

BENNIE: I talk to you.

ARLIE: Where's Frankie Hill?

BENNIE: Gone.

ARLIE: Out?

BENNIE: Pretty soon.

ARLIE: When.

BENNIE: Miss her don't you? Ain't got nobody to bullshit with. Stories you gals tell . . . whoo-ee!

ARLIE: Get to cut that grass now, Frankie, honey.

BENNIE: Huh?

ARLIE: Stupidest thing she said. *(Gently)* Said first thing she was gonna do when she got out—

Arlene leaves the apartment.

BENNIE: Get laid.

ARLIE: Shut up. First thing was gonna be going to the garage. Said it always smelled like car grease an turpur . . . somethin'.

BENNIE: Turpentine.

ARLIE: Yeah, an gasoline, wet. An she'll bend down an squirt oil in the lawnmower, red can with a long pointy spout. Then cut the grass in the backyard, up an back, up an back. They got this grass catcher on it. Says she likes scoopin' up that cut grass an spreadin' it out under the trees. Says it makes her real hungry for some lunch. *(A quiet curiosity about all this)*

BENNIE: I got a power mower, myself.

ARLIE: They done somethin' to her. Took out her nerves or somethin'. She . . .

BENNIE: She jus' got better, that's all.

ARLIE: Hah. Know what else? They give her a fork to eat with last week. A fork. A fuckin' fork. Now how long's it been since I had a fork to eat with?

BENNIE *(Getting ready to leave the cell)*: Wish I could help you with that, honey.

ARLIE *(Loud)*: Don't call me honey.

BENNIE *(Locks the door behind him)*: That's my girl.

ARLIE: I ain't your girl.

BENNIE *(On his way back up the stairs)*: Screechin' wildcat.

ARLIE *(Very quiet)*: What time is it?

Arlene walks back into the apartment. She is out of breath and has some trouble getting the door open. She is carrying a big sack of groceries. As she sets the bag on the counter, it breaks open, spilling cans and packages all over the floor. She just stands and looks at the mess. She takes off her scarf and sets down her purse, still looking at the spilled groceries. Finally, she bends down and picks up the package of pickle loaf. She starts to put it on the counter, then turns suddenly and throws it at the door. She stares at it as it falls.

ARLENE: Bounce? *(In disgust)* Shit.

Arlene sinks to the floor. She tears open the package of pickle loaf and eats a piece of it. She is still angry, but is completely unable to do anything about her anger.

ARLIE: Who's out there? Is anybody out there? *(Reading)* Depart from evil and do good. *(Yelling)* Now, you pay attention out there 'cause this is right out of the Lord's mouth. *(Reading)* And dwell, that means live, dwell for-ever-more. *(Speaking)* That's like for longer than I've been in here or longer than . . . this Bible the chaplain give me's got my name right in the front of it. Hey! Somebody's s'posed to be out there watchin' me. Wanna hear some more? *(Reading)* For the Lord for . . . *(The word is forsaketh)* I can't read in here, you turn on my light, you hear me? Or let me out and I'll go read it in the TV room. Please let me out. I won't scream or nuthin'? I'll just go right to sleep, okay? Somebody! I'll go right to sleep. Okay? You won't even know I'm there. Hey! Goddammit, somebody let me out of here, I can't stand it in here anymore. Somebody! *(Her spirit finally broken)*

ARLENE *(She draws her knees up, wraps her arms around them and rests her head on her arms)*: Jus' gotta git a job an make some money an everything will be all right. You hear me, Arlene? You git yourself up an go find a job. *(Continues to sit)* An you kin start by cleanin' up this mess you made 'cause food don't belong on the floor.

Arlene still doesn't get up. Carl appears in the doorway of the apartment. When he sees Arlene on the floor, he goes into a fit of vicious, sadistic laughter.

CARL: What's happenin', mama? You havin' lunch with the bugs?
ARLENE *(Quietly)*: Fuck off.
CARL *(Threatening)*: What'd you say?
ARLENE *(Reconsidering)*: Go away.
CARL: You watch your mouth or I'll close it up for you.

Arlene stands up now. Carl goes to the window and looks out, as if checking for someone.

ARLENE: They after you, ain't they?

Carl sniffs, scratches at his arm. He finds a plastic bag near the bed, stuffed with brightly colored knitted things. He pulls out baby sweaters, booties and caps.

CARL: What the fuck is this?
ARLENE: You leave them be.
CARL: You got a baby hid here somewhere? I found its little shoes. *(Laughs, dangling them in front of him)*
ARLENE *(Chasing him)*: Them's mine.

CARL: Aw sugar, I ain't botherin' nuthin'. Just lookin'. *(Pulls more out of the sack, dropping one or two booties on the floor, kicking them away)*

ARLENE *(Picking up what he's dropped)*: I ain't tellin' you again. Give me them.

CARL *(Turns around quickly, walking away with a few of the sweaters)*: How much these go for?

ARLENE: I don't know yet.

CARL: I'll jus' take care of 'em for you—a few coin for the trip. You *are* gonna have to pay your share, you know.

ARLENE: You give me them. I ain't goin' with you. *(She walks toward him)*

CARL: You ain't?

Mocking, Arlene walks up close to him now, taking the bag in her hands. He knocks her away and onto the bed.

CARL: Straighten up, girlie. *(Now kneels over her)* You done forgot how to behave yourself. *(Moves as if to threaten her, but kisses her on the forehead, then moves out into the room)*

ARLENE *(Sitting up)*: I worked hard on them things. They's nice, too, for babies and little kids.

CARL: I bet you fooled them officers good, doin' this shit. *(Throws the bag in the sink)*

ARLENE: I weren't—

CARL: I kin see that scene. They sayin' . . . *(Puts on a high southern voice)* "I'd jus' love one a them nice yella sweaters."

ARLENE: They liked them.

CARL: Those turkeys, sure they did. Where else you gonna git your free sweaters an free washin' an free step-right-up-git-your-convict-special-shoe-shine. No, don't give me no money, officer. I's jus' doin' this 'cause I likes you.

ARLENE: They give 'em for Christmas presents.

CARL *(Checks the window again, then peers into the grocery sack)*: What you got sweet, mama? *(Pulls out a box of cookies and begins to eat them)*

ARLIE: I'm sweepin', Doris, 'cause it's like a pigpen in here. So you might like it, but I don't, so if you got some mops, I'll take one of them too.

ARLENE: You caught another habit, didn't you?

CARL: You turned into a narc or what?

ARLENE: You scratchin' an sniffin' like crazy.

CARL: I see a man eatin' cookies an that's what you see too.

ARLENE: An you was laughin' at me sittin' on the floor! You got cops lookin' for you an you ain't scored yet this morning. You better get yourself back to prison where you can git all you need.

CARL: Since when Carl couldn't find it if he really wanted it?

ARLENE: An I bought them cookies for me.

CARL: An I wouldn't come no closer if I's you.

ARLENE *(Stops, then walks to the door)*: Then take the cookies an git out.

CARL *(Imitating Bennie)*: Oh, please, Miss Arlene, come go with Carl to the big city. We'll jus' have us the best time.

ARLENE: I'm gonna stay here an git a job an save up money so's I kin git Joey. *(Opening the door)* Now, I ain't s'posed to see no ex-cons.

CARL *(Big laugh)*: You don't know nobody else. Huh, Arlie? Who you know ain't a con-vict?

ARLENE: I'll meet 'em.

CARL: And what if they don't wanna meet you? You ain't exactly a nice girl, you know. An you gotta be jivin' about that job shit. *(Throws the sack of cookies on the floor)*

ARLENE *(Retrieving the cookies)*: I kin work.

CARL: Doin' what?

ARLENE: I don't know. Cookin', cleanin', somethin' that pays good.

CARL: You got your choice, honey. You can do cookin' an cleanin' *or* you can do somethin' that pays good. You ain't gonna git rich working on your knees. You come with me an you'll have money. You stay here, you won't have shit.

ARLENE: Ruby works an she does okay.

CARL: You got any Kool-Aid? *(Looking in the cabinets, moving Arlene out of his way)* Ruby who?

ARLENE: Upstairs. She cooks. Works nights an has all day to do jus' what she wants.

CARL: And what, exactly, do she do? See flicks take rides in cabs to pick up see-through shoes?

ARLENE: She watches TV, plays cards, you know.

CARL: Yeah, I know. Sounds just like the day room in the fuckin' joint.

ARLENE: She likes it.

CARL *(Exasperated)*: All right. Say you stay here an *finally* find yourself some job. *(Grabs the picture of Jesus off the wall)* This your boyfriend?

ARLENE: The chaplain give it to me.

CARL: Say it's dishwashin', okay? *(Arlene doesn't answer)* Okay?

ARLENE: Okay. *(Takes the picture, hangs it back up)*

CARL: An you git maybe seventy-five a week. Seventy-five for standin' over a sink full of greasy gray water, fishin' out blobs of bread an lettuce. People puttin' pieces of chewed-up meat in their napkins and you gotta pick it out. Eight hours a day, six days a week, to make seventy-five lousy pictures of Big Daddy George. Now, how long it'll take you to make seventy-five workin' for me?

ARLENE: A night.

She sits on the bed, Carl pacing in front of her.

CARL: Less than a night. Two hours maybe. Now, it's the same fuckin' seventy-five bills. You can either work all week for it or make it in two hours. You work two hours a night for me an how much you got in a week? *(Arlene looks puzzled by the multiplication required. He sits down beside her, even more disgusted)* Two seventy-five's is a hundred and fifty. Three hundred-and-fifties is four hundred and fifty. You stay here you git seventy-five a week. You come with me an you git four hundred and fifty a week. Now, four hundred and fifty, Arlie, is *more* than seventy-five. You stay here you gotta work eight hours a day and your hands git wrinkled and your feet swell up. *(Suddenly distracted)* There was this guy at Bricktown had webby toes like a duck. *(Back now)* You come home with me you work two hours a night an you kin sleep all mornin' an spend the day buyin' eyelashes and tryin' out perfume. Come home, have some guy openin' the door for you sayin', "Good evenin', Miss Holsclaw, nice night now ain't it?" *(Puts his arm around her)*

ARLENE: It's Joey I'm thinkin' about.

CARL: If you was a kid, would you want your mom to git so dragged out washin' dishes she don't have no time for you an no money to spend on you? You come with me, you kin send him big orange bears an Sting-Ray bikes with his name wrote on the fenders. He'll like that. Holsclaw. *(Amused)* Kinda sounds like coleslaw, don't it? Joey be tellin' all his friends 'bout his mom livin' up in New York City an bein' so rich an sendin' him stuff all the time.

ARLENE: I want to be with him.

CARL *(Now stretches out on the bed, his head in her lap)*: So, fly him up to see you. Take him on that boat they got goes roun' the island. Take him up to the Empire State Building, let him play King Kong. *(Rubs her hair, unstudied tenderness)* He be talkin' 'bout that trip his whole life.

ARLENE *(Smoothing his hair)*: I don't want to go back to prison, Carl.

CARL *(Jumps up, moves toward the refrigerator)*: There any chocolate milk? *(Distracted again)* You know they got this motel down in Mexico named after me? Carlsbad Cabins. *(Proudly)* Who said anything about goin' back to prison? *(Slams the refrigerator door, really hostile)* What do you think I'm gonna be doin'? Keepin' you out, that's what!

ARLENE *(Stands up)*: Like last time? Like you gettin' drunk? Like you lookin' for kid junkies to beat up?

CARL: God, ain't it hot in this dump. You gonna come or not? You wanna wash dishes, I could give a shit. *(Yelling)* But you comin' with me, you say it right now, lady! *(Grabs her by the arm)* Huh?

There is a knock on the door.

RUBY'S VOICE: Arlene?

CARL *(Yelling)*: She ain't here!

RUBY'S VOICE *(Alarmed)*: Arlene! You all right?

ARLENE: That's Ruby I was tellin' you about.

CARL (*Catches Arlene's arm again, very rough*): We ain't through!

RUBY (*Opening the door*): Hey! (*Seeing the rough treatment*) Goin' to the store. (*Very firm*) Thought maybe you forgot somethin'.

CARL (*Turns Arlene loose*): You this cook I been hearin' about?

RUBY: I cook. So what?

CARL: Buys you nice shoes, don't it, cookin'? Why don't you hock your watch an have somethin' done to your hair? If you got a watch.

RUBY: Why don't you drop by the coffee shop. I'll spit in your eggs.

CARL: They let you bring home the half-eat chili dogs?

RUBY: You . . . you got half-eat chili dogs for brains. (*To Arlene*) I'll stop by later. (*Contemptuous look for Carl*)

ARLENE: No. Stay.

Carl gets the message. He goes over to the sink to get a drink of water out of the faucet, then looks down at his watch.

CARL: Piece a shit. (*Thumps it with his finger*) Shoulda took the dude's hat, Jack. Guy preachin' about the end of the world ain't gonna own a watch that works.

ARLENE (*Walks over to the sink, bends over Carl*): You don't need me. I'm gittin' too old for it, anyway.

CARL: I don't discuss my business with strangers in the room. (*Heads for the door*)

ARLENE: When you leavin'?

CARL: Six. You wanna come, meet me at this bar. (*Gives her a brightly colored matchbook*) I'm havin' my wheels delivered.

ARLENE: You stealin' a car?

CARL: Take a cab. (*Gives her a dollar*) You don't come . . . well, I already laid it out for you. I ain't never lied to you, have I girl?

ARLENE: No.

CARL: Then you be there. That's all the words I got. (*Makes an unconscious move toward her*) I don't beg nobody. (*Backs off*) Be there.

He turns abruptly and leaves. Arlene watches him go, folding up the money in the matchbook. The door remains open.

ARLIE (*Reading, or trying to, from a small Testament*): For the Lord forsaketh not his saints, but the seed of the wicked shall be cut off.

Ruby walks over to the counter, starts to pick up some of the groceries lying on the floor, then stops.

RUBY: I 'magine you'll want to be puttin' these up yourself. (*Arlene continues to stare out the door*) He do this?

ARLENE: No.

RUBY: Can't trust these sacks. I seen bag boys punchin' holes in 'em at the store.

ARLENE: Can't trust anybody. *(Finally turning around)*

RUBY: Well, you don't want to trust him, that's for sure.

ARLENE: We spent a lot of time together, me an Carl.

RUBY: He live here?

ARLENE: No, he jus' broke outta Bricktown near where I was. I got word there sayin' he'd meet me. I didn't believe it then, but he don't lie, Carl don't.

RUBY: You thinkin' of goin' with him?

ARLENE: They'll catch him. I told him but he don't listen.

RUBY: Funny ain't it, the number a men come without ears.

ARLENE: How much that dishwashin' job pay?

RUBY: I don't know. Maybe seventy-five.

ARLENE: That's what he said.

RUBY: He tell you you was gonna wear out your hands and knees grubbin' for nuthin', git old an be broke an never have a nice dress to wear? *(Sitting down)*

ARLENE: Yeah.

RUBY: He tell you nobody's gonna wanna be with you 'cause you done time?

ARLENE: Yeah.

RUBY: He tell you your kid gonna be ashamed of you an nobody's gonna believe you if you tell 'em you changed?

ARLENE: Yeah.

RUBY: Then he was right. *(Pauses)* But when you make your two nickels, you can keep both of 'em.

ARLENE *(Shattered by these words)*: Well, I can't do that.

RUBY: Can't do what?

ARLENE: Live like that. Be like bein' dead.

RUBY: You kin always call in sick . . . stay home, send out for pizza an watch your Johnny Carson on TV . . . or git a bus way out Preston Street an go bowlin'.

ARLENE *(Anger building)*: What am I gonna do? I can't git no work that will pay good 'cause I can't do nuthin'. It'll be years fore I have a nice rug for this place. I'll never even have some ol' Ford to drive around, I'll never take Joey to no fair. I won't be invited home for pot roast and I'll have to wear this fuckin' dress for the rest of my life. What kind of life is that?

RUBY: It's outside.

ARLENE: Outside? Honey I'll either be *inside* this apartment or *inside* some kitchen sweatin' over the sink. Outside's where you get to do what you want, not where you gotta do some shit job jus' so's you can eat worse than you did in prison. That ain't why I quit bein' so hateful, so I could come back and rot in some slum.

RUBY *(Word "slum" hits hard)*: Well, you can wash dishes to pay the rent on your "slum," or you can spread your legs for any shit that's got the ten dollars.

ARLENE *(Not hostile)*: I don't need you agitatin' me.

RUBY: An I don't live in no slum.

ARLENE *(Sensing Ruby's hurt)*: Well, I'm sorry . . . it's just . . . I thought . . . *(Increasingly upset)*

RUBY *(Finishing her sentence)*: . . . it was gonna be different. Well, it ain't. And the sooner you believe it, the better off you'll be.

A guard enters Arlie's cell.

ARLIE: Where's the chaplain? I got somethin' to tell him.

ARLENE: They said I's . . .

GUARD (CALDWELL): He ain't comin'.

ARLENE: . . . he tol' me if . . . I thought once Arlie . . .

ARLIE: It's Tuesday. He comes to see me on Tuesday.

GUARD (CALDWELL): Chaplain's been transferred, dollie. Gone. Bye-bye. You know.

ARLENE: He said the meek, meek, them that's quiet and good . . . the meek . . . as soon as Arlie . . .

RUBY: What, Arlene? Who said what?

ARLIE: He's not comin' back?

ARLENE: At Pine Ridge there was . . .

ARLIE: He woulda told me if he couldn't come back.

ARLENE: I was . . .

GUARD (CALDWELL): He left this for you.

ARLENE: I was . . .

GUARD (CALDWELL): Picture of Jesus, looks like.

ARLENE: . . . this chaplain . . .

RUBY *(Trying to call her back from this hysteria)*: Arlene . . .

ARLIE *(Hysterical)*: I need to talk to him.

ARLENE: This chaplain . . .

ARLIE: You tell him to come back and see me.

ARLENE: I was in lockup . . .

ARLIE *(A final, anguished plea)*: I want the chaplain!

ARLENE: I don't know . . . years . . .

RUBY: And . . .

ARLENE: This chaplain said I had . . . said Arlie was my hateful self and she was hurtin' me and God would find some way to take her away . . . and it was God's will so I could be the meek . . . the meek, them that's quiet and good an git whatever they want . . . I forgit that word . . . they git the earth.

RUBY: Inherit.

ARLENE: Yeah. And that's why I done it.

RUBY: Done what?

ARLENE: What I done. 'Cause the chaplain he said . . . I'd sit up nights waitin' for him to come talk to me.

RUBY: Arlene, what did you do? What are you talkin' about?

ARLENE: They tol' me . . . after I's out an it was all over . . . they said after the chaplain got transferred . . . I didn't know why he didn't come no more till after . . . they said it was three whole nights at first, me screamin' to God to come git Arlie an kill her. They give me this medicine an thought I's better . . . then that night it happened, the officer was in the dorm doin' count . . . an they didn't hear nuthin' but they come back out where I was an I'm standin' there tellin' 'em to come see, real quiet I'm tellin' 'em, but there's all this blood all over my shirt an I got this fork I'm holdin' real tight in my hand . . . *(Clenches one hand now, the other hand fumbling with the front of her dress as if she's going to show Ruby)* this fork, they said Doris stole it from the kitchen an give it to me so I'd kill myself and shut up botherin' her . . . an there's all these holes all over me where I been stabbin' myself an I'm sayin' Arlie is dead for what she done to me, Arlie is dead an it's God's will . . . I didn't scream it, I was jus' sayin' it over and over . . . Arlie is dead, Arlie is dead . . . they couldn't git that fork outta my hand till . . . I woke up in the infirmary an they said I almost died. They said they's glad I didn't. *(Smiling)* They said did I feel better now an they was real nice, bringing me chocolate puddin' . . .

RUBY: I'm sorry, Arlene.

Ruby reaches out for her, but Arlene pulls away sharply.

ARLENE: I'd be eatin' or jus' lookin' at the ceiling an git a tear in my eye, but it'd jus' dry up, you know, it didn't run out or nuthin'. An then pretty soon, I's well, an officers was sayin' they's seein' such a change in me an givin' me yarn to knit sweaters an how'd I like to have a new skirt to wear an sometimes lettin' me chew gum. They said things ain't never been as clean as when I's doin' the housekeepin' at the dorm. *(So proud)* An then I got in the honor cottage an nobody was foolin' with me no more or nuthin'. An I didn't git mad like before or nuthin'. I jus' done my work an knit . . . an I don't think about it, what happened, 'cept . . . *(Now losing control)* people here keep callin' me Arlie an . . . *(Has trouble saying "Arlie")* I didn't mean to do it, what I done . . .

RUBY: Oh, honey . . .

ARLENE: I did . . . *(This is very difficult)* I mean, Arlie was a pretty mean kid, but I did . . . *(Very quickly)* I didn't know what I . . .

Arlene breaks down completely, screaming, crying, falling over into Ruby's lap.

ARLENE *(Grieving for this lost self)*: Arlie!

Ruby rubs her back, her hair, waiting for the calm she knows will come.

RUBY *(Finally, but very quietly)*: You can still . . . *(Stops to think of how to say it)* . . . you can still love people that's gone.

Ruby continues to hold her tenderly, rocking as with a baby. A terrible crash is heard on the steps outside the apartment.

BENNIE'S VOICE: Well, chicken-pluckin', hog-kickin' shit!

RUBY: Don't you move now, it's just somebody out in the hall.

ARLENE: That's—

RUBY: It's okay Arlene. Everything's gonna be just fine. Nice and quiet now.

ARLENE: That's Bennie that guard I told you about.

RUBY: I'll get it. You stay still now. *(She walks to the door and looks out into the hall, hands on hips)* Why you dumpin' them flowers on the stairs like that? Won't git no sun at all! *(Turns back to Arlene)* Arlene, there's a man plantin' a garden out in the hall. You think we should call the police or get him a waterin' can?

Bennie appears in the doorway, carrying a box of dead-looking plants.

BENNIE: I didn't try to fall, you know.

RUBY *(Blocking the door)*: Well, when you git ready to *try*, I wanna watch!

ARLENE: I thought you's gone.

RUBY *(To Bennie)*: You got a visitin' pass?

BENNIE *(Coming into the room)*: Arlie . . . *(Quickly)* Arlene. I brung you some plants. You know, plants for your window. Like we talked about, so's you don't see them bars.

RUBY *(Picking up one of the plants)*: They sure is scraggly-lookin' things. Next time, git plastic.

BENNIE: I'm sorry I dropped 'em, Arlene. We kin get 'em back together an they'll do real good. *(Setting them down on the trunk)* These ones don't take the sun. I asked just to make sure. Arlene?

RUBY: You up for seein' this petunia killer?

ARLENE: It's okay. Bennie, this is Ruby, upstairs.

BENNIE *(Bringing one flower over to show Arlene, stuffing it back into its pot)*: See? It ain't dead.

RUBY: Poor little plant. It comes from a broken home.

BENNIE *(Walks over to the window, getting the box and holding it up)*: That's gonna look real pretty. Cheerful-like.

RUBY: Arlene ain't gettin' the picture yet. *(Walking to the window and holding her plant up too, posing)* Now.

Arlene looks, but is not amused.

BENNIE *(Putting the plants back down)*: I jus' thought, after what I done last night . . . I jus' wanted to do somethin' nice.

ARLENE *(Calmer now)*: They is nice. Thanks.

RUBY: Arlene says you're a guard.

BENNIE: I was. I quit. Retired.

ARLENE: Bennie's goin' back to Alabama.

BENNIE: Well, I ain't leavin' right away. There's this guy at the motel says the bass is hittin' pretty good right now. Thought I might fish some first.

ARLENE: Then he's goin' back.

BENNIE *(To Ruby as he washes his hands)*: I'm real fond of this little girl. I ain't goin' till I'm sure she's gonna do okay. Thought I might help some.

RUBY: Arlene's had about all the help she can stand.

BENNIE: I got a car, Arlene. An money. An . . . *(Reaching into his pocket)* I brung you some gum.

ARLENE: That's real nice, too. An I 'preciate what you done, bringin' me here an all, but . . .

BENNIE: Well, look. Least you can take my number at the motel an give me a ring if you need somethin'. *(Holds out a piece of paper)* Here, I wrote it down for you. *(Arlene takes the paper)* Oh, an somethin' else, these towel things . . . *(Reaching into his pocket, pulling out a package of towelettes)* they was in the chicken last night. I thought I might be needin' 'em, but they give us new towels every day at that motel.

ARLENE: Okay then. I got your number.

BENNIE *(Backing up toward the door)*: Right. Right. Any ol' thing, now. Jus' any ol' thing. You even run outta gum an you call.

RUBY: Careful goin' down.

ARLENE: Bye Bennie.

BENNIE: Right. The number now. Don't lose it. You know, in case you need somethin'.

ARLENE: No.

Bennie leaves, Arlene gets up and picks up the matchbook Carl gave her and holds it with Bennie's piece of paper. Ruby watches a moment, sees Arlene trying to make this decision, knows that what she says now is very important.

RUBY: We had this waitress put her phone number in matchbooks, give 'em to guys left her nice tips. Anyway, one night this little ol' guy calls her and comes over and says he works at this museum an he don't have any money but he's got this hat belonged to Queen Victoria. An she felt real sorry for him so she screwed him for this little ol' lacy hat. Then she takes the hat back the next day to the museum thinkin' she'll git a reward or somethin' an you know what they done? *(Pause)* Give her a free membership. Tellin' her thanks so much an we're so grateful an wouldn't she like to see this mummy they got downstairs . . . an all the time jus' stallin' . . . waiting 'cause they called the police.

ARLENE: You do any time for that?

RUBY *(Admitting the story was about her)*: County jail.

ARLENE *(Quietly, looking at the matchbook)*: County jail. *(She tears up the matchbook and drops it in the sack of trash)* You got any Old Maids?

RUBY: Huh?

ARLENE: You know.

RUBY *(Surprised and pleased)*: Cards?

ARLENE *(Laughs a little)*: It's the only one I know.

RUBY: Old Maid, huh? *(Not her favorite game)*

ARLENE: I gotta put my food up first.

RUBY: 'Bout an hour?

ARLENE: I'll come up.

RUBY: Great. *(Stops by the plants on her way to the door, smiles)* These plants is real ugly.

Ruby exits. Arlene watches her, then turns back to the groceries still on the floor. Slowly, but with great determination, she picks up the items one at a time and puts them away in the cabinet above the counter. Arlie appears on the catwalk. There is one light on each of them.

ARLIE: Hey! You 'member that time we was playin' policeman an June locked me up in Mama's closet an then took off swimmin'? An I stood around with them dresses itchin' my ears an crashin' into that door tryin' to git outta there? It was dark in there. So, finally, *(Very proud)* I went around an peed in all Mama's shoes. But then she come home an tried to git in the closet only June taken the key so she said, "Who's in there?" an I said, "It's me!" and she said, "What you doin' in there?" an I started gigglin' an she started pullin' on the door an yellin', "Arlie, what you doin' in there?" *(Big laugh)*

Arlene has begun to smile during the story. Now they speak together, both standing as Mama did, one hand on her hip.

ARLIE AND ARLENE: Arlie, what you doin' in there?

ARLENE *(Still smiling and remembering, stage dark except for one light on her face)*: Aw shoot.

Light dims on Arlene's fond smile as Arlie laughs once more.

End of Play

THIRD
AND OAK

breakable. Clean it up, that's all. You've been up this late before. Nothing the matter with you, just nerves . . . and gravity.

Alberta bends down and begins to put the things back in her purse. She cannot see as Deedee backs in the door of the laundromat. Deedee is a wreck. She carries her clothes tied up in a man's shirt. She trips over a wastebasket and falls on her laundry as it spills out of the shirt.

DEEDEE: Well, poo-rats!

Alberta stands up, startled, hesitates, then walks over to where Deedee is still sprawled on the floor.

ALBERTA: Are you all right? *(She is angry that Deedee is there at all, but polite nevertheless)*

DEEDEE *(Grudgingly)*: Cute, huh?

ALBERTA *(Moving the wastebasket out of the way)*: Probably a wet spot on the floor. *(Goes back to her wash)*

DEEDEE: I already picked these clothes off the floor once tonight. *(No response from Alberta)* We been in our apartment two years and Joe still ain't found the closets. He thinks hangers are for when you lock your keys in your car. *(Still no response, though she is expecting one)* I mean, he's got this coat made of sheep's fur or somethin' and my mom came over one day and asked where did we get that fuzzy little rug. *(She is increasingly nervous)* Joe works at the Ford plant. I asked him why they call it that. I said, "How often do you have to water a Ford plant?" It was just a little joke, but he didn't think it was very funny.

ALBERTA *(Her good manners requiring her to say something)*: They probably do have a sprinkler system.

DEEDEE: Shoulda saved my breath and just tripped over the coffee table. He'd laughed at that. *(No response)* Well, *(Brightly)* I guess it's just you and me.

ALBERTA: Yes. *(Makes a move to get back to her wash)*

DEEDEE: Guess not too many people suds their duds in the middle of the night.

ALBERTA: Suds their duds?

DEEDEE: I do mine at Mom's. *(She begins to put her clothes in two washers, imitating Alberta)* I mean, I take our stuff over to Mom's. She got matching Maytags. She buys giant-size Cheer and we sit around and watch the soaps till the clothes come out. Suds the duds, that's what she says. Well, more than that. She wrote it on a little card and sent it in to Cheer so they could use it on their TV ads.

ALBERTA *(Pleasantly)*: Gives you a chance to talk, I guess. Visit.

DEEDEE: She says, "Just leave 'em, I'll do 'em," but that wouldn't be right, so I stay. Course she don't ever say how she likes seeing me, but she holds back, you know. I mean, there's stuff you don't have to say when it's family.

ALBERTA: Is she out of town tonight?

DEEDEE: No, probably just asleep. *(Alberta nods. She reads from the top of the washer)* Five cycle Turbomatic Deluxe. *(Punching buttons)* Hot wash-warm rinse, warm wash-warm rinse, warm wash-cold rinse, cold wash-cold rinse, cold wash, delicate cycle. *(Now lifts the lid of the washer)* What's this? Add laundry aids.

ALBERTA: Your mother does your laundry.

DEEDEE: You don't have a washer either, huh?

ALBERTA *(Too quickly)*: It's broken.

DEEDEE: Get your husband to fix it. *(Looking at Alberta's mound of shirts)* Got a heap of shirts, don't he?

ALBERTA: It can't be fixed.

DEEDEE: Where are *your* clothes?

ALBERTA: Mine are mostly hand wash.

DEEDEE: We just dump all our stuff in together.

ALBERTA: That's nice.

DEEDEE: Joe can fix just about anything. He's real good with his hands. *(Relaxing some now)* I've been saying that since high school. *(Laughs)* He makes trucks. God, I'd hate to see the truck I'd put together. *(Now a nervous laugh)* He had to work the double shift tonight. *(Going on quickly)* They do all kinds out there. Pickups, dump trucks . . . they got this joke, him and his buddies, about what rhymes with pickle truck, but I don't know the end of it, you know, the punch line. Goes like . . . "I'll come to get you baby in a pickle truck, I'll tell you what I'm wantin' is a—*(Stops, but continues the beat with her foot or by snapping her fingers)* See, that's the part I don't know. The end. *(Shrugs)*

ALBERTA: Overtime pays well, I imagine.

DEEDEE: It's all-the-time, here lately. He says people are buyin' more trucks 'cause farmers have to raise more cows 'cause we got a population explosion going on. Really crummy, you know? People I don't even know having babies means Joe can't come home at the right time. Don't seem fair.

ALBERTA: Or true.

DEEDEE: Huh?

ALBERTA: The population explosion is over. The birthrate is very stable now.

DEEDEE: Oh.

ALBERTA: Still, it's no fun to be in the house by yourself.

DEEDEE: See, we live right over there, on top of the Mexican restaurant. *(Going over to the window)* That window with the blue light in it, that's ours. It's a bunch of blueberries on a stalk, only it's a light. Joe gave it to me. He thinks blue is my favorite color.

ALBERTA: So the restaurant noise was bothering you.

DEEDEE: They got this bar that stays open till four. That's how Joe picked the apartment. He hates to run out for beer late. He don't mind running down. *(Broadly)* Old Mexico Taco Tavern. Except Joe says it's supposed to be Olé Mexico, like what they say in bullfights.

ALBERTA: Bullfights are disgusting.

DEEDEE: You've seen a real bullfight?

ALBERTA: We used to travel quite a bit.

DEEDEE *(Excited, curious, demanding)*: Well, tell me about it.

ALBERTA: There's not much to tell. The bull comes out and they kill it.

DEEDEE: What for? *(Putting her clothes in the washer)*

ALBERTA *(Pleased at the question)*: Fun. Doesn't that sound like *fun* to you?

DEEDEE *(Encouraged)*: Your husband works nights too?

ALBERTA: Herb is out of town. Did you mean to put that in there?

DEEDEE *(Peering into her washer)*: Huh?

ALBERTA: Your whites will come out green.

DEEDEE *(Retrieving the shirt)*: Joe wouldn't like that. No sir. Be like when Mom's washer chewed this hole in his bowling shirt. Whoo-ee! Was he hot. Kicked the chest of drawers, broke his toe. *(No response from Alberta)* And the chest of drawers too. *(No response)* Is Herb picky like that?

ALBERTA: Herb likes to look nice. *(Reaches for her soap)*

DEEDEE: Hey! You forgot one. *(Picking the remaining shirt out of Alberta's basket)* See? *(Opens it out, showing an awful stain)* Yuck! Looks like vomit.

ALBERTA: It's my cabbage soup.

DEEDEE: Well, *(Helping)* in it goes. *(Opening one of Alberta's washers)*

ALBERTA: No!

DEEDEE: The other one? *(Reaching for the other washer)*

ALBERTA *(Taking the shirt away from her)*: I don't want to . . . it's too . . . that stain will never . . . *(Enforcing a calm now)* It needs to presoak. I forgot the Woolite.

DEEDEE: Sorry.

ALBERTA: That's quite all right. *(Folding the shirt carefully, putting it back in the basket. Wants Deedee to vanish)*

DEEDEE: One of those machines give soap?

Alberta points to the correct one and Deedee walks over to it.

DEEDEE: It takes nickels. I only got quarters.

ALBERTA: The attendant will give you change. *(Pointing to the open attendant door, putting her own coins in her washers)*

DEEDEE *(Looking in the door)*: He's asleep.

ALBERTA: Ah.

DEEDEE: Be terrible to wake him up just for some old nickels. Do you have any change?

ALBERTA: No.

DEEDEE: Looks like he's got a pocket full of money. Think it would wake him up if I stuck my hand in there? *(Enjoys this idea)*

ALBERTA *(Feeling bad about not helping and also not wanting the attendant awake)*: Twenty years ago, maybe. *(Deedee laughs)* Here, I found some.

Deedee walks back, gives Alberta the quarters; she counts out the change.

ALBERTA: That's ten, twenty, thirty, forty, fifty.

DEEDEE *(Putting the nickels in the soap machine)*: He shouldn't be sleeping like that. Somebody could come in here and rob him. You don't think he's dead or anything, do you? I mean, I probably wouldn't know it if I saw somebody dead.

ALBERTA: You'd know. *(Starts her washers)*

DEEDEE *(Pushing in the coin trays, starting her washers)*: Okay. Cheer up! *(Laughs)* That's what Mom always says, "Cheer up." *(Looks at Alberta)* Hey, my name is Deedee. Deedee Johnson.

ALBERTA: Nice to meet you.

DEEDEE: What's yours?

ALBERTA: Alberta.

DEEDEE: Alberta what?

ALBERTA *(Reluctantly)*: Alberta Johnson.

DEEDEE: Hey! We might be related. I mean, Herb and Joe could be cousins or something.

ALBERTA: I don't think so.

DEEDEE: Yeah. I guess there's lots of Johnsons.

ALBERTA *(Looking down at the magazine)*: Yes.

DEEDEE: I'm botherin' you, aren't I? *(Alberta smiles)* I'd talk to somebody else, but there ain't nobody else. 'Cept Sleepy back there. I talk in *my* sleep sometimes, but him, he looks like he's lucky to be breathin' in his. *(Awkward)* Sleep, I mean.

ALBERTA: Would you like a magazine?

DEEDEE: No thanks. I brought a Dr. Pepper. *(Alberta is amazed)* You can have it if you want.

ALBERTA: No thank you.

DEEDEE: Sleepy was one of the seven dwarfs. I can still name them all. I couldn't tell you seven presidents of the United States, but I can say the dwarfs. *(Very proud)* Sleepy, Grumpy, Sneezy, Dopey, Doc and Bashful. *(Suddenly very low)* That's only six. Who's the other one?

ALBERTA *(Willing to help)*: You could name seven presidents.

DEEDEE: Oh no.

ALBERTA: Try it.

DEEDEE: Okay. *(Takes a big breath)* There's Carter, Nixon, Kennedy, Lincoln, Ben Franklin, George Washington . . . uh . . .

ALBERTA: Eleanor Roosevelt's husband.

DEEDEE: Mr. Roosevelt.

ALBERTA: Mr. Roosevelt. That's seven. Except Benjamin Franklin was never president.

DEEDEE: You're a teacher or something, aren't you?

ALBERTA: I was. Say Mr. Roosevelt again.

DEEDEE: Mr. Roosevelt.

ALBERTA: There. Teddy makes seven.

DEEDEE: Around here? *(Alberta looks puzzled)* Or in the county schools?

ALBERTA: Ohio. Columbus.

DEEDEE: Great!

ALBERTA: Do you know Columbus?

DEEDEE: Not personally.

ALBERTA: Ah.

DEEDEE: I better be careful. No ain'ts or nuthin'.

ALBERTA: You can't say anything I haven't heard before.

DEEDEE: Want me to try?

ALBERTA: No.

DEEDEE: What does Herb do?

ALBERTA *(Too quickly)*: Is Deedee short for something? Deirdre, Deborah?

DEEDEE: No. Just Deedee. The guys in high school always kidded me about my name. *(Affecting a boy's voice)* Hey, Deedee, is Deedee your name or your bra size?

ALBERTA: That wasn't very nice of them.

DEEDEE: That ain't the worst. Wanna hear the worst? *(Alberta doesn't respond)* Ricky Baker, Icky Ricky Baker and David Duvall said this one. They'd come up to the locker bank, David's locker was right next to mine and Ricky'd say, "Hey, did you have a good time last night?" And David would say, "Yes. In Deedee." Then they'd slap each other and laugh like idiots.

ALBERTA: You could've had your locker moved.

DEEDEE: I guess, but see, the basketball players always came down that hall at the end of school. Going to practice, you know.

ALBERTA: One of the basketball players I taught . . . *(Begins to chuckle)*

DEEDEE *(Anxious to laugh with her)*: Yeah?

ALBERTA: . . . thought Herbert Hoover invented the vacuum cleaner.

Alberta waits for Deedee to laugh. When she doesn't, Alberta steps back a few steps. Deedee is embarrassed.

DEEDEE: Why did you quit . . . teaching.

ALBERTA: Age.

DEEDEE: You don't look old enough to retire.

ALBERTA: Not my age. Theirs.

DEEDEE: Mine, you mean.

ALBERTA: Actually, Mother was very sick then.

DEEDEE: Is she still alive?

ALBERTA: No.

DEEDEE: I'm sorry.

ALBERTA: It was a blessing, really. There was quite a lot of pain at the end.

DEEDEE: For her maybe, but what about you?

ALBERTA: She was the one with the pain.

DEEDEE: Sounds like she was lucky to have you there, nursing her and all.

ALBERTA: I read her *Wuthering Heights* five times that year. I kept checking different ones out of the library, you know, *Little Women, Pride and Prejudice,* but each time she'd say, "No, I think I'd like to hear *Wuthering Heights.*" Just like she hadn't heard it in fifty years. But each time, I'd read the last page and look up, and she'd say the same thing.

DEEDEE: What thing?

ALBERTA: She'd say, "I still don't see it. They didn't have to have all that trouble. All they had to do was find Heathcliff someplace to go every day. The man just needed a job. *(Pause)* But maybe I missed something. Read it again."

DEEDEE: My mom thinks Joe's a bum. *(Somehow she thinks this is an appropriate response, and Alberta is jolted back to the present)* No really, she kept paying this guy that worked at Walgreen's to come over and strip our wallpaper. She said, "Deedee, he's gonna be manager of that drugstore someday." Hell, the only reason he worked there was getting a discount on his pimple cream. She thought that would get me off Joe. No way. We've been married two years last month. Mom says this is the itch year.

ALBERTA: The itch year?

DEEDEE: When guys get the itch, you know, to fool around with other women. Stayin' out late, comin' in with stories about goin' drinkin' with the boys or workin' overtime or . . . somethin'. Is that clock right?

ALBERTA: I think so.

DEEDEE: Bet Herb never did that, huh?

ALBERTA: Be unfaithful, you mean? *(Deedee nods)* No.

DEEDEE: How can you be so sure like that? You keep him in the refrigerator?

ALBERTA: Well, I suppose he could have . . . *(Doesn't believe this for a minute)*

DEEDEE: Like right now, while he's up in wherever he is . . ..

ALBERTA: Akron. *(Surprised at her need to say this)*

DEEDEE: Akron, he could be sittin' at the bar in some all-night bowling alley polishin' some big blonde's ball.

ALBERTA: No.

DEEDEE: That's real nice to trust him like that.

ALBERTA: Aren't you afraid Joe will call you on his break and be worried about where you are?

DEEDEE: You got any kids?

ALBERTA: No.

DEEDEE: Didn't you want some?

ALBERTA: Oh yes.

DEEDEE: Me too. Lots of 'em. But Joe says he's not ready. Wants to be earning lots of money before we start our family.

ALBERTA: That's why he works this double shift.

DEEDEE: Yeah. Only now he's fixin' up this '64 Chevy he bought to drag race. Then when the race money starts comin' in, we can have them kids. He's really lookin' forward to that—winnin' a big race and havin' me and the kids run out on the track and him smilin' and grabbin' up the baby and pourin' beer all over us while the crowd is yellin' and screamin' . . .

ALBERTA: So all his money goes into this car.

DEEDEE: Hey. I love it too. Sundays we go to the garage and work on it. *(Gets a picture out of her wallet)* That devil painted there on the door, that cost two hundred dollars!

ALBERTA: You help him?

DEEDEE: He says it's a real big help just havin' me there watchin'.

ALBERTA: I never understood that, men wanting you to watch them do whatever it is . . . I mean . . . . Well *(Deciding to tell this story, a surprise both to her and to us)* every year at Thanksgiving, Herb would watch over me, washing the turkey, making the stuffing, stuffing the turkey. Made me nervous.

DEEDEE: You coulda told him to get lost. *(Offers fabric softener)* Downy?

Alberta nods yes, accepting Deedee's help, but is still nervous about it.

ALBERTA: Actually, the last ten years or so, I sent him out for sage. For the dressing. He'd come in and sit down saying "Mmm boy was this ever going to be the best turkey yet" and rubbing his hands together and I'd push jars around in the cabinet and look all worried and say "Herb, I don't think I have enough sage." And he'd say, "Well, Bertie, my girl, I'll just go to the store and get some."

DEEDEE *(Jittery when someone else is talking)*: I saw white pepper at the store last week. How do they do that?

ALBERTA: I don't know.

DEEDEE: Is Dr. Pepper made out of pepper?

ALBERTA: I don't know.

DEEDEE: And what did Herb do, that you had to watch, I mean.

ALBERTA: He gardened. I didn't have to watch him plant the seeds or weed the plants or spray for pests or pick okra. But when the day came to turn over the soil, that was the day. Herb would rent a rototiller and bring out a lawn chair from the garage. He'd wipe it off and call in the kitchen window, "Alberta, it's so pleasant out here in the sunshine." And when he finished, he'd bring out this little wooden sign and drive it into the ground.

DEEDEE: What'd it say?

ALBERTA: Herb Garden. *(Pauses)* He thought that was funny.

DEEDEE: Did you laugh?

ALBERTA: Every year.

DEEDEE: He's not doing one anymore? *(Walking to the window)*

ALBERTA: No.

DEEDEE *(Looks uneasy, still staring out the window)*: Why not?

ALBERTA: What's out there?

DEEDEE: Oh nothing.

ALBERTA: You looked like—

DEEDEE: Joe should be home soon. I turned out all the lights except the blueberries so I could tell if he comes in, you know, when he turns the lights on.

ALBERTA: When is the shift over?

DEEDEE *(Enforced cheer now)*: Oh, not for a long time yet. I just thought . . . . He might get through early, he said. And we could go have a beer. Course, he might stop off and bowl a few games first.

Alberta gets up to check on her wash. Deedee walks to the bulletin board.

DEEDEE *(Reading)*: "Typing done, hourly or by the page. Cheer." What on earth?

ALBERTA: Must be cheap. *(Laughs a little)* It better be cheap.

DEEDEE *(Taking some notices down)*: Most of this stuff is over already. Hey! Here's one for Herb. "Gardening tools, never used. Rake, hoe, spade and towel."

ALBERTA: Trowel.

DEEDEE *(Aggravated by the correction)*: You got great eyes, Alberta. *(Continues reading)* "459–4734. A. Johnson." You think this A. Johnson is related to us? *(Laughs)* No, that's right, you said Herb wasn't doing a garden anymore. No, I got it! This A. Johnson is you. And the reason Herb ain't doin' a garden is you're selling his rakes. But this says "never used." Alberta, you shouldn't try to fool people like that. Washin' up Herb's hoe and selling it like it was new. Bad girl.

ALBERTA: Actually, that is me. I bought Herb some new tools for his birthday and then he . . . gave it up . . . gardening.

DEEDEE: Before his birthday?

ALBERTA: What?

DEEDEE: Did you have time to go buy him another present?

ALBERTA: Yes . . . well, no. I mean, he told me before his birthday, but I didn't get a chance to get him anything else.

DEEDEE: He's probably got everything anyhow.

ALBERTA: Just about.

DEEDEE: Didn't he get his feelings hurt?

ALBERTA: No.

DEEDEE: Joe never likes the stuff I give him.

ALBERTA: Oh, I'm sure he does. He just doesn't know how to tell you.

DEEDEE: No. He doesn't. For our anniversary, I planned real far ahead for this one, I'm tellin' you. I sent off my picture, not a whole body picture, just my face real close up, to this place in Massachusetts, and they painted, well I don't know if they really painted, but somehow or other they *put* my face on this doll. It was unbelievable how it really looked like me. 'Bout this tall *(Indicates about two feet)* with overalls and a checked shirt. I thought it was real cute, and I wrote this card sayin' "From one livin' doll to another. Let's keep playin' house till the day we die."

ALBERTA: And he didn't like it?

DEEDEE: He laughed so hard he fell over backward out of the chair and cracked his head open on the radiator. We had to take him to the emergency room.

ALBERTA: I'm sorry.

DEEDEE: We was sittin' there waitin' for him to get sewed up and this little kid comes in real sick and Joe he says to me, *(Getting a candy bar out of her purse and taking a big anxious bite out of it)* I brought this doll along, see, I don't know why, anyway Joe says to me . . . "Deedee, that little girl is so much sicker than me. Let's give her this doll to make her feel better." And they were takin' her right on in to the doctors 'cause she looked pretty bad, and Joe rushes up and puts this doll in her arms.

ALBERTA: They let her keep it?

DEEDEE: Her mother said, "Thanks a lot." Real sweet like they didn't have much money to buy the kid dolls or something. It made Joe feel real good.

ALBERTA: But it was your present to him. It was your face on the doll.

DEEDEE: Yeah, *(Pause)* but I figure it was his present as soon as I gave it to him, so if he wanted to give it away, that's his business. But *(Stops)* he didn't like it. I could tell. *(Walks to the window again)* They need to wash this window here.

ALBERTA: I gave Herb a fishing pole one year.

DEEDEE *(Not interested)*: He fishes.

ALBERTA: No, but I thought he wanted to. He'd cut out a picture of this husky man standing in water practically up to his waist, fishing. I thought he left it out so I'd get the hint.

DEEDEE: But he didn't?

ALBERTA: Oh, it was a hint all right. He wanted the hat.

DEEDEE: Right.

ALBERTA *(Seeing that Deedee is really getting upset)*: Do you like the things Joe gives you?

DEEDEE: I'd like it if he came home, that's what I'd like.

ALBERTA: He'll be back soon. You'll probably see those lights go on as soon as your clothes are dry.

DEEDEE: Sure.

ALBERTA: People just can't always be where we want them to be, when we want them to be there.

DEEDEE: Well, I don't like it.

ALBERTA: You don't have to like it. You just have to know it.

DEEDEE *(Defensive)*: Wouldn't you like for Herb to be home right now?

ALBERTA: I certainly would.

DEEDEE: 'Cause if they were both home where they should be, we wouldn't have to be here in this crappy laundromat washin' fuckin' shirts in the middle of the night!

Deedee kicks a dryer. Alberta is alarmed and disturbed at the use of the word "fuckin'."

DEEDEE: I'm sorry. You probably don't use language like that, well, neither do I, very often, but I'm *(Now doing it on purpose)* pissed as hell at that sunuvabitch.

Alberta picks up a magazine, trying to withdraw completely. She is offended, but doesn't want to appear self-righteous. Now, Shooter pushes open the front door. Deedee turns sharply and sees him. She storms back and sits down beside Alberta. Both women are somewhat alarmed at a black man entering this preserve so late at night. Shooter is poised and handsome. He is dressed neatly, but casually. He is carrying an army duffel bag full of clothes, a cue case and a sack of tacos. He has a can of beer in one pocket. He moves toward a washer, sets down the duffel bag, opens the cap on the beer. He is aware that he has frightened them. This amuses him, but he understands it. Besides, he is so goddamned charming.

SHOOTER *(Holding the taco sack so they can see it)*: Would either of you two ladies care to join me in a taco?

ALBERTA *(Finally)*: No thank you.

SHOOTER *(As though in an ad)*: Freshly chopped lettuce, firm vine-ripened New Jersey beefsteak tomatoes, a-ged, shred-ded, ched-dar cheese, sweet slivers of Bermuda onion and Ole Mexico's very own, very hot taco sauce.

DEEDEE: That's just what they say on the radio.

SHOOTER: That's because I'm the "they" who says it on the radio.

DEEDEE: You are?

SHOOTER *(Walking over)*: Shooter Stevens. *(Shakes her hand)*

ALBERTA *(As he shakes her hand)*: Nice to meet you.

DEEDEE: You're the Number One Night Owl?

SHOOTER *(As he said it at the beginning of the act)*: . . . sayin' it's three o'clock, all right, and time to rock your daddy to dreams of de-light.

DEEDEE: You are! You really are! That's fantastic! I always listen to you!

SHOOTER *(Walking back to his laundry)*: Yeah?

DEEDEE: Always. Except when . . . I mean, when I get to pick, I pick you. I mean, your station. You're on late.

SHOOTER: You got it.

DEEDEE *(To Alberta)*: Terrific. *(Disgusted with herself)* I'm telling him he's on late. He knows he's on late. He's the one who's on late. Big news, huh?

SHOOTER: You a reporter?

DEEDEE *(Pleased with the question)*: Oh no. *(Stands up, stretches)* Gotten so stiff sitting there. *(Walks over)* Don't you know what they put in those things?

SHOOTER: The tacos?

DEEDEE: Dog food.

SHOOTER *(Laughing)*: Have to eat 'em anyway. Good business. I keep stoppin' in over there, they keep running the ad. Gonna kill me.

DEEDEE: No kidding. We take our . . . *(Quickly)* My garbage cans are right next to theirs and whatta theirs got in 'em all the time? Dog-food cans.

SHOOTER *(He smiles)*: Maybe they have a dog.

ALBERTA: It could be someone else in the building.

SHOOTER: See?

DEEDEE: She didn't mean they have a dog. She meant some old person in the building's eatin' dog food. It happens. A lot around here.

SHOOTER *(To Alberta)*: You her mom?

ALBERTA: No.

DEEDEE: We just met in here. She's Alberta Johnson. I'm Deedee Johnson.

ALBERTA: Shooter is an unusual name.

SHOOTER *(Nodding toward the pool hall next door)*: I play some pool.

DEEDEE *(Pointing to the cue case)*: What's that?

SHOOTER: My cue.

DEEDEE: You any good?

SHOOTER: At what?

DEEDEE: At pool, dummy.

SHOOTER *(Putting his clothes in the washer)*: I do okay.

DEEDEE: You must do better than okay or else why would you have your own cue?

SHOOTER: Willie says, Willie's the guy who owns the place, Willie says pool cues are like women. You gotta have your own and you gotta treat her right.

DEEDEE *(Seeing a piece of clothing he's dropped in)*: Did you mean to put that in there?

SHOOTER *(Pulling it back out)*: This?

DEEDEE: Your whites will come out green.

SHOOTER *(Dropping it back in the washer)*: Uh-uh. It's nylon.

ALBERTA: Your work sounds very interesting.

SHOOTER: Yes, it does.

DEEDEE: What's your real name?

SHOOTER: G.W.

DEEDEE: That's not a real name.

SHOOTER: I don't like my real name.

DEEDEE: Come on . . .

SHOOTER *(Disgusted)*: It's Gary Wayne. Now do I look like Gary Wayne to you?

DEEDEE *(Laughs)*: No.

SHOOTER: Mom's from Indiana.

ALBERTA: From Gary or Fort Wayne?

DEEDEE: Alberta used to be a teacher.

SHOOTER: It coulda been worse. She coulda named me Clarksville. *(Deedee laughs)* Hey! Now why don't the two of you come over and join us for a beer?

ALBERTA: No thank you.

SHOOTER *(Pouring in the soap)*: It's just Willie and me this time of night.

ALBERTA: No.

DEEDEE *(With a knowing look at Alberta)*: And watch you play pool?

SHOOTER: Actually, what we were planning to do tonight was whip us up a big devil's food cake and pour it in one of the pool tables to bake. Turn up the heat real high . . . watch it rise and then pour on the creamy fudge icing with lots of nuts.

DEEDEE: *You're* nuts.

SHOOTER: Get real sick if we have to eat it all ourselves . . .

DEEDEE: I've never seen anybody play pool.

SHOOTER: The key to pool's a . . . *(Directly seductive now)* real smooth stroke . . . the feel of that stick in your hand . . .

DEEDEE: Feels good?

SHOOTER: You come on over, I'll show you just how it's done.

DEEDEE: Pool.

SHOOTER: Sure. *(Smiles, then turns sharply and walks back to Alberta, depositing an empty soap box in the trash can)* Willie always keeps hot water. You could have a nice cup of tea.

ALBERTA *(A pointed look at Deedee)*: No.

DEEDEE: Our wash is almost done. We have to—

SHOOTER: We'll be there quite a while. Gets lonesome this late, you know.

DEEDEE: We know.

And suddenly, everybody feels quite uncomfortable.

SHOOTER *(To Alberta)*: It was nice meeting you. Hope I didn't interrupt your reading or anything.

DEEDEE: She used to be a teacher.

SHOOTER: That's what you said. *(Walking toward the door)* Right next door, now. Can't miss it. *(To Deedee)* Give you a piece of that fudge cake.

DEEDEE: Yeah, I'll bet you would.

SHOOTER *(Closing the door)*: Big piece.

Alberta watches Deedee watch to see which direction Shooter takes.

DEEDEE *(After a moment)*: I thought we'd had it there for a minute, didn't you? *(Visibly cheered)* Coulda been a murderer, or a robber or a rapist, just as easy! *(Increasingly excited)* We coulda been hostages by now!

ALBERTA: To have hostages you have to commit a hijacking. You do not hijack a laundromat.

DEEDEE: Depends how bad you need clean clothes.

ALBERTA: I didn't like the things he said to you.

DEEDEE: He was just playin'.

ALBERTA: He was not playing.

DEEDEE: Well, what does it hurt? Just words.

ALBERTA: Not those words.

DEEDEE: You don't miss a thing, do you?

ALBERTA: I'm not deaf.

DEEDEE: Just prejudiced.

ALBERTA: That's not true.

DEEDEE: If that was a white DJ comin' in here, you'd still be talkin' to him, I bet. Seein' if he knows your "old" favorites.

ALBERTA: If you don't want to know what I think, you can stop talking to me.

DEEDEE: What you think is what's wrong with the world. People don't trust each other just because they're some other color from them.

ALBERTA: And who was it who said he could be a murderer? That was you, Deedee. Would you have said that if he'd been white?

DEEDEE: It just makes you sick, doesn't it. The thought of me and Shooter over there after you go home.

ALBERTA: It's not my business.

DEEDEE: That's for sure.

Alberta goes back to reading her magazine. Deedee wanders around.

DEEDEE: You don't listen to him on the radio, but I do. And you know what he says after "rock your daddy to dreams of de-light"? He says, "And mama, I'm comin' home." Now, if he has a "mama" to go home to, what's he doing washing his own clothes? So he don't have a "mama," and that means lonely. And he's loaded, too. So if he's got a wife, she's got a washer, so don't say maybe they don't have a washer. Lonely.

ALBERTA: All right. He's a nice young man who washes his own clothes and is "friendly" without regard to race, creed or national origin.

DEEDEE: I mean, we're both in here in the middle of the night and it don't mean we're on the make, does it?

ALBERTA: It's perfectly respectable.

DEEDEE: You always do this when Herb is out of town?

ALBERTA: No.

DEEDEE: You don't even live in this neighborhood, do you?

ALBERTA: No.

DEEDEE: Know how I knew that? That garden. There ain't a garden for miles around here.

ALBERTA: You've been reading Sherlock Holmes.

DEEDEE *(Knows Alberta was insulting her)*: So why did you come over here?

ALBERTA *(Knows she made a mistake)*: I came for the same reason you did. To do my wash.

DEEDEE: In the middle of the night? Hah. It's a big mystery, isn't it? And you don't want to tell me. Is some man meetin' you here? Yeah, and you can't have your meetin' out where you live 'cause your friends might see you and give the word to old Herb when he gets back.

ALBERTA: No. *(Pauses)* I'm sorry I said what I did. Go on over to the pool hall. I'll put your clothes in the dryer.

DEEDEE *(Easily thrown off the track)*: And let him think I'm all hot for him. No sir. Besides, Joe might come home.

ALBERTA: That's right.

DEEDEE: Might just serve him right, though. Come in and see me drinkin' beer and playin' pool with Willie and Shooter. Joe hates black people. He says even when they're dancin' or playin' ball, they're thinkin' about killin'. Yeah, that would teach him to run out on me. A little dose of his own medicine. Watch him gag on it.

ALBERTA: So he *has* run out on you.

DEEDEE: He's workin' the double shift.

ALBERTA: That's what you said.

DEEDEE: And you don't believe me. You think he just didn't come home, is that it? You think I was over there waitin' and waitin' in my new nightgown and when the late show went off I turned on the radio and ate a whole pint of chocolate ice cream, and when the radio went off I couldn't stand it anymore so I grabbed up all these clothes, dirty or not, and got outta there so he wouldn't come in and find me cryin'. Well, *(Firmly)* I wasn't cryin'!

ALBERTA *(After a considerable pause)*: I haven't cried in forty years.

DEEDEE: Just happy I guess.

ALBERTA *(With a real desire to help now)*: I had an Aunt Dora, who had a rabbit, Puffer, who died. I cried then. I cried for weeks.

DEEDEE: And it wasn't even your rabbit.

ALBERTA: I loved Aunt Dora and she loved that rabbit. I'd go to visit and she'd tell me what Puffer had done that day. She claimed he told her stories, Goldilocks and the Three Hares, The Rabbit Who Ate New York. Then we'd go outside and drink lemonade while Puffer ate lettuce. She grew lettuce just for him. A whole backyard of it.

DEEDEE: Little cracked, huh?

ALBERTA: I helped her bury him. Tears were streaming down my face.

"Bertie," she said, "stop crying. He didn't mean to go and leave us all alone and he'd feel bad if he knew he made us so miserable." But in the next few weeks, Aunt Dora got quieter and quieter till finally she wasn't talking at all and Mother put her in a nursing home.

DEEDEE: Where she died.

ALBERTA: Yes.

DEEDEE: Hey! Our wash is done. *(Alberta seems not to hear her)* Look, I'll do it. You go sit.

ALBERTA *(Disoriented)*: No, I . . .

DEEDEE: Let me, really. I know this part. Mom says you can't blow this part, so I do it. She still checks, though, finds some reason to go downstairs and check the heat I set. I don't mind, really. Can't be too careful.

Deedee unloads the washers and carries the clothes to the dryers. Alberta walks to the window, seeming very far away.

DEEDEE *(Setting the heat)*: Regular for you guys, warm for permos and undies. Now Herb's shirts and shorts get hot. Pants and socks get . . .

ALBERTA: Warm.

DEEDEE: What's Herb got left to wear anyhow?

ALBERTA: His gray suit.

DEEDEE *(Laughs at how positive Alberta is about this)*: What color tie?

ALBERTA: Red with a silver stripe through it.

DEEDEE *(Still merry)*: Shirt?

ALBERTA: White.

DEEDEE: Shoes?

ALBERTA *(Quiet astonishment)*: I don't know.

DEEDEE: Well I'm glad. Thought you were seeing him all the way to Akron, X-ray eyes or something weird. Alberta . . .

ALBERTA: Yes? *(Worried, turning around to face her now, afraid Deedee will know her secret)*

DEEDEE: You got any dimes?

ALBERTA *(Relieved)*: Sure. *(Walks to her purse)* How many do we need?

DEEDEE: Two each, I guess. Four dryers makes eight. *(As Alberta is getting them out of her wallet)* I don't know what I'd have done if you hadn't been here. I didn't think . . . before I . . .

ALBERTA: You'd have done just fine. Don't forget Sleepy back there.

DEEDEE: I wish Mom were more like you.

ALBERTA: Stuck up?

DEEDEE: Smart. Nice to talk to.

ALBERTA: Thank you, but . . .

DEEDEE: No, really. You've been to Mexico and you've got a good man.

Alberta takes off her glasses, still very upset.

DEEDEE: Mom's just got me and giant-size Cheer. And she don't say two words while I'm there. Ever. I don't blame her I guess.

ALBERTA: Well . . .

DEEDEE: Yeah.

ALBERTA *(Back in balance now)*: But you're young and pretty. You have a wonderful sense of humor.

DEEDEE: Uh-huh.

ALBERTA: And you'll have those children someday.

DEEDEE: Yeah, I know. *(Gloomily)* I have my whole life in front of me.

ALBERTA: You could get a job.

DEEDEE: Oh, I got one. This company in New Jersey, they send me envelopes and letters and lists of names and I write on the names and addresses and Dear Mr. Wilson or whatever at the top of the letter. I do have nice handwriting.

ALBERTA: I'm sure.

DEEDEE: I get so bored doing it. Sometimes I want to take a fat orange crayon and scribble *(Making letters in the air)* EAT BEANS, FATSO, and then draw funny faces all over the letter.

ALBERTA: I'm sure the extra money comes in handy.

DEEDEE: Well, Joe don't know I do it. I hide all the stuff before he comes home. And I keep the money at Mom's. She borrows from it sometimes. She says that makes us even for the water for the washing machine. See, I can't spend it or Joe will know I got it.

ALBERTA: He doesn't want you to work.

DEEDEE *(Imitating Joe's voice)*: I'm the head of this house.

ALBERTA: He expects you to sit around all day?

DEEDEE: I guess. *(With good-humored rage)* Oh, I can wash the floor if I want.

ALBERTA: You should tell him how you feel.

DEEDEE: He'd leave me.

ALBERTA: Maybe.

DEEDEE *(After a moment)*: So what, right?

ALBERTA: I just meant, if you give him the chance to understand—

DEEDEE: But what would I say?

ALBERTA: You'd figure something out. I'm sure.

DEEDEE: I don't want to start it. I don't want to say I want a real job, 'cause then I'll say the reason I want a real job is I gotta have something to think about besides when are you coming home and how long is it gonna be before you don't come home at all. And he'll say what do you mean don't come home at all and I'll have to tell him I know what you're doing, I know you're lying to me and going out on me and he'll say what are you gonna do about it. You want a divorce? And I don't want him to say that.

ALBERTA: Now . . . you don't know—

DEEDEE (*Firmly*): I called the bowling alley and asked for him and the bartender said, "This Patsy? He's on his way, honey." I hope he falls in the sewer.

ALBERTA: Deedee!

DEEDEE: I hope he gets his shirt caught in his zipper. I hope he wore socks with holes in 'em. I hope his Right Guard gives out. I hope his baseball cap falls in the toilet. I hope she kills him. (*Pushing one of the carts, hard*)

ALBERTA: Deedee!

DEEDEE: I do. Last night, I thought I'd surprise him and maybe we'd bowl a few games? Well, I was gettin' my shoes and I saw them down at lane twelve, laughin' and all. He had one of his hands rubbing her hair and the other one rubbing his bowling ball. Boy did I get out of there quick. I've seen her there before. She teaches at the Weight Control upstairs, so she's probably not very strong but maybe she could poison him or something. She wears those pink leotards and even her hair looks thin. I hate him.

ALBERTA: I'm sure you don't really.

DEEDEE: He's mean and stupid. I thought he'd get over it, but he didn't. Mean and stupid. And I ain't all that smart, so if I know he's dumb, he must really be dumb. I used to think he just acted mean and stupid. Now, I know he really *is* . . .

ALBERTA: . . . mean and stupid.

DEEDEE: Why am I telling you this? You don't know nuthin' about bein' dumped.

ALBERTA: At least you have some money saved.

DEEDEE: For what?

ALBERTA: And your mother would let you stay with her till you got your own place.

DEEDEE: She's the *last* person I'm tellin'.

ALBERTA: I'll bet you'd like being a telephone operator.

DEEDEE: But how's he gonna eat? The only time he ever even fried an egg, he flipped it over and it landed in the sink. It was the last egg, so he grabbed it up and ate it in one bite.

ALBERTA: One bite?

DEEDEE: I like how he comes in the door. Picks me up, swings me around in the air . . .

ALBERTA (*Incredulous*): He stuffed a whole egg in his mouth?

DEEDEE: You're worse than Mom. (*Angrily*) He's gonna be a famous race car driver someday and I want to be there.

ALBERTA: To have him pour beer all over you.

DEEDEE: Yes, to have him pour beer all over me.

ALBERTA (*Checking the clothes in one of her dryers, knowing she has said too much*): He could have come in without turning on the lights. If you want to go check, I'll watch your things here.

DEEDEE: You want to get rid of me, don't you?

ALBERTA: I do not want to get rid of you.

DEEDEE: So why don't *you* go home? Go get the Woolite for that yucky shirt you didn't wash. You not only don't want to talk to me, you didn't even want me to touch that shirt. Herb's shirt is too nice for me to even touch. Well, I may be a slob, but I'm clean.

ALBERTA: I didn't want to wash it.

DEEDEE: That ain't it at all. Herb is so wonderful. You love him so much. You wash his clothes just the right way. I could never drop his shirt in the washer the way you do it. The stain might not come out and he might say what did you do to my shirt and you might fight and that would mess up your little dream world where everything is always sweet and nobody ever gets mad and you just go around gardening and giving each other little pecky kisses all the time. Well, you're either kidding yourself or lying to me. Nobody is so wonderful that somebody else can't touch their shirt. You act like he's a saint. Like he's dead and now you worship the shirts he wore.

ALBERTA: What do I have to do to get you to leave me alone?

DEEDEE *(Feeling very bad)*: He is dead, isn't he?

ALBERTA: Yes.

DEEDEE: I'm so stupid.

ALBERTA: You . . .

DEEDEE: What? Tell me. Say something horrible.

ALBERTA *(Slowly, but not mean)*: You just don't know when to shut up.

DEEDEE: Worse than that. I don't know how. *(Hates what she has done)*

ALBERTA: But you are not dumb, child. And don't let anybody tell you you are, okay? *(Takes off her glasses and rubs her eyes)*

DEEDEE: I'm sorry, Mrs. Johnson, I really am sorry. You probably been plannin' this night for a long time. Washin' his things. And I barged in and spoiled it all.

ALBERTA: I've been avoiding it for a long time.

Deedee feels terrible, she wants to ask questions, but is trying very hard, for once, to control her mouth.

ALBERTA: Herb died last winter, the day before his birthday.

DEEDEE: When you got him the rakes.

ALBERTA: He was being nosy, like I told you before, in the kitchen. I was making his cake. So I asked him to take out the garbage. He said, "Can't we wait till it's old enough to walk?"

DEEDEE: How . . .

ALBERTA: I didn't miss him till I put the cake in the oven. Guess I thought he was checking his seedbeds in the garage. I yelled out, "Herb, do you want butter cream or chocolate?" And then I saw him. Lying in the alley, covered in my cabbage soup. It was his heart.

DEEDEE: Did you call the . . .

ALBERTA: I picked up his head in my hand and held it while I cleaned up as much of the stuff as I could. A tuna can, coffee grounds, eggshells . . .

DEEDEE *(Carefully)*: You knew he was dead, not just knocked out?

ALBERTA: He'd hit his head when he fell. He was bleeding in my hand. I knew I should get up, but the blood was still so warm.

DEEDEE: I'm so sorry.

ALBERTA: I don't want you to be alone, that's not what I meant before.

DEEDEE: Looks like I'm alone anyway.

ALBERTA: That's what I meant.

DEEDEE: Sometimes I bring in a little stand-up mirror to the coffee table while I'm watching TV. It's my face over there when I look, but it's a face just the same.

ALBERTA: Being alone isn't so awful. I mean, it's awful, but it's not that awful. There are hard things.

The dryers stop. Deedee watches Alberta take a load of clothes from the dryer, holding them up to smell them.

DEEDEE: I'd probably eat pork and beans for weeks.

ALBERTA *(Her back to Deedee)*: I found our beachball when I cleaned out the basement. I can't let the air out of it. It's *(Turning around now)* his breath in there. *(Sees Deedee is upset)* Get your clothes out. They'll wrinkle. That's amazing about the shoes.

DEEDEE: The shoes?

ALBERTA: Remember I was telling you what Herb had on? Gray suit . . .

DEEDEE: . . . white shirt, red tie with a silver stripe through it . . .

ALBERTA: I hang onto the shirt he died in, and I don't even know if he's got shoes on in his coffin.

DEEDEE: Well, if he's flyin' around heaven, he probably don't need 'em. *(Pauses)* You bought him all black socks.

ALBERTA: It was his idea. He thought they'd be easier to match if they were all the same color.

DEEDEE: Is it?

ALBERTA: No. Now I have to match by length. They may be all black, but they don't all shrink the same. I guess I don't really have to match them now, though, do I? *(Continues to match them)*

DEEDEE: I'd like to lose all Joe's white ones. *(Holding them up over the trash can, then thinking maybe it's not such a good idea)*

ALBERTA *(Going back for her last load of clothes, looking toward the window)*: Deedee . . . your lights are on. In your apartment. All the lights are on now.

DEEDEE: You sure?

ALBERTA: Come see.

Deedee walks over to the window.

DEEDEE: You're right.

ALBERTA: Yes.

DEEDEE: So what do I do now?

ALBERTA: I don't know.

DEEDEE: Should I rush right home? Ask Joe did he have a good time bowling a few games after his double shift? Listen to him brag about his score? His score he didn't make in the games he didn't bowl after the double shift he didn't work? Well I don't feel like it. I'm going next door. Play some pool. Make him miss me.

ALBERTA: You should go home before you forget how mad you are. You don't have to put up with what he's doing. You can if you want to, if you think you can't make it without him, but you don't have to.

DEEDEE: But what should I say? Joe, if you don't stop going out on me, I'm not ever speaking to you again? That's exactly what he wants.

ALBERTA: What you say isn't that important. But there is something you have to remember while you say it.

DEEDEE: Which is?

ALBERTA: Your own face in the mirror is better company than a man who would eat a whole fried egg in one bite. *(Deedee laughs)* But it won't be easy.

DEEDEE *(Cautiously)*: Are you gonna wash that other shirt ever?

ALBERTA: The cabbage-soup shirt? No, I don't think so.

DEEDEE: Yeah.

ALBERTA *(Loading up her basket)*: Maybe, in a few months or next year sometime, I'll be able to give these away. They're nice things.

DEEDEE: People do need them. Hey! *(Leaving her laundry and going to the bulletin board)* I told you there ain't a garden for miles around here. You better hang onto these hoes. It's gettin' about time to turn over the soil, isn't it?

ALBERTA: Another two weeks or so, yes it is. Well, *(Taking the card)* that's everything. I'll just get my soap and . . .

DEEDEE *(Hesitantly)*: Mrs. Johnson?

ALBERTA: Alberta.

DEEDEE: Alberta.

ALBERTA: Yes?

DEEDEE: I'm really lonely.

ALBERTA: I know.

DEEDEE: How can you stand it?

ALBERTA: I can't. *(Pauses)* But I have to, just the same.

DEEDEE: How do I . . . how do you do that?

ALBERTA: I don't know. You call me if you think of something. *(Gives her a small kiss on the forehead)*

DEEDEE: I don't have your number.

ALBERTA *(Backing away toward the door)*: I really wanted to be alone tonight.

DEEDEE: I know.

ALBERTA: I'm glad you talked me out of it.

DEEDEE: Boy, you can count on me for that. Hey! Don't go yet. I owe you some money.

ALBERTA: No. *(Fondly)* Everybody deserves a free load now and then.

DEEDEE *(Trying to reach across the space to her)*: Thank you.

ALBERTA: Now, I suggest you go wake up Sleepy back there and see if there's something he needs to talk about.

DEEDEE: Tell you the truth, I'm ready for a little peace and quiet.

ALBERTA: Good night. *(Leaves)*

DEEDEE *(Reaching for the Dr. Pepper she put on the washer early on)*: Yeah, peace and quiet. *(Pops the top on the Dr. Pepper)* Too bad it don't come in cans.

Lights go down as she stands there looking out the window.

End of Act One

ACT
TWO

The Pool Hall

The pool hall is small and seedy. Plastic beer ads cover the walls. Talc is kept in empty candy-bar boxes along the window sills. There is an old bar with sacks of potato chips and other snacks. Tacky ashtrays and calendars litter the room. There is one television set and one pool table. "The Star-Spangled Banner" is playing on the television as the lights come up.

Willie is wiping off the bar. As the song ends, he turns off the TV and opens a beer. He pulls out a racing form and sits down. He looks at the clock. Shooter enters, carrying a sack of tacos, his cue case and a beer.

SHOOTER *(In greeting)*: Willie.

WILLIE *(Not looking up from the form)*: It's the man from the radio.

SHOOTER: How's it goin'?

WILLIE: Gets any busier I'll have to stand up.

SHOOTER: Or at least *look* up.

WILLIE *(Looking up now)*: Sondra just called.

SHOOTER: She knows when I get off.

WILLIE: She sure does.

SHOOTER: Where else would I be?

WILLIE: Somethin' like that.

SHOOTER: Somebody did one helluva job teaching that girl to tell the time. Tells me the time to come home, tells me the time to eat, tells me the time to go to bed.

WILLIE: Well, I told her I'd send you on soon's you finished your beer.

SHOOTER *(Indicating the racing form)*: Got any winners tomorrow?

WILLIE: Till tomorrow, they're all winners.

SHOOTER: Still betting those grays?

WILLIE: Yeah, the older I get, the more I love them gray horses.

SHOOTER: Trouble is, most of the ones you pick, gray isn't so much their color as an indication of their age.

WILLIE: Yeah, that one horse, Dusty Days, he's still runnin' from the first time I bet on him. *(Laughs)* 'Bout eight years now. I sit here and handicap 'em, he always comes out the winner. I can't figure it out.

SHOOTER: It's some other dude does the handicappin', Willie. Back in the stable. Finds out which ones you're layin' your money on, then ties lead weights to their legs. That's handicappin', man.

WILLIE: You're tellin' me.

SHOOTER: George go home already?

WILLIE: Sick.

SHOOTER: Bad?

WILLIE: You know any that's good? Doc says circulation.

SHOOTER: I thought I improved his circulation with that wheelchair I gave him.

WILLIE: Callin' himself the stick-shift cripple. That was nice, boy. End of the world wouldn't keep ol' George from comin' in here every night, but he sure does like havin' that motor do the work. Last six months, he gets real tired, real quick.

SHOOTER: Sondra said he wouldn't even know it was real leather, but I figured, what the hell, it's only money.

WILLIE: Oh he knew. Said, "Willie, cows got it rough, don't they? Folks lookin' at 'em seein' steak dinners and upholstery." You shoulda seen him, George doin' this dumb cow voice, "Hey, man, you don't love me for what I am. You love me for what I'm gonna be—your suede leather shoes that walk you to get your all-beef cheeseburger which you pay for outta your genuine cowhide wallet."

SHOOTER: This dude at the surgical supply says, "Who's this for, son?" I started into this whole number like I had to explain, "Well, George, see, he's Sondra's father. Sondra, that's my wife. But George, he's also, well, my dad and George and this other man Willie, Willie he owns a pool hall, the three of them were real tight, and since Dad's gone now, one helluva pool player, my dad, anyway, George and Willie are like, well, George is family about five ways, see?" And on and on like that till finally he was givin' me this crazy look so I slapped down all those hundreds and said, "Hey, man, just give me the chair, okay?"

WILLIE: White boy in here the other night wouldn't let me lift George up to the rail to shoot. Said he had to keep one wheel on the floor.

SHOOTER: Just letting anybody in here these days.

WILLIE: Yeah. Even DJs.

SHOOTER: Little kid called me up tonight, wanted to talk to the record player. I said it don't talk, kid. He said, "No, man, you man, the record player." Over the air he said that. (*And he sets his cue case on the bar*)

WILLIE: The record player.

SHOOTER: Very funny.

WILLIE: Oh come on, boy, it don't matter what you say over the air.

SHOOTER: Thanks.

WILLIE: Folks turn on the radio to hear the music, remember?

SHOOTER *(Opening the cue case)*: I'll try to keep that in mind.

WILLIE *(Closing the cue case)*: You're hidin' out tonight, aren't you? Well, you ain't hidin' *here*.

SHOOTER *(Getting his cue out of the case)*: What you mean is you don't want nobody else hidin' in your hole. Well, the "hole" population looks pretty sparse to me.

WILLIE: Then what are you doin' here? Run outta skinny white girls?

SHOOTER: What's with you, man?

WILLIE: Go home, boy. Get outta my hall. Go home. See your wife.

SHOOTER: Ah, now we're gettin'—

WILLIE: Yeah, we're gettin'—

SHOOTER *(Looking for the felt brush)*: Nowhere, man. I've had enough of this mother-hen shit.

WILLIE: Then quit playin' rooster.

A big laugh from Shooter.

SHOOTER: Oh I'm so sorry. Did I interrupt your nap? Did I disturb your dust?

WILLIE: You're sorry all right. Did I pay for you to be born? Did I scrape up what was left of your old man when he died? Now you go home when I tell you.

SHOOTER: I'm what's left of my old man.

WILLIE: Yeah. *(Unfortunately)*

SHOOTER: And I didn't plan to be in Miami Beach when he died, it just happened. So, I'd have done it.

WILLIE: But you didn't. I identified him. I carried him to the ambulance. I bought his buryin' suit. I paid for his funeral.

SHOOTER: You got a plot out back for George when he goes? Way you tell it, those guys can't even die without you.

WILLIE: Man in here the other night said you better not die without payin' him his six thousand dollars you owe him. Said he'd come to hell to get it. Left you this note.

SHOOTER *(Crumpling up the note)*: Least thanks to me, you won't have to carry George. Just dig the hole, then wheel him outta here some night, bury him wheelchair and all.

WILLIE: You can have your chair back, boy. He don't need your four-speed charity.

SHOOTER: Listen to you, giving away the cripple's chair. And charity, my man, is building a ramp *(Pointing to the door)* up to a pool hall.

WILLIE *(Pointing to the cue)*: What you think you're doin' with that?

SHOOTER *(Swinging it around in a showy move)*: Gonna pick my teeth.

WILLIE: Might as well, G.W., 'cause you sure as hell don't know nothin' else to do with it.

SHOOTER: Least I ain't forgot what it's for. *(And he sets the cue ball on the head spot, taps it down to the foot rail so it rolls back to hit the tip of the cue in follow-through position)*

WILLIE: And I ain't tryin' to be somethin' I ain't.

SHOOTER: I'm his kid.

WILLIE: You got his name.

SHOOTER: Yes sir. I've got the prize-winning best of the Three Blind Mice. I've got ol' Shooter's name, I've got George's only child, Sondra. And now I've got my own private pool palace.

WILLIE: Think so, huh?

SHOOTER: But not for long, right, Willie? You ain't the only nigger got spies. Man down at the station owns a part of Baskin-Robbins told me the chain needs a downtown shop and they got their eye on this place. I hear Mr. Rum Raisin makes a nice offer.

WILLIE: You heard wrong. I ain't sellin'.

SHOOTER: The hell you ain't. Come on, Willie, all the old pool players go to Asbury Park to die. Pool player's paradise. Big tournaments, best players coming through all the time. Then just eight miles up the Jersey coast you got the ponies running at Monmouth Park. And gambling in Atlantic City. Don't blame you for goin', Willie.

WILLIE: This place is a firetrap. Who'd want it?

SHOOTER: You might as well tell me, Willie, 'cause I got the picture already. Wake up about noon, spend a coupla hours with the racing form, then go for a swim, well, more like a walk in the pool. Then drive up to Monmouth, catch the daily double, collect your money and get back in time to see the hustlers do business down at Hopkins Billiards. Yes sir, racing, roulette and rack 'em up, boys, Willie's retirin' to Asbury Park. I hear they even got green felt carpet in the nursing homes.

WILLIE: I'd sell this place in a minute just to keep you outta here, get you home at night.

SHOOTER: This place, got your "friend" Shooter's tracks all over the floor? This place, the only place your "friend" George got to go every night? You'd sell the only thing you got to show for your whole life just to keep me paying Sondra's cleaning lady?

WILLIE: I sure would.

SHOOTER *(As he puts the balls on the table)*: Married her to please Dad and George and now I gotta keep her 'cause of you?

WILLIE: Catch right on, don't you.

SHOOTER: You're talking crazy, man.

WILLIE: You talk crazy for a living. Man gets famous talking to the air.

SHOOTER: I'm not famous.

WILLIE: But you do talk to the air.

SHOOTER: And get paid for it.

WILLIE: Well, it ain't improved your personality.

SHOOTER: When you *are* a personality, you don't have to *have* a personality.

WILLIE: Good thing.

SHOOTER: What's between Sondra and me is between Sondra and me. What do you care? She's not your baby.

WILLIE: She's George's baby and that's enough for me. And if Shooter was here—

SHOOTER: He'd be shootin' pool and that's all. 'Cause he knew—

WILLIE: 'Cause that's all he could do. Never had a job in his life. I paid for you to be born.

SHOOTER: We know.

WILLIE *(Refuses to stop)*: George paid the electric, and I paid the phone bill. George kept the grocery sendin' ham hocks, and I bought his beer.

SHOOTER: So what's that come to? I'm good for my old man's bills. *(Getting out his wallet)* You take MasterCharge?

WILLIE: It comes to more than you'll ever have.

SHOOTER: I'm rich, remember?

WILLIE: Too bad you ain't blond. I hear that's a terrific combination.

SHOOTER: Couldn't you take care of that for me, Willie? I mean, you're takin' care of George and takin' care Sondra gets her new Lincoln every year.

WILLIE: Whatever she wants. *(Then quickly)* Don't you rack those balls, boy.

SHOOTER: Uh-uh. *(Racking the balls)* What she wants, my man, is everything there is. Sable coats, suede chairs, a Cuisinart and a cook to run it, trips to wherever-it-is Hong Kong, five-hundred-dollar shoes, and fourteen-carat-gold fingernails.

WILLIE: Just things, kid. Everybody needs some things. You, you could even do with a few things.

SHOOTER: I don't need any things.

WILLIE: Your things are how you know it's your house.

SHOOTER: Then my house . . . is one of her things. I bought myself a re-cliner . . .

WILLIE: Yeah?

SHOOTER: She gave it away. *(Pauses)* Said it didn't go with the rest of the "things" I paid for. Marrying her was like cosigning for the national debt.

WILLIE: Marrying her was what you did.

SHOOTER: Unfortunately.

WILLIE: And you are going to stay married to her or you are going to have to answer to me.

SHOOTER: Well, the answer is no.

WILLIE: And you are going to keep her happy or you are gonna stay outta my sight. You gonna grow up if it kills you. And don't you think you can get away with one thing because I know every move you make. You screw a sheep and I'll know it.

SHOOTER: Sure you will. What else you got to do?

WILLIE: You're the one needs somethin' else to do. Somethin' else besides that gambling or dope or whatever you s'posed to owe that greasy white boy that six thousand dollars for. He shows up again, I'll kill him.

SHOOTER: It's an investment, man.

WILLIE: The hell it is.

SHOOTER: Yeah. I'm buying a mountain, a great big mountain covered in pretty red flowers. None of your business.

WILLIE: You're my business. You want somethin' I can get for you, I'll get it. Till then, I'm keepin' you from makin' the mistake of your life. You lose Sondra . . . she's a real classy lady and you like the way she looks and you know it. She reminds you where you want to get to in this world. You lose her and you're gonna lose it all. Then all you'll have left is some lousy grams of cocaine and pictures of your daddy.

SHOOTER: And won't you be happy then?

WILLIE: I will be happy—no, happy ain't got nuthin' to do with it. I will let you back in here when you stop messin' around and stay where you belong. At home. With Sondra. Your wife.

SHOOTER: Till depth do us part.

WILLIE: Now that is all I have to say to you. Get outta my hall.

SHOOTER: I don't believe you. I mean, did somebody make you Resident Caretaker and Marvelous Little Yard Man for the whole world?

WILLIE: If you don't get outta my hall—

SHOOTER: What? Huh? *(Taking his practice strokes)* What you gonna do, man? You gonna prune my hedge and trim the edges of my mile-long circular driveway? *(Now gets up quickly, poses, in an old move of his father's)* Give me a break! *(And he gets in position just as quickly and breaks the racked balls with a powerful stroke)*

WILLIE *(Has to laugh)*: Give me a break.

SHOOTER *(Pleased with his shot)*: Yeah.

WILLIE: Shooter always said that.

SHOOTER *(After a moment)*: Yeah. Give me a break.

WILLIE: Hadn't been funny for years.

SHOOTER: He's probably still sayin' it. *(And now he proceeds to run the balls in rotation)*

WILLIE *(Starting to clean up now)*: Yeah. Beer's probably hot in hell, but they got all the best pool players down there. Greenleaf, Hoppe . . . Shooter takin' 'em all on, dollar a game and the loser runs up to heaven for the cold Falls City. *(Laughs)* He was the best.

SHOOTER: Nobody even close.

WILLIE: One night he puts on this cowboy hat and glasses, wraps his left arm in a sling, rents a tux, figures to hop on down to South Side, Owensboro, pick up some fast cash. Borrows George's car, gets the word about the shortstop* there, how much money he's carrying, where he'll be standin' in the room—

SHOOTER: Who's runnin' that place now?

WILLIE: Lookin' for some one-pocket, see? So he's got on this rig. I swear he looks so strange, and walks in this joint and the bartender, swingin' a pretzel around his finger and openin' a beer, looks up, sees this bifocaled, broken-armed cowboy wearin' a tux, and says, "Hey boys, it's Shooter Stevens!" Like to died. He like to died. Got on all that crap and the first guy sees him says, "Hey boys, it's Shooter Stevens! Trip the alarm, the robber has arrived." *(Shakes his head)* Nothin', but nothin' so goddamned sad as a pool player can't get a game.

SHOOTER *(Referring to the fact that Willie won't play with him)*: Know what you mean.

WILLIE: But God, the thing he said the last night he . . . well . . .

SHOOTER: You can say it. You can say "the last night before the leap." Before the final, flyin' leap of his life.

WILLIE: Walked in. Right by a big money nine-ball goin' over there. *(Points)* Whistlin'. Not a good sign, whistlin'. Meant trouble when he was shootin', but just walkin' whistlin', I didn't worry, see?

SHOOTER: Wish you had, Willie.

WILLIE: Gets a Falls City and goes back to the nine-ball. Man with white shoes and his own stick, blue knitty pants says, "You in, buddy?" Man, I heard that word, "buddy," and I knew it was all over. Shooter backs up to the cues there, picks a stick not even lookin'. Mr. White Shoes says, "You don't even look?" Your ol' man gives him the ugliest scariest straight-on stare you ever seen in your life and says, "Buddy, if you can't play with any of 'em, you can't play with any of 'em." *(He laughs)* Whole place cracked up.

SHOOTER: And sure enough that night . . .

WILLIE: He couldn't play with any of 'em.

SHOOTER: Well, it had to be something else, Willie. My old man did not jump off of that bridge because of a lousy run here.

WILLIE: Sorry, boy. He did. He really did. Oh sure, maybe he knew he was losin' it, shaky stroke, no games. Hell, George was even beatin' him. So no, it wasn't this one night, but it was this goddamn game and you can bet all your fancy DJ bucks on that.

SHOOTER: All right, then, since you know so much about *my* old man, why'd he pick that side? *(He has been wanting to know the answer to this for a long time, but would prefer to have Willie think he has asked out of anger)*

WILLIE: Go for the salvage yard instead of the water?

*The shortstop is the best local player, the hustler's target.

SHOOTER: Why did he land on the '56 Chevy?

WILLIE: I got a thought about it.

SHOOTER: Well, let's hear it, Willie.

WILLIE: He was a helluva swimmer.

SHOOTER: Nice try, man.

WILLIE: I'm tellin' you, boy, your old man was so stubborn, I mean, he didn't want to give himself the slightest chance of pullin' outta that dive alive. He'd never lived it down. George'd been on him somethin' awful.

Shooter takes a shot and misses. Willie laughs.

SHOOTER: What's so funny?

WILLIE: I'm sorry. See, they called me to come get him. One of the cops knew us. Got there, nice bright mornin', spotted him soon's I got outta the car. Been layin' there all night, flat on his back, arms stretched out, legs hangin' down over the windshield. That far away, I swear to God, he looked like he was gettin' himself a suntan.

SHOOTER: Just what he always wanted.

WILLIE: Close up was different. *(Points but Shooter doesn't see him)* Needed a shorter bridge.

SHOOTER: That's enough about it, okay?

WILLIE: I'm talkin' your bridge, not his. *(Starts to walk over)* Six inches, fingers to cue tip.

SHOOTER: You start playing again, I'll start listening.

WILLIE: Shooter was the only game I had in this town. So he's gone, so why bother?

SHOOTER: It's your game, man.

WILLIE: It was his game. It killed him.

SHOOTER: You don't keep in shape, he'll be ashamed of you down at hell's pool hall. Make you watch. "But I been waitin' to play you, Shooter," you'll say, and he'll say, "Willie, I'm real glad to see you and you look real good for an old man, but this is a serious game, you know?"

WILLIE: I'll keep this place open, I'll tell you to bend from the knees and stroke from the shoulder, but unless I get some all-fired good reason, like my life depended on it, I ain't playin'.

SHOOTER: It's gonna kill you to play with me?

WILLIE: You want a beer?

SHOOTER: You just couldn't stand losin' to me.

WILLIE: What I couldn't stand, is a game that didn't mean nothin'. Don't take it personal, boy, but I went fifteen rounds with the champ, so I ain't got nothin' to prove to the challengers. Now do you want a beer or not?

SHOOTER *(Miscues)*: No.

WILLIE: Boy.

SHOOTER *(Belligerent, expecting more advice)*: Yeah?

WILLIE: What are you doing here?

Shooter doesn't answer. Willie turns away.

SHOOTER *(Finally)*: Workin' on this bank shot.

WILLIE *(Louder)*: Boy . . .

SHOOTER *(Stands up, leans on his stick)*: What?

WILLIE: Look . . . *(Then deciding not to go on with this)* Don't lean on your . . . *(Tired of this too)* Oh hell. Did you ever see him shoot with an umbrella?

SHOOTER *(Going back to his game)*: No.

WILLIE *(Laughs)*: He lost your crib one night before he figured it out.

SHOOTER: Huh?

WILLIE: Havin' us a helluva storm, your old man comes in soaked, carryin' his umbrella, still all folded up perfect. George busts out laughin', says, "Why didn't you use that thing? Shooter you the dumbest nigger." And Shooter says, just like always, first thing popped into his head, says, " 'Cause I'm runnin' the rack with it, mother." So George says, "Let's see your green, man." Well, Shooter didn't have any, of course, so he says, "Bet the boy's bed, buddy." Now he goes real good for a while, but then he gets to the seven, and it's plumb froze to the rail. He looks it over, checks the line, sets him a sweet rail bridge, pulls back to shoot. George waits for just the right moment and says, "Do de name Ruby Begonia ring a bell?"

SHOOTER: And Dad miscued.

WILLIE: Then he hit George upside of the head.

SHOOTER: Then George went over and got my crib.

WILLIE: Bet's a bet, boy. Came draggin' it back in here, said your mama said, "George I am so tired of seein' your face carryin' out my furniture."

SHOOTER: Uh-huh.

WILLIE: So then Shooter has to learn how to shoot with that umbrella 'cause that's the only way George will give the crib back. Run the rack you get it back. Run the rack, you get it back. Wonder old George didn't die off of that bet. He could be awful mean, your daddy.

SHOOTER: The Three Blind Mice.

WILLIE: Well that's what your mama thought all right.

SHOOTER *(Singing)*: They all ran after the farmer's wife.

WILLIE: You use a wafer on that tip?

SHOOTER *(Still singing)*: She cut off their tails with a carving knife.

WILLIE: Need about five more pounds over your right foot.

SHOOTER *(Singing)*: Did you ever see such a sight in your life as three blind mice.

WILLIE: God, your mama, that night down at the jail. *(Laughing)* God almighty.

SHOOTER: I heard that story so many times. I don't know anything like I know that story.

WILLIE: So do it.

SHOOTER *(As Mama did it, more music than narration)*: See, I'm pregnant with you, boy, and paintin' on your crib one night, while your daddy and George and Willie are busy beatin' up on each other down at Willie's pool hall.

WILLIE *(Loving this)*: Yeah!

SHOOTER: And I pick up the phone and, Lord have mercy, it's the police and they say they got three beat-up black men, all callin' my name. And they said would I gather up some money and come relieve them of their prisoners. And they said, it's gonna be dark when you get here, honey, 'cause the 'lectric's knocked out and the stoves ain't workin', but we fed 'em Velveeta just to hold 'em till you get here, girl.

WILLIE: She took one look at us, drunk as shit, sittin' on the floor, in the dark, eatin' cheese. She said, "I drive myself all the way down here, I give them all my money, and what do I get?"

SHOOTER AND WILLIE *(As Mama said it)*: The Three Blind Mice. *(They laugh)*

WILLIE: Shooter turns on the radio on the way home and she says, "I ain't through screamin' at you yet, turn that thing off. And George, if you don't stop bleedin' on my Buick, you gonna walk!"

SHOOTER: It's a wonder she didn't drive him straight to the Red Cross, sayin', "George here's so anxious to give blood, he done started without you. Just catch a coupla pints and send him over to Willie's when he dries up."

WILLIE *(Beginning to recover from the laughing)*: I'd like to see your mama again. Maybe she'll come visit. She would've walked to China for your daddy. Nearly did a coupla times. But God, did she hate George.

SHOOTER: Remember George's stick at the wedding?

WILLIE: And that big fudge cake sittin' on the table here?

SHOOTER: Mom wanted the reception at the church.

WILLIE: Sure she did.

SHOOTER: Sondra wanted it at the Palm Room.

WILLIE: Not a bad place.

SHOOTER: Her mom wanted it at the Galt House.

They both laugh.

WILLIE *(Proudly)*: But we had it . . . here.

SHOOTER: Got a great picture of Dad and George holdin' their cues lookin' down real serious at this what was always their table, but what is now a high-rise fudge cake, you pourin' champagne on their heads.

WILLIE: Oh, Sondra was beautiful that day. She's the best shot ol' George ever made.

SHOOTER: She's still beautiful, man. That's not the problem.

WILLIE: She really wants a new Lincoln?

SHOOTER: Silver.

WILLIE: Used to look like the Lincoln dealership in front of this place.

SHOOTER: We can't even go to Sears driving my BMW. Gotta arrive in her Linc.

WILLIE *(Proudly)*: She just looks like money.

SHOOTER: Which is why I don't have any.

WILLIE: George says they raised you to thirty grand.

SHOOTER *(Opening his sack of tacos)*: Want a taco?

WILLIE: Says you can expect sixty maybe seventy in five years.

SHOOTER: And then what? You ever seen any old DJs man? You watch those records go around long enough, you start thinkin' in circles, walkin' in circles, talkin' in circles. All I learned in five years is the names of eight hundred and ninety-two singing groups and how many people don't have anybody to talk to late at night so they call up the "record player."

WILLIE: So quit.

SHOOTER: And do what?

WILLIE: You tell me.

SHOOTER: I don't know.

WILLIE: There's gotta be somethin' you like to do.

SHOOTER: I like to play pool.

WILLIE: That's not what I mean. Somethin' else.

SHOOTER: There isn't anything else.

WILLIE: Then you got a real problem, boy, 'cause pool just ain't your game.

SHOOTER: I see.

WILLIE: I mean, you do okay, but I gotta tell you—

SHOOTER *(Quietly)*: No you don't.

WILLIE: Good. So tell me somethin' else you like to do.

And Willie's helpful tone only intensifies Shooter's realization.

SHOOTER *(In complete emotional panic)*: There isn't anything else I like to do.

Willie backs off, stunned, but knows not to wait too long before he starts to talk again.

WILLIE: There's about a billion jobs in this world. You think there ain't one or two might make you happy?

SHOOTER *(Angry now)*: How am I supposed to know what makes me happy? And what difference does it make? You don't work to be happy. You work to make money. Happy, my man . . . was one of the seven dwarfs.

WILLIE: Well, either you really do like what you do, in which case you can shut up bitchin' about it, or you hate what you do so you quit.

SHOOTER: I don't like it and I don't hate it. It pays the bills.

WILLIE: Fryin' fish would pay the bills.

SHOOTER: Not her bills.

WILLIE: I'm sick to death of you blaming her for spendin' the money you make. You quit makin' it, she'll quit spendin' it. She'd do anything for you, but you ain't told her anything except don't buy fur coats. So she's doin' what she can. Makin' you look good, and makin' your house look good. You quit work, she'll make poor look good. So you shut up about you have to work to pay her bills. Her bills are all you got to show for your work . . . *(Pauses)* best I can tell.

SHOOTER *(Stops shooting)*: Well, I got something to tell you. *(Calm but firm)* And I got the chain burns to prove it. I am a certified, wholly owned, shipped-to-the-plantation slave boy, property of . . . MasterCharge. *(And he takes a bite of his taco now)*

WILLIE: You shouldn't eat that crap.

SHOOTER: Girl next door says they're made out of dog food.

WILLIE: White girl?

SHOOTER: Come on, man, I stopped in the laundromat next door, put my clothes in the wash, and this white girl talked to me, okay?

WILLIE: Makes me sick just to look at those tacos. But George eats so many of 'em, he starts speakin' Spanish around midnight.

SHOOTER: I keep tellin' Sondra to come see him.

WILLIE: She should. He's her father. She should come in here some night and see him.

SHOOTER: I know. I told her.

WILLIE: Yeah? So tell her not to. Tell her this is the last place you want to see her sweet face. Look ugly mean. Hit the table. She'll sneak right over soon's you look the other way.

SHOOTER: Yeah. Like this other routine she's got asking should I wear the green or should I wear the red. I say green, she puts on the red. I say red—

WILLIE: On go the green.

SHOOTER: I mean, why does she bother to ask?

WILLIE: It ain't just her, boy. They all do it.

SHOOTER: Yeah, but why?

WILLIE: Well if I knew that, I'd be on Johnny Carson 'stead of runnin' this place.

SHOOTER: Yeah.

WILLIE: You get Sondra down here to see George. He needs it, but he won't ask for it, and he won't get himself over to her . . . your place, 'cause he don't feel . . . he hates that white rug.

SHOOTER: Who doesn't?

WILLIE: I know she don't feel safe comin' down, and I don't exactly blame her, it ain't safe, and she is good about callin', but you bring her down here, you hear?

SHOOTER *(Throwing away the taco sack)*: Right.

Willie watches him, perhaps begins to feel a little of Shooter's pain. Suddenly, Willie shouts.

WILLIE: Shooter! Shooter Stevens! *(And now he lines up the balls)* Wipe the sweat outta your eyes and pay attention up here, man. The boy's gonna try your favorite trick! Shooter! Hey!

Shooter doesn't understand at first, then sees that Willie is preparing one of his father's old shots.

SHOOTER: Come on . . .

WILLIE: I'll set it up for you. You can do it.

SHOOTER: This ain't my game, remember?

WILLIE *(Pointing out what should happen)*: Cue ball here, hit top center, like a clean follow. No English. Hit the one about half-ball, it goes here . . . *(Points to the middle left-hand pocket)* while the two is rotatin' its way up there. *(Points to the top right-hand pocket)* And, not to leave anybody out in the cold, the cue ball rolls across the table and drops the three in the middle. *(Middle right-hand pocket)* And, don't scratch.

SHOOTER: Of course.

WILLIE *(Reviewing)*: One to here, two up there, three over there.

SHOOTER: Yeah. *(Studying the shot)* Okay. I'm ready.

WILLIE *(As Shooter is about to shoot)*: Now, what about kids?

SHOOTER: Christ! You got a shopping list for my life. Milk, bread, wife, kids . . .

WILLIE: Then read me your list. What do you want?

SHOOTER: Her exact words, Willie, about kids? Her exact words, "I'm gonna blow up like a whale? Not this body, baby. Uh-uh, honey." I mean, if you could buy 'em, she'd have 'em, but she ain't buyin' havin' 'em.

WILLIE: Probably thinks she'd have to raise it by herself.

SHOOTER: If she'd have a baby, I'd stay.

WILLIE: Does she know that?

SHOOTER: But how long am I supposed to wait? If she had the boy today, I'd be forty when he's ten. He's ready to go play ball and I'm workin' up a sweat gettin' outta my chair.

WILLIE: And what you're doin' now, goin' out on her all over town, that's supposed to convince her to have your boy for you?

SHOOTER: Whoever's playing records in your head's asleep at the deck, man. Got a broken one, goin' around and around.

WILLIE: You shape up, you'll get your boy.

SHOOTER: Wanna bet?

WILLIE: Wanna try?

SHOOTER: I want to try this shot, okay?

WILLIE: Keep your stick level.

SHOOTER: All right. One for the old man. *(Shoots and misses)* Shit.

WILLIE: One to nothin', favor of the ol' man.

SHOOTER: He really could make this?

WILLIE: This shot bought you strained carrots, boy. Lotta folks thought he couldn't make this shot. Lotta folks and lotta their money said he'd miss. But he never did.

SHOOTER: Then we'll just give it another shot.

And Shooter goes around, replacing the balls. Willie adjusts them so they're in the right position.

WILLIE *(Trying another approach)*: There's nothin' wrong, I mean, with you or Sondra? Doctor's got all kinds of—

SHOOTER: No.

WILLIE: There's tests.

SHOOTER: Look, Willie, she's taking the pill, using a diaphragm, I have to wear a rubber. Keeps foam just in case, I mean, this lady does not want any kids, okay?

WILLIE: Then you gotta change her mind. George needs a grandbaby.

SHOOTER: Tell that to her. Have George tell that to her.

WILLIE: Shooter needs a grandbaby.

SHOOTER: Shooter is dead. *(Now turning to face him)* Willie needs the grandbaby.

WILLIE *(As Shooter is ready to try the shot again)*: You don't have any children, it's the end of the line for the Three Blind Mice.

SHOOTER: You're talking to the wrong person, Willie. I want kids. But I'll tell you something, Sondra could care less about the Three Blind Mice. Here we go. *(Shoots and misses again)*

WILLIE: That's two. Three and the ol' man crosses you off his visitin' list.

SHOOTER: Have your own kid. You got a coupla good shots left, huh?

WILLIE: I'm old, G.W.

SHOOTER: Ain't a question of old. It's a question of aim. Concentration. Bend from the hips, steady stroke, you know.

WILLIE *(Laughs)*: I know.

SHOOTER: How long's it been?

WILLIE: None of your damned business.

SHOOTER: That long, huh?

Willie gets out his keys and walks to the door.

SHOOTER: Okay. Here goes. Watch.

WILLIE: I'm watchin'.

SHOOTER *(As he misses again)*: Shit.

WILLIE: That's three.

As Willie gets to the back door, it opens, and Deedee steps in carrying a stack of folded clothes.

DEEDEE: Hello?

WILLIE: Laundry's next door, miss.

DEEDEE *(Steps in, very uncomfortable)*: Yeah, but I'm lookin' for the pool hall.

WILLIE: We're closed.

DEEDEE: Are you Willie?

WILLIE *(Grudgingly)*: Yes.

DEEDEE: See? I got Shooter Stevens' clothes. Shooter Stevens? He put 'em in over there and I figured since I didn't really have—

WILLIE: Shooter Stevens? *(Turning around to look at Shooter)* You got Shooter Stevens' clothes?

DEEDEE: It's his nickname.

WILLIE: Girl's got your old man's clothes, Gary Wayne. *(Very bitter)* Shooter Stevens' clothes.

SHOOTER *(Walking over)*: Hey, thanks.

Shooter takes the clothes from her. Deedee follows him into the room, then stops as though Willie had grabbed her.

DEEDEE: I thought they were yours, oh well, guess it don't matter now.

WILLIE: Nope. It don't matter now.

SHOOTER: You didn't have to bring me these.

DEEDEE: Your dad has nice stuff.

SHOOTER: They're mine.

DEEDEE: Can I come in?

SHOOTER: Sure. I invited you, didn't I?

DEEDEE: Don't you just love the way they smell when they come out of the dryer?

SHOOTER: You thirsty?

DEEDEE: I put in a Cling-Free. That's the smell. There any tacos left?

SHOOTER *(Walking toward the bar)*: Sorry. Chips though.

WILLIE: Dollar a bag.

Shooter stops. Willie shouldn't have said that.

DEEDEE: Mind if I look around?

WILLIE: Not much to see.

SHOOTER: Sure. I'll set up so you can see how the game goes.

DEEDEE *(To Willie)*: My name's Deedee. *(No response from Willie)* Hard to tell what year it is in here. *(Picking up an ashtray)* Hey! I been there! *(Reading from the ashtray)* See Rock City! *(Then remembering)* It wasn't much. Only thing I really wanted to see, we couldn't stop for. On the way there, kept seein' these signs . . . Giant Jungle Rat. Sure wish I coulda seen that Giant Jungle Rat.

WILLIE *(In Shooter's direction)*: Oh we got 'em come in here all the time.

SHOOTER: Really just old jungle mice.

DEEDEE: Shooter, are you hungry? There's this pancake place down on Broadway . . .

WILLIE: His name is Gary Wayne.

SHOOTER: I always wondered if that place was any good. I haven't had any pancakes since—

DEEDEE: You'd love it. They're open all night too.

WILLIE: Oh, I thought the Board of Health closed it down.

SHOOTER: Now, first you have to break. *(Gets into position, Deedee comes over to watch)* Like this.

WILLIE: Or somethin' like that. Stop by some day when we're open, you'll see what a real—

Shooter gives her the cue, and gives Willie a fierce look.

SHOOTER: This is a game of rotation. You have to hit the one ball first. Then every shot after that, you have to hit the lowest numbered ball on the table. You can sink other balls with the shot, but if you don't hit the low ball first, the other balls come out and you lose your turn. *(Now showing her how to stand)* Bend like this, let the cue just rest in your hand, somewhere around here, or so. Now . . . stand up a minute. *(Showing her a beginner's bridge)* Put your hand out on the table flat like this. Ease it up, like how an inchworm . . .

DEEDEE *(Doing it)*: That?

SHOOTER: Perfect. Now curl your index finger and slip the cue through it. *(Reaching around her to show her how it's done)* Take some practice strokes. Eye on the ball.

DEEDEE *(Straightening up suddenly)*: I got it! Your dad's name was the same as yours.

SHOOTER: Yeah.

DEEDEE: Shooter.

WILLIE: No. Stevens.

SHOOTER: And he was one helluva pool player. *(Trying to appease Willie)* Dad and Willie, here, and this other man, George—

WILLIE: The father of G.W.'s wife—

SHOOTER: Were real tight.

Deedee gets back in position and takes practice strokes.

DEEDEE: Friends.

SHOOTER: More like triplets. I ever needed anything, lunch money, rubbers, anything, didn't matter which one I asked. Seemed like it all came out of the same pocket.

WILLIE *(Not to Deedee)*: It did.

SHOOTER: Gave the same advice, wore the same clothes, drove the same cars, drank the same beer, 'bout the same age, called themselves the Three Blind Mice.

Willie does not appreciate Shooter giving away this information. That name was something they called themselves, not something they would let anybody else call them.

DEEDEE *(A little bored by this information)*: This place we did stop in, on that trip where we didn't stop in to see the Giant Jungle Rat, this place, Pete's, had this three-headed mouse in a jar. It was dead, though. A freak. *(Now concentrating on the table)* I'm ready. *(She shoots and miscues)* What happened?

SHOOTER: Aim for the middle of the ball. Loosen up your finger a little.

DEEDEE: They said it had, I mean, they, the heads . . . only had one heart. That's what killed them, it, the mouse.

SHOOTER: Yeah.

And Deedee tries to shoot on her own now, Shooter backing off a little to watch.

DEEDEE: How does this end, this rotation?

WILLIE: I could turn out the lights.

SHOOTER: First person to get sixty-one points wins the game.

DEEDEE: Could be real soon, huh?

SHOOTER: What kind of pancakes do you like?

DEEDEE: Strawberry, with whipped cream.

SHOOTER: I'll just call and have them save us some. Wouldn't want them running out before we get there.

DEEDEE *(Handing him the cue)*: Here. You get the rest of them, okay?

WILLIE: Her mother's probably worried about her, G.W.

DEEDEE: It must feel real good to like somethin' this much.

And Shooter is putting on a real show now, getting all the balls in as quickly as possible.

DEEDEE: Mom likes TV.

SHOOTER: Yeah?

DEEDEE: Joe loves his '56 Chevy.

WILLIE *(In Shooter's direction)*: Joe loves his '56 Chevy.

DEEDEE: I must love somethin'.

WILLIE: Miss . . .

SHOOTER *(Indicating, somehow, himself)*: Giant Jungle Rats?

WILLIE: Deedee . . . that's your name, Deedee?

DEEDEE: Yes.

WILLIE: Go home.

SHOOTER: Willie!

WILLIE: The pool hall is closed. And Gary Wayne has a wife to go home to, and I'm gonna see that he gets there. Now go home.

DEEDEE: No, see, we're gonna—

WILLIE: Good night.

Deedee looks at Shooter as if asking whether she should go or not. Shooter looks at Willie, then back to Deedee. This is an awkward moment, to say the least. Finally, Shooter shrugs his shoulders.

SHOOTER: It's his hall.

DEEDEE: Yeah.

SHOOTER: Need a cab?

DEEDEE *(As she walks to the door)*: I just live across the street.

SHOOTER: I'll watch you out the window.

DEEDEE: That's us. *(Pointing)* See those blueberries in the window? It's a light. They're a light. I mean, I like blue, it's not my favorite color, but I like it a lot, and somebody gave it to me for, well, if the other lights were out, then you could see it real good, no, not it, them, no, it, the light better, the vines on it and everything. *(She's really chattering here)* I can't ever, well, I have to hunt all over town to find blue bulbs. I tried painting one blue, but something in the paint, I guess, made the bulb break. No, it didn't break, but it got these little holes all over the . . . *(Smacks herself to stop talking)* Don't you ever shut up, Deedee? *(Embarrassed laugh)* Mom says I could find somethin' to say to a head of cabbage.

SHOOTER: You got a cabbage at home to talk to?

DEEDEE: Yeah. I do. *(She laughs)* 'Night.

SHOOTER *(Stepping back in, door still open)*: Thanks again for the laundry. Good night.

Shooter closes the door, but he is still watching her. He yells at Willie, who is returning the pool cue to its place on the wall.

SHOOTER *(Fiercely)*: Just who do you think you are, man?

WILLIE: Messed up your plans, huh, boy?

SHOOTER: I can make them again, you know.

WILLIE: Not in here.

SHOOTER: It's a free country.

WILLIE: Not in here.

SHOOTER: And who knows, if she'd stayed here a little longer, you might have even picked up a cue and played with me. Anything, you'd have done just about anything to keep me from sharing a stack of strawberry pancakes with a dumb little blonde who talks to cabbages. I mean, you tell me why it is I am not allowed to talk to other people in this world without you standing there like Moses heaving your stone-tablet ten commandments down on my head. You do this to Dad? That your deal with him? I'll pay your bills, you do what I say? And when he couldn't make your trick shots anymore, he had to jump off that bridge because he never found anything else satisfying in his life 'cause you already done it all for him. Is that the real story?

WILLIE: Shooter was my friend. And I don't see that you got any friends, so you don't know nothin' about friends, so you shut up.

SHOOTER: He was my father and I'll say whatever I want. And I'll call myself Shooter if I want. And I'll dump Sondra if I want and I'll screw white women if I want.

WILLIE *(Very cold)*: Go to hell.

SHOOTER: I mean, what gives you the right to run my life?

WILLIE: I'll tell you what it is, you little—

SHOOTER *(Boiling)*: The Gospel According to Willie:

> Thou shalt not call thyself by thy father's name because it is a holy name.
>
> Thou shalt not try to play thy father's game because it is a holy game.
>
> Thou shalt not give thy father-in-law George a motorized wheelchair because I, Willie, am the giver of all good things.
>
> Thou shalt not make thy living at a radio station.
>
> Thou shalt not refuse thy wife a new Lincoln or any other damn fool thing she wants.
>
> Thou shalt not go home at night except that thou go straight home.
>
> Thou shalt not talk to any other women.
>
> Thou shalt especially not talk to white women.

WILLIE: Eight.

SHOOTER: Thou shalt not get old enough to make thy own decisions.

WILLIE *(Almost a dare)*: Nine?

SHOOTER *(Particularly intense)*: That's all of your gospel, Willie. The last two are mine. The last two are for you. Thou shalt not forsake, desert, skip out on, run away from, break promises to, or leave behind to die . . . thy friends.

WILLIE *(Truly confused)*: What?

SHOOTER: What do you mean "What?" Thou shalt not sell this pool hall!

WILLIE: I told you—

But Shooter can't stop now. He's been wanting to deliver this lecture ever since he got here tonight. This is why he came here.

SHOOTER: Don't you know what it's going to do to George when you split for New Jersey? It's going to kill him. Where's he got to go? Nowhere. What's he got to do? Nothing. Who does he care about in the world? Nobody . . . except you. And you're selling this place, and too cheap at that, so you can go live it up at Asbury Park. *(Now as if Willie were saying it)* Well, George, old friend, I hate to leave you like this, in the wheelchair and all, but listen, you call me up sometime and we'll talk about the good old days.

WILLIE *(Calmly)*: George . . .

SHOOTER: George will understand? George will not understand! Only two of the Three Blind Mice left as it is, and Willie wants to sell the hole. And you were giving me that shit about Sondra. Do your duty, keep your promises. Hang in there with those commitments, G.W., and all the time, you're deciding whether to pack your black shoes and wondering if they got Senior Citizens swimming pools.

WILLIE: Are you through?

SHOOTER: No. All my life I watched Dad and George depend on you. And maybe you got a rest coming, but you can't do it yet. If you leave now, while he's sick, then all that friends talk was just talk, and all those friends stories must be made up, and all that you-be-good-to-Sondra-because-she's-my-friend-George's-little-girl lecture is nothing but lies, because if you leave him all alone, you are not his friend and you never were.

WILLIE: My friend, George . . .

SHOOTER: Your "friend," George . . .

WILLIE: My . . . friend . . . George . . . is . . . dying.

SHOOTER: No.

WILLIE: Yes. And I am not going to Asbury Park. I am going to stay here and watch my friend George die.

SHOOTER: You said sick.

WILLIE: Yeah I said sick. Why didn't you go home when I first told you to, boy?

SHOOTER *(More gentle now)*: I didn't want to.

WILLIE *(Wearily)*: Would you go home now?

SHOOTER: No. *(Walks behind the bar)* Beer?

WILLIE: Yeah.

And Shooter opens two beers, puts one in front of Willie.

WILLIE: And a bag of chips. *(As Shooter gets one)* Uh-uh. The one at the top.

SHOOTER *(Reaching for it)*: This one?

WILLIE: Yeah. *(Taking the bag and looking at it)* We been watchin' this bag, me and George. *(Pauses)* We figure it's about a year old now.

SHOOTER: How long does he have?

WILLIE: Six months, maybe.

SHOOTER: That's not much.

WILLIE: Nope.

SHOOTER: Hospital?

WILLIE: Friday. They said he'd be more comfortable.

SHOOTER: That bad.

WILLIE: Right.

SHOOTER: And this place . . . selling this place . . . is going to pay for it.

WILLIE: Just about. *(Pause)* If he really drags his feet, it might take my car, too. *(Then standing up)* Shit, the pool hall on the mall's gettin' all the business anyway. Got pinball machines and air hockey.

SHOOTER *(With contempt)*: Pink felt tables and a ladies' john.

WILLIE *(Laughs)*: Real clean.

SHOOTER: Safe.

WILLIE: Then there's the jukebox, here. Don't exactly draw the crowd, you know.

SHOOTER: Huh?

WILLIE: Day George got his first wheelchair, hit him pretty hard, you know. I thought I told you this. *(Shooter shakes his head no)* Had me stop by Vine Records, buy all his favorites, coupla Chubby Checkers, lotta Tennessee Ernie Ford, Christ! *(Shooter laughs)* Filled up the jukebox with 'em. Left on the labels, up top here, like they were, just changed the records. Now, see, no matter what somebody picks out, they get one of George's oldies but goodies. Makes people mad. Makes me mad. Got lousy taste in music, George. Likes real crap, you know. *(Pats the machine)* Isn't all that bad, though. Funny sometimes. People punchin' up Aretha Franklin, gettin' Pat Boone.

SHOOTER: Pat Boone?

WILLIE: I told you he was sick.

SHOOTER: Know what he told me the day we got married?

WILLIE: Little fatherly advice?

SHOOTER: He said, "Boy, there's somethin' you got to know about women. *(Conspiratorial tone)* You want 'em to act nice, you want to stay outta trouble with 'em, you want 'em to love you forever?" *(Now in his own voice)* "Yeah," I'm sayin', "yeah, George, how do I do that?" And he says, "Well, when you get undressed at night . . . you got to hang up your clothes."

WILLIE: Goddamn him.

SHOOTER: Sondra must've guessed. She said George was smelling funny and that's why she wouldn't come see him.

WILLIE: She's just scared of it.

SHOOTER: Aren't you?

WILLIE: George ain't got a smell on him I ain't smelled. *(Shooter laughs)* She just don't want to know about it.

SHOOTER: Maybe.

WILLIE: She's afraid she'll be with him when it happens. He'll say somethin' smart like, "If you'll excuse me, girl, I gotta be goin'." Close his eyes and split. Go. Die.

SHOOTER: Maybe. *(Gentler about her now)* And maybe she's just a selfish, silly girl who started buying grown-up clothes but never grew into them.

WILLIE: She'll get there.

SHOOTER: I could help, with George.

WILLIE: Save it.

SHOOTER: For you?

WILLIE: I want a table, set right next to my casket, so right after "Don't he look nice," I'll hear "Little nine-ball?" I mean, if I gotta lay there dyin' for a beer, least I can have a game to watch. Boys cussin' and carryin' on, balls flyin' off the table, crushin' carnations in my wreath I'm wearin' says "Bartender."

SHOOTER: If that's the way you want it.

WILLIE: You know what I want. I want you and Sondra—

SHOOTER: Yeah, I know.

WILLIE: Right.

SHOOTER: I heard you, okay?

WILLIE: So?

SHOOTER: So what?

WILLIE: So are we gonna play or not?

Willie's offer is so unexpected, it triggers an overwhelming emotional response in both of them. They embrace, acknowledging at last their desperate need, their mutual loss, and their pure and lasting love for each other.

SHOOTER: Oh man.

WILLIE: Thought you were too old to hug me, didn't you.

SHOOTER *(Fondly)*: Just get off my neck and chalk your cue. Nine-ball. Dollar a game.

WILLIE: You're on, buddy.

Shooter gets out the balls and racks them in silence as Willie gets his cue and chalks it. Willie takes his practice, then looks up at Shooter.

WILLIE: I got to see this dollar, boy.

SHOOTER: Give me a break. *(And he slaps his dollar down on the table)*

WILLIE: What did you say? *(And he stands up, assumes old Shooter's pose)*

WILLIE AND SHOOTER *(As Shooter would have said it)*: Give me a break.

And Willie breaks the balls with a powerful shot and the lights come down immediately. We hear the beginning of ad-lib exchanges as the game starts.

End of Play

THE
HOLDUP

ABOUT THE PLAY

The Holdup was developed in a 1980 Actors Theatre of Louisville workshop directed by the author, and then as part of Circle Repertory Company's 1982 summer residency at Saratoga, New York, in a production directed by Rod Marriott. Under the direction of Edward Hastings, the play officially premiered at San Francisco's American Conservatory Theatre in April 1983.

CHARACTERS

THE OUTLAW, a worn, grizzled desperado, now approaching fifty. He is fearless and mean-tempered, a wily survivor of the Hole-in-the-Wall era, who never says more than is necessary and who generally gets what he wants because he knows how to stand there and mean business.

LILY, a frontier beauty, a little past her prime. She has graciously accepted the wisdom and perspective that have replaced her once startling appearance. In the old days she was a dance-hall favorite. Now she owns the finest hotel east of Albuquerque.

ARCHIE TUCKER, a green Clovis boy of seventeen. Archie's open face and simple enthusiasm seem quite out of place in this barren country. He talks too much and smiles too much and complains too much and, all in all, doesn't belong here. He's eager to find a way out but is held back by his mother and his age and his fear.

HENRY TUCKER, Archie's hothead rancher brother. Henry is mean and tough, a foul-mouthed, heavy-drinking cattleman, a bit embarrassed to be supplementing his income by working this wheat-threshing crew. He is thirty years old but still lives at home. His youth was baked dry in the sun of too many days doing his endless, lifeless work. His sole entertainment is reading outlaw books. He is an expert in their methods and manners.

TIME AND PLACE

The play takes place around a cookshack belonging to a wheat-threshing crew working a field in northern New Mexico in the fall of 1914. It is miles from nowhere and long past sundown.

ACT ONE

Night in New Mexico is dark and flat. And if you are alone, you are always lost, even if you think you know where you are going.

   There are two strays in this night, headed straight for each other, but they don't know that. We see their faces but we don't know where they are. We only know that they are alone, and they are dealing with their respective problems as best they can, determined to reach what they think is a safe place, the company of other humans.

   The Outlaw takes his saddle off the horse and ties up the cinches so he can carry it. And he talks.

OUTLAW: Well, old girl, I've shot better horses than you, but never one I felt so kin to, at the moment.

   And now, from another part of the blackness comes a terrified voice, a shaky praying voice.

ARCHIE: Jesus God in heaven, it's Archie Tucker from Clovis, New Mexico. I know you can see me, so I know you can see that coyote that's following me and I don't know if he's alone, but I'm alone and I need you to keep him back there till I can run for the cookshack, which shouldn't be too much longer, now, thank you so much, Amen.

OUTLAW *(Taking off the bridle)*: I just don't have any choice about shootin' you, see. I can't just leave you here to die by *yourself.* And I can't hobble along with you or I'll miss Lily. I told her I'd be there at midnight, sharp. Nice and easy, girl, here it comes.

   And we hear the gunshot, and Archie hears it too, but he has other concerns.

ARCHIE: Uh, Lord, you gave me a gun, I know, but Henry, that's my brother, he's got it standing guard back at the cookshack. So it's just you and me and that coyote. I'd stand and fight him but I imagine I'd die, if you know what I mean. People die out here all the time and nobody ever knows. Tell you what, I'll run when I can.

OUTLAW: You know who I miss? That gelding. Suzy. Snaggle-tooth horse. She was! Who am I talking to. Just pick up your gear and walk, old man. Just another mile, buddy. Lily always had an eye for horseflesh, didn't she? She'll bring you somethin' sweet to ride, you can count on that, at least. *(And we hear him begin to walk)*

ARCHIE: Uh, Lord, in case you saw me ride into town today, maybe you got me mixed up with the rest of the boys stayed in town to . . . all right, but I don't like to even *say* it. They stayed in town to drink beer and abuse women. I am *not* one of them, I am *saved* and I need some help here. Oh boy. I bet you hear that a lot. Well, listen, forget about everybody else for a while. This is serious.

OUTLAW: Well what have we got up here? Looks like some kind of cookshack, some wheat-threshing crew I guess. Well sure it is. It's the water hole, isn't it? Only water for twenty miles, as I remember. Think she's here yet? Think she's as old as you are? Think she's gonna show up at all? What do you do if she don't, huh?

ARCHIE *(His voice showing his relief)*: Oh now, there's the cookshack, I can just about make it now. Thank you so much. *(Screaming)* Run, Archie!

OUTLAW *(Hearing Archie)*: What the hell?

And now we see the cookshack and the barrels and benches that huddle around it. It is a small wood building on wheels with one door, one window and a metal chimney for ventilation. There are heavy cloth flaps hanging down to the ground on all sides protecting the sleeping area underneath it. You wonder how it continues to stand up, but you have no doubt that it does. There are some curiously modern-looking machine parts lying around, but otherwise, the scene looks almost pre-Civil War. And Archie runs up to the cookshack, terrified.

ARCHIE: Henry! Hey in there, Henry Tucker! *(Banging on the cookshack door)* You gotta hear what just happened to me when I'm coming back from town just now. *(Jumps up to the window, trying to wake Henry)* Henry! Wake up! I know you're in there, Henry, and you know who this is so you open this door, Henry. *(Still no answer)* Did you know they were gonna stay in town all night? Get cleaned up, that's what they said. But then . . . *(Screaming)* Henry! *(And the door finally opens)* Nobody acts right out here. I hate this place!

HENRY: So leave, priss, the train runs both ways, Archie.

ARCHIE: You're not gonna believe what happened, Henry!

HENRY *(Starting to build the fire back up, not eager to hear anything)*: It won't be worth wakin' up for, I can tell that already.

ARCHIE: I jumped off the train, only right away I'm not alone, see. I turn around and there he was, standing sideways in the road, the biggest coyote I ever saw. So I started up walking again, but when I speeded up, he speeded up and when I slowed down, he slowed down and finally, I got where I could see the cookshack and took off running and here I am.

HENRY: And that's your big story?

ARCHIE: I mean, I could hardly breathe there for a while.

HENRY: You ran away? Damn right it's your big story. Got a problem? Call Henry or run away. Runt coward. You make me sick, Archie. I don't know what I was doing, bringing you along. Dad's probably still laughing at me stuck out here with you.

ARCHIE: I've got as much right to be here as you do. They hired us both. Mr. White says I'm a good worker.

HENRY: They hired you because they couldn't get me unless they took you. What do you know about threshing wheat, Archie? They all laugh at you, you know. You're a joke, Archie.

ARCHIE: Well just how hard do you think the boys would laugh if they saw your pillow full of outlaw books, huh? Every spare minute you get, sneaking off to ride with the Wild Bunch, fighting the Johnson County War.

HENRY: The Wild Bunch didn't fight the Johnson County War.

ARCHIE: Well who cares whether they did or they didn't? That stuff is made up, Henry. People write those books just to find out if anybody's dumb enough to believe it.

HENRY: 'Bout like the Bible, I guess.

ARCHIE: The Bible is the truth.

HENRY: People walk out on the water and get swallowed by whales, Archie?

ARCHIE: It has to be the truth, Henry. What do you think God's trying to do, entertain?

HENRY: Just leave me alone, okay. Just go to bed, Diddly.

ARCHIE: Don't call me that!

HENRY: Just don't say one more word to me, you think you can do that? I get rid of you for one night in my whole life and what do you do? Take the train right on back here.

ARCHIE: You're just mad about Corbin in town spendin' all your pay you gambled off last night. It serves you right, pulling your gun like one of your outlaws, for God's sake. I hope you learned your lesson.

HENRY: They've had it in for me since the beginning of this job, Archie. I don't know who they think they are, these cowboys, they're just as dumb and just as worn out as everybody else I know. Bunch of sheepherders, if you ask me. So I showed 'em, that's all. Now, you just watch and see if anybody ever tries to cheat Henry Tucker again. What do I want to go into town for anyway? Have a good time with that bunch of know-it-alls? Fat chance.

ARCHIE: Oh I almost forgot! Guess what else I saw in town? Marines signing up men for the war. It's all over the papers too. Some Archduke Somebody-or-other got killed and it's all about to blow up!

HENRY (Not the least bit interested): What is?

ARCHIE: The world, Henry! Unless we get there in time!

HENRY: So why didn't you join up?

ARCHIE: Mother would *kill* me!

HENRY: So would a war, Archie.

ARCHIE: You could go! You're exactly who they're lookin' for! They're gonna fly airplanes in this war, Henry! You'd like that, zoomin' around the sky. You could be The Outlaw of the Air, Henry!

HENRY: Well, they better not take you, Archie. You'd be out there on the front lines, walk over to the enemy and say, "Hi there, my name is Archie and these are my buddies, this is Ralph and this is Joey and we're from New Mexico," and you'd be the first marine who ever died in the middle of a sentence. *(Archie turns away)* What's the matter with you? Guys like us go to war and we don't get to fly airplanes. We just stand on the ground and get shot. Don't make any sense at all, Archie. I can do that here.

ARCHIE: He told me I could learn to fly a plane. I asked him and he said, "Come on."

HENRY: Just shut up. You don't know what you're talking about.

ARCHIE: Okay. Okay.

And then, in a moment of silence, they hear a twig break just behind the cookshack.

ARCHIE *(Whispering)*: What was that?

HENRY *(Covering his fear)*: Well, it sure as hell ain't the marines.

Henry picks up a stick of wood from the fire and Archie backs away, toward Henry for protection. The Outlaw appears, gun raised, from the other direction, surprising them both. The Outlaw looks quite different than when we saw him before. Maybe it's the effect of the gun in his hand. Maybe he likes horses better than people. Whatever it is, this is somebody you don't want to fool around with. This man looks dangerous.

OUTLAW: Keep on talking, boy. *(Waving the pistol at Henry)* Hands high, cowboy.

Henry is reluctant. Archie raises his hands.

OUTLAW: Not you, boy. You sit. Over there. Him. Up.

ARCHIE: Henry!

OUTLAW: That's better. Don't need any heroes here. Just a little hospitality. *(Starts to search Henry)*

HENRY: What do you want, gramps?

OUTLAW *(Not easing the tension one bit)*: Oh, I don't know. What have you got?

ARCHIE: Anything you want. You just name it.

HENRY *(Turning quickly)*: Shut up, Archie.

OUTLAW *(Poking Henry with the gun, not liking that fast turn)*: Careful, cowboy.

ARCHIE: His name's Henry.

HENRY: Shut up, Archie! *(Then quickly)* How long have you been out there?

OUTLAW *(Still very threatening)*: Long enough. You don't look a thing alike.

ARCHIE: He takes after Dad. That whole side of the family is—

HENRY: Shut up, Archie. The man's not here to get a family history. What do you want, mister?

OUTLAW: Eggs. Cooked.

HENRY: No.

ARCHIE: I'll make 'em, Henry, if you want me to.

HENRY: I said no.

OUTLAW: Yes. And if you got a gun in the cookshack, there, you just bring it right on out here.

HENRY: Maybe I will.

OUTLAW: Yeah, you go get it and then you'll draw on me and I'll kill you. Won't be anything personal, just how it happens to me anymore. I get what I want. Now, I want some eggs.

HENRY: Any man can walk in hungry and ask for eggs and I'll make 'em, any day, but you ain't asked.

OUTLAW: Are we gonna fight over a mess of eggs?

ARCHIE *(Trying to be reasonable)*: I said I'd make the eggs. The man's a stranger here and we should—

HENRY *(Stops him, rough)*: Don't you move. You do what I say.

ARCHIE: Then you do what he says.

HENRY: Don't tell me what to do!

ARCHIE: I'm not. What do I know? It's just . . . you do see the gun, don't you, Henry? We're just talking about some old eggs, Henry.

OUTLAW: Don't you want to get your gun?

HENRY: I'll cook. *(And he heads for the cookshack)*

OUTLAW: And bring me some whiskey.

ARCHIE: We don't have any whiskey. We got a rule about it.

OUTLAW: If you didn't have any whiskey, you wouldn't have a rule about it.

And now, the Outlaw walks behind the water barrels to retrieve his saddle and a leather satchel. He puts the saddle over a bale of hay to make a kind of seat, but he doesn't sit on it. Archie watches as long as he can before he talks.

ARCHIE: Are you gonna kill us?

OUTLAW: I'm gonna eat first.

ARCHIE: That's not fair! We're minding our own business. It's Saturday night. We threshed wheat all week, we work hard. Then we get a night off and you come up and shoot us. It's not fair. It's not civilized. We're a state now. It's 1914.

OUTLAW: Do you know what a joke is? You know, one person says a funny thing to some other person and the other person laughs? *(No response)* Do you? Joke? Ha-ha?

ARCHIE: I know that.

OUTLAW: Then why didn't you laugh at my joke?

ARCHIE: Are you gonna kill us or not?

OUTLAW: Are you always like this? *(No response)* What time is it?

ARCHIE: Oh, you're meeting somebody here! What a good idea. It's a perfect place for it. Why didn't you say that in the first place. Maybe we've seen 'em already. Nope. Nobody for hours now, well, what do I know? I just got back myself. Maybe Henry saw somebody. Who're we lookin' for? Tall? Thin?

OUTLAW: I just asked you what time it was.

ARCHIE: Oh. Right. I don't know. Dark.

OUTLAW: What does Henry do? How come he's out here with everybody else on the town for the night?

ARCHIE: The crew could come back anytime, you know. There's twenty-five or more. Big men.

OUTLAW *(Screaming)*: I want those eggs, cowboy! *(Then normally)* They call you Archie?

ARCHIE: Or Doc. Some of 'em call me Doc. *(The Outlaw nods, but doesn't ask why)* I was sweet on Doc Porter's girl, Sarah. They started calling me Doc because, well, Doc Porter runs the drugstore in Clovis. I'm courting a Doc's daughter so they call me Doc. It's a joke.

OUTLAW: It isn't very funny for a joke.

ARCHIE: Or fork-pitcher. It's what I do. I fork up the wheat and—

OUTLAW: —pitch it on the wagon, I know. What's that big machine out there?

ARCHIE: It's a brand-new separator. Thing threshes ten times as much wheat as the old one in half the time. Gonna change everything.

OUTLAW: It takes up too much room. It's ugly.

Henry comes out of the cookshack carrying a steaming plate of eggs, and now wearing a light jacket.

HENRY *(Heartily, as though he'd cooked for a friend)*: Six eggs. Hot and ready!

ARCHIE: I told you he'd make the eggs.

OUTLAW *(Referring to the coat)*: Got your gun, I see.

HENRY: Cold out here. Eat up. That's a clean fork.

OUTLAW *(Walking toward Archie, picking up a forkful of eggs)*: I was asking Archie, how come you pulled this guard duty while the rest of the boys are in raisin' hell tonight. *(He pushes the bite of eggs in Archie's mouth)*

HENRY: Somebody has to.

OUTLAW: Yeah, but why you, cowboy? What happened last night?

HENRY: It's none of your business.

OUTLAW: Oh yes it is, too. I want to hear it. Archie will tell me, won't you boy? Eggs taste good, cowboy.

HENRY *(To Archie)*: You do and I'll—

OUTLAW *(Demanding)*: Archie!

ARCHIE *(Beginning rather helplessly)*: It was just another stupid poker game.

Corbin was cheating and I saw it. I told Henry and Henry drew on him. That's all.

OUTLAW: If that was all, Archie, Mr. Corbin would be out here eatin' hay, not Henry.

HENRY *(Before Archie can start)*: You shut your mouth, priss.

The Outlaw plays with his gun, just to terrify Archie.

ARCHIE: The gun is why Henry's out here. Not supposed to have guns in camp, that's all.

OUTLAW *(Not satisfied)*: Go on.

ARCHIE *(Compulsively)*: All right! When Henry drew his gun he dropped his cards and there's not supposed to be two ace of hearts either! *(The Outlaw laughs)* They woulda killed each other if Mr. White hadn't been here. They woulda both lost their jobs, too, if this wasn't twenty square miles of wheat to thresh next week. They were acting like some saloon characters from twenty years ago.

OUTLAW: Man's got to protect himself, Archie.

ARCHIE: Yeah, but he's supposed to use his brain, not his gun.

OUTLAW: Well, you want to use the quickest thing you got, whatever that is.

ARCHIE: You shouldn't cheat till you learn how to play, Henry.

HENRY: You started it all, Archie. I'd be spendin' his money right now if it wasn't for you and your big mouth. "Corbin's cheatin', Henry," like a damn idiot.

OUTLAW: Henry's right, Archie. You talk too much.

HENRY: There's a horse comin'.

OUTLAW *(Quite calm, having heard it already)*: Uh-huh.

HENRY *(Nodding in agreement)*: Sounds like a Morgan horse to me.

OUTLAW *(Watching Archie, playing along)*: Black, with . . . white feet.

HENRY: Seven, eight years old maybe.

OUTLAW *(Knows it isn't a horse by now)*: Still got all his teeth, though.

And they laugh and Archie was completely taken in.

ARCHIE: It's the rest of your gang, I guess. *(Then quite dispirited, to Henry)* He asked me while ago what time it was, Henry.

HENRY: Relax, Archie. It's just Mother comin' to collect you for prayer meeting.

ARCHIE: I hear it now. It doesn't sound like a horse at all. It sounds like an automobile! *(They laugh)* It does!

HENRY: Archie, the closest road is five miles from here.

OUTLAW *(Very concerned by now)*: So if it is a car, it's a damn fool drivin' it.

ARCHIE *(Feeling quite anxious)*: How did *you* get here? Where's your horse?

OUTLAW: 'Bout a mile back.

ARCHIE: I could get him for you.

OUTLAW: You could have her for breakfast.

ARCHIE: She's dead.

OUTLAW: I shot her.

ARCHIE: You saw the fire and walked to here.

OUTLAW: Oh there's no foolin' you, is there Archie?

ARCHIE *(Staring out into the night)*: It sure is a car all right. Are they lost or what? Who'd come out here in a car?

Then as Henry and the Outlaw are both very anxious, and clearly not willing to speculate about who this might be, Archie goes on babbling.

ARCHIE: Was she a good horse?

HENRY: Would you shoot a good horse, Archie? Yes, you would. Archie would shoot a good horse if Mother told him to.

ARCHIE: Good horses get sick.

HENRY *(Testing the Outlaw)*: A man shoots his horse is shootin' off his pecker, Archie.

OUTLAW: Shut up, cowboy.

HENRY: I was saying not to ask about it. It ain't your business, Archie. It makes you feel bad to shoot your horse. As bad as *(Turning around to face the Outlaw)* shootin' off your pecker so don't make jokes about it.

ARCHIE: I wasn't joking, I was asking.

OUTLAW *(As the car stops)*: Archie don't use his pecker anyway, so he wouldn't know.

ARCHIE: I do too. Use it. *(Henry and the Outlaw laugh)* I water the garden. *(They laugh and he continues)* I put out fires. *(More laughter)* Cuts the dust right off a wagon wheel.

OUTLAW *(Getting his gun out again)*: Go on.

ARCHIE: That's all.

OUTLAW *(Covering his nervousness about who's coming)*: You just been doin' chores with it? You ain't had any fun with it?

ARCHIE: Leave me alone.

OUTLAW: Any girls took a peek at it?

HENRY: Hell, he doesn't even look at it.

ARCHIE: Whose side are you on, Henry?

And now, from offstage, we hear a voice full of anticipation.

LILY: Tom? Tom?

HENRY: What is this?

OUTLAW: Sounds like a lady came in a car.

ARCHIE: Tom? Is that your name, Tom?

And Lily rushes onstage, wearing a Barney Oldfield-type duster over her long split riding skirt. It all looks very expensive, but is clearly western and meant for hard use.

LILY: Tom!

OUTLAW (*Reacting to the duster*): What the hell?

LILY (*Thrilled to see him, but stops herself from running to him once she sees Archie and Henry*): You are! You're still alive!

OUTLAW (*Concealing whatever he feels*): Well I wouldn't write you to tell you I was dead!

LILY: But anybody could've written that letter. Your handwriting's not as—

OUTLAW: Take that thing off. Let me look at you.

LILY (*Delighted to*): Just a minute. I almost didn't find this place, you know. They cut down that cottonwood tree. Good thing the water hole's still here. (*The jacket is off now*) Now!

OUTLAW: Oh that's much better. You haven't changed a bit.

LILY (*Walking into his arms*): It's going to work out just fine, isn't it? I'm getting old and you're going blind.

And the Outlaw turns Lily around to them, not able to give her quite the greeting he wanted to, but still obviously desperate to touch her.

ARCHIE: Did you really come all the way out here in a car?

LILY: Big black Buick. Go see for yourself!

Archie starts off toward the car, but Henry stops him.

OUTLAW: Lily, this is the Tucker Brothers. Archie and Cowboy.

ARCHIE: His name's Henry.

OUTLAW: Boys, meet Lily.

LILY (*She nods to them, but talks to the Outlaw*): What a ride! That's at least forty miles! And there's no road at all for the last five!

OUTLAW (*Starting for the bench now*): Well, here, why don't you sit down a minute and—

HENRY (*Disgusted*): Look, folks. This ain't exactly Main Street out here. Could you take your visit on down the road so we can get some sleep?

OUTLAW (*Ignoring Henry and walking her to the bench*): There's no road, remember?

LILY: Boy, we're in big trouble if we have a blowout out here, I guess I could have rented a horse, but oh, Tom, (*In a mock scolding*) where have you been?

HENRY (*Irritated, but beginning to be curious*): How come he couldn't meet you in town? Been a helluva lot easier to find.

OUTLAW (*Breaking away from Lily*): Can you shut your mouth and do whatever I tell you to do? Can you get the lady a drink and not ask any stupid questions, cowboy? (*Henry doesn't move*) And I told you while ago I wanted some whiskey but I don't see it out here, now, do I? Move!

HENRY: One drink and you go?

OUTLAW: Get it.

And Henry goes into the cookshack and the Outlaw turns back to Lily.

OUTLAW: Why the hell did you buy an automobile?

LILY: For the horn. I like the horn. A little man brought it. I kept him too. He . . . works on it.

ARCHIE: That's where I saw you! Outside that fancy hotel in town.

LILY: Oh Tom, you wouldn't know the old place now. It's solid white paint, no wallpaper. There's actually trees growing in barrels all along that front hall. Oh and the dining room is this bright green and Roy Luther hooked me up a waterfall, inside the dining room. And I'm about ready to go order another automobile to pick up my guests at the train station. They come in hot and thirsty and see those trees and that waterfall and they feel like staying a *week*.

ARCHIE: I saw that car too. That's some car all right.

OUTLAW: You think she's pretty?

ARCHIE: She's pretty.

OUTLAW: You got any money?

ARCHIE: I worked hard for it, if I do, and I'm not handing it over, no sir.

OUTLAW: Money for the lady. How much you got?

ARCHIE: I'm not interested in that.

LILY: And the price has gone way up, mister.

OUTLAW: You squirmy little mole. Tell me how much money you got!

ARCHIE: Twenty-eight dollars.

OUTLAW: You could have this pretty lady, all day, all night for a solid month with that money. All to yourself, just you and her. You ever thought about that?

ARCHIE: No.

Henry comes out with the whiskey.

OUTLAW: Do you know what you're going to be when you grow up?

ARCHIE: No.

OUTLAW: Sorry, that's what.

And the Outlaw and Henry have a good laugh about that.

LILY: Do you know what year this is? I'm not a whore. It's not a whorehouse. It's a hotel now and I own it.

OUTLAW *(Clearly annoyed)*: A little pride goes a long way, girl.

LILY: I *told* them you were still alive. I just *knew* it. Roy Luther said Bob Ford got you.

HENRY: Bob Ford got Jesse James.

LILY: Daisy said it was Frank Canton.

HENRY *(More energy than we've seen from him all night)*: He got Nate Champion at the Johnson County War.

LILY: Gus figured it was the Pinkertons. Chase you down like Kid Curry.

HENRY: Kid Curry killed himself.

OUTLAW: And I bet you know where.

HENRY: I do, that's true. Parachute, Colorado.

ARCHIE: Henry believes in outlaws.

HENRY: Shut up, Archie.

LILY *(Laughs)*: Roy Luther swore he saw it in the papers.

OUTLAW: He saw Bill and Fred. They got Bill and Fred.

HENRY: Bill Carver?

OUTLAW: Bill my brother. His boy Fred. Nice boy, big hands.

LILY: Guess he just saw the name then.

HENRY: What name?

OUTLAW *(Ignoring Henry)*: Well, how do I look? Old?

HENRY: Hey, your eggs got cold before you finished them. How 'bout some more eggs.

OUTLAW: We aren't gonna be here long enough for that, cowboy.

HENRY: Sure you are. The lady's tired and you could use some more food, pops. It looks like it's been a while. You want anything, ma'am? Might be a corn stick left from supper.

LILY: No thank you.

HENRY: Well, you just let me know if you change your mind. And just take your time there. We're glad to have you. Gets awful lonely out here.

ARCHIE *(Dumbfounded but pleased by this change in Henry)*: See how nice Henry can be when he wants to?

LILY: Have you seen Bub Meeks?

OUTLAW: Lost a leg in prison, last I heard.

HENRY: They shot him trying to escape. Climbing up the walls at Idaho Federal.

OUTLAW: Well you're a real outlaw expert, aren't you cowboy?

HENRY: Want your eggs sunny-side up this time?

OUTLAW *(Now eager to get rid of him)*: That sounds good.

HENRY: Comin' right up. *(He goes into the cookshack)*

LILY: Anybody else?

OUTLAW: They're in Bolivia, you know. Butch is alive.

ARCHIE: That's in South America.

OUTLAW: Thank you.

ARCHIE: I go to school.

OUTLAW: Or dead. Bolivia or dead.

ARCHIE: I don't get it.

OUTLAW: I wasn't talking to you.

ARCHIE: Your folks, is that it?

OUTLAW: Yeah, boy. My folks all died.

ARCHIE: Or went to Bolivia.

OUTLAW *(Ignoring Archie)*: I've got a new picture with me. I want you to take it to the Western Union and switch it. Burn that one from Telluride.

LILY: I always thought it was better of Butch than you.

OUTLAW: This is a much better picture.

LILY: I had my picture made for my birthday. Beside my Buick. In front of my hotel. Wearing my duster and goggles. Looks like I cut it out of a magazine but it's me all right.

ARCHIE: Are we talking about a wanted poster?

OUTLAW: *We* were.

LILY: Well actually, *he* was.

ARCHIE: You want them to catch you?

OUTLAW: No, I don't want them to catch me. But I do want them to know what I look like now. I got my pride. *(To Lily)* You're prettier than you were.

LILY: It's the money. Are you going to Bolivia?

OUTLAW: It's a long trip, but I bet they'd make you the goddamn queen of Bolivia.

ARCHIE: Do you speak Spanish? They speak Spanish.

OUTLAW *(Furious with him)*: If I want to go to Bolivia, I'll go to Bolivia. They have tin mines there. Did you learn that in school? I'll rob mine payrolls. And I'll eat those green bananas and I'll lay around with this lady and have our dinner cooked by some mountain kid about your age who knows not to say a goddamned thing like who are you or what do you want. Except he will say good morning and thank you, muchas gracias. And we'll have a wonderful time and we won't think about you or all the people like you back here building houses and running for mayor.

ARCHIE: This is the best country in the world! I could be president!

OUTLAW: That's why we're talking about Bolivia! What's the matter with you?

LILY: You can't go to Bolivia either. The trip alone would kill you. And how do you know you *like* bananas?

OUTLAW: Don't you want to see the lady's car, boy?

And Archie gets out of there quickly, knowing they want to be alone.

OUTLAW: Got a kiss for the old man?

They kiss and we see him relax for just a moment.

LILY *(Tenderly)*: You look awfully tired, Tom. I heard you were working horses in Montana, but you look like you've been living in a cave.

OUTLAW *(A sense of purpose now)*: I've been . . . seeing your face.

LILY: This face? Or the old one. The young one?

OUTLAW: I mean . . . I think about you.

LILY: I waited for you to come back, you know. I kept eggs in the house for two years for you.

OUTLAW: Well, here I am, girl.

LILY *(She has a small laugh)*: So I see.

OUTLAW *(Impatient as always)*: You know what I want. Yes or no?

LILY: Yes or no what? I've seen you one day in the last twenty years!

OUTLAW: Helluva day.

LILY: What do you want, Tom?

OUTLAW *(Her directness backs him off)*: Well, like I said in my letter, I . . . *(The more he looks at her, the more he can't say what he's come all these miles to say)* I had some business down this way.

LILY: What business? Twenty years is a long time. Things happen. Tell me what your business is. Tell me what you want me to say yes or no to. Then ask me. A girl needs to hear a man talk a little.

OUTLAW: About what?

LILY: No, don't say anything now. I'm rested enough, I think. Come back to town with me. You'll be safe enough. They all think you're dead anyway. And if anybody asks who you are, which they won't, I'll say you're my father. *(He backs off even further)* I'll get you whatever you want to eat and you can stay as long as you like. You'll like the hotel, there's lots of fancy eastern folks coming through all the time and we're getting our telephone next month so—

OUTLAW: Whatever happened to your rancher friend?

LILY: You shot him.

OUTLAW: Oh that's right I did.

LILY *(Trying to regain his attention)*: He died. Tom. Roy Luther is dying to see you. It'll be just like you remember. You'll get a bath and some sleep and you can tell me everything you've done for the last—

OUTLAW: You want to hear me *talk?*

LILY: I want to know if you're still the man I knew, that's all.

OUTLAW: Well, the girl I knew . . .

LILY: Is right here, Tom.

OUTLAW: Woulda brought me a horse.

And the Outlaw stands up now, and Henry opens the cookshack door, and Archie returns from looking at the car.

ARCHIE *(Running up to Henry, a conspiratorial tone in his voice)*: He's an outlaw, Henry. They've got his picture at the Western Union.

HENRY: He's no outlaw, Archie. Just some old prospector lost track of the mother lode, huh, pops? You were pannin' for gold and you lost your pan. Well, we got plenty more inside. Take this one when you're through with the eggs.

ARCHIE: Henry, he's with Butch Cassidy in this picture. They're at Telluride in this picture.

HENRY *(Appreciating the clue)*: Is that so? Well, Cassidy's in Bolivia, now, Archie, and if this guy was anybody he'd be down there with him, so maybe they were just in a bar together sometime or Cassidy sold him a horse.

LILY: Butch sold *you* a horse, oh that's funny.

HENRY *(Very cagey)*: Yeah, Cassidy didn't know much about horses, did he ma'am. The real expert was that doctor's son in the gang. What did your old man do, mister?

ARCHIE: They're *going* to Bolivia, Henry. That's what he came to ask her.

HENRY: Only she won't go. Or I know, she won't go on a horse and he won't go in a car! Is that the holdup, pops?

ARCHIE: Don't give him any ideas, Henry.

The Outlaw laughs.

OUTLAW: Would you like to see a holdup, Archie?

LILY: Come on. Eat your eggs and let's get out of here.

HENRY: Relax, Archie. A holdup is quick. A holdup would be over by now. Unless of course, you forgot how to pull one.

ARCHIE *(Trying to stay in Henry's good graces)*: Yeah, you're supposed to bust in here. No, first you ride up on your horse. You don't shoot your horse first. *(Expecting Henry to be pleased)* You ride up on your horse, you slam open the doors, you say everybody does what I say and nobody gets hurt. *(The Outlaw laughs)* And then you say up against the wall.

HENRY: No wall, Archie.

ARCHIE: The cookshack and spread your arms.

OUTLAW: Situation like this, I'd say down on the ground, Archie.

ARCHIE: Then it's throw your money over here.

OUTLAW *(Pointing the gun at them)*: All right. Down on the ground, boys. *(They hesitate)* Now!

LILY: What are you doing?

ARCHIE: Her too?

OUTLAW: I rode a thousand miles to see her. I don't want her dirty.

LILY: If this is for my benefit, you can stop right now because I've seen it, outlaw. Get up, you two. We're leaving right this minute.

And as Lily starts to move, the Outlaw grabs her, rough, and pushes her back down on the bench. Archie sees this and ducks his head even further into the ground.

ARCHIE: Throw our money over to you?

HENRY: Why don't you just shut up, Archie.

OUTLAW: Yeah, let's have your money.

HENRY: Don't have mine on me.

ARCHIE: Mine's in my bedroll, inside.

OUTLAW: See, Archie? I knew that already.

ARCHIE: She could get it for you.

OUTLAW: I don't need your money.

HENRY: So what are we doin' with our face in the dirt?

OUTLAW *(Laughs)*: Ask Archie. It was his idea.

Henry sits up, furious with Archie, and slaps him hard with his hat.

ARCHIE: Can we sit up?

OUTLAW: Sure.

ARCHIE *(Aware of Henry's rage)*: Could you just tell us what you want so we could give it to you so you could go on, wherever you're goin'?

OUTLAW: Who says I'm goin' anywhere? I'm gettin' what I want. A visit. Hear some stories, see some people. I haven't seen any people for a long time.

ARCHIE: Why not?

LILY: Because he acts like this, Archie.

ARCHIE: I mean, what is this? Who are you?

HENRY: You mind your own business.

ARCHIE: This feels like my business to me.

HENRY: It's his past, it's his business.

ARCHIE: I can ask the man.

HENRY: You can shut up!

ARCHIE: Why should I? So he won't know we're scared?

HENRY: I'm not scared. I'm sick to death of you.

ARCHIE: Me? What about him? He's the one ordered you around all night. He's got his gun in our face and you're sick to death of me? I don't get you, Henry.

HENRY: You never have. You don't know a thing about me.

ARCHIE: Oh I get it. If she won't go with him, you will, is that it? You'll just disappear to Bolivia like one of your books come to life and I'll have to tell Mr. White what happened in the morning? Let Dad sit around the rest of his life wondering whatever happened to Henry while I'm out doing your work on the ranch? Well, why don't you tell him how many shots it took you to nail that coyote in the barn last year.

HENRY *(Slaps him hard)*: And why don't you just remember we're all alone out here. And I've had you hanging around my neck as long as I can remember and if I decide to cut you loose, Diddly, nobody's ever gonna know.

ARCHIE: What does that mean?

OUTLAW: It means he's not on your side, Archie. Nobody is really, when you get right down to it, out here.

LILY *(Trying a different approach)*: Look, I'm sorry you two got in the middle of this. It's just two old friends getting together someplace safe, all right? We'll be on our way now.

HENRY: He can't go into town, girl. His draw's so shaky he wouldn't last two minutes.

OUTLAW *(Drawing his gun as he turns)*: Shoot him first?

HENRY *(Grabbing Archie like a shield)*: Him first!

OUTLAW: That's fine. Get you both with one shot.

HENRY *(Jumping away from Archie)*: God that was fast! You've still got it all, don't you! Now. Let's see if the kid can dance!

LILY: Now you look here!

OUTLAW *(Laughs)*: Shoot at his feet, you mean?

ARCHIE: Henry! You're not reading this in some book. What the hell are you doing?

HENRY: Something I should've done a long time ago. Looking out for myself. He needs somebody to ride with him and I'm it! We'll take two of the horses off this place and be on our way.

OUTLAW *(Quickly throwing Henry a rope)*: You better tie him up so he don't follow us.

HENRY *(Catches the rope and grabs Archie)*: Yeah boy!

LILY: Tom! Put that gun away! This is ridiculous!

The Outlaw is just as surprised as Lily is that Henry is willing to tie Archie up, but he doesn't show Henry that.

ARCHIE: What did I ever do to you?

HENRY: Are you kidding? My whole life I spent so you could go to school, so you could dream about airplanes, so you could go to church. I'm out there feedin' half-starved cattle and raisin' scrub crops, still workin' for Dad when I oughta be long gone all because you can't do nuthin' and never could. The most help you can ever be is just get out of my way, Archie. All you ever think about is where your next bath is comin' from and tell 'em, Archie, what are you saving your money for?

LILY *(Furious)*: I'm leaving right this minute and Archie's coming with me. Get whatever you need and let's get out of here.

Henry trips Archie to make him fall down and to make it clear that Archie's not going anywhere. Henry starts to tie Archie up, and he's real rough about it.

ARCHIE *(An appeal to Lily)*: I'm saving for a buggy. I already ordered the lap robe and harness. *(Then to Henry)* You watch. You'll want to borrow it. Well don't even ask. I'm gonna be somebody.

HENRY: Somebody's aunt, that's what you'll be. Dad took Archie to the Hart Ranch. They brought in forty-eight hundred head of cattle, Dad picked the hundred he wanted, then they rode with the drivers bringing the cattle back to Clovis. Know what Archie had to say about the trip? The ranch house was dirty.

ARCHIE: Noisy. We slept in a room where a man was killed. There was a bullet hole in the door!

HENRY *(To the Outlaw)*: See what I mean?

ARCHIE: You coulda gone on that trip except Dad knew you'd get drunk.

HENRY: You ain't goin' nowhere now, kid.

LILY: What kind of man ties up his brother? *(To the Outlaw)* And you! You ask me to meet you out here in the middle of nowhere after twenty years and then you won't even talk to me. And they don't play this kind of game even in bars anymore. I see this, all right, but it's when the school lets out for recess. Or when we celebrate Frontier Day.

HENRY: There. Done and tight! That's what I felt like my whole life, Archie. How do you like it, huh? *(Kicks him)*

Henry is proud of his work. The Outlaw takes his time coming over to him.

OUTLAW: Now, who are you?

HENRY: What?

OUTLAW: You heard me.

ARCHIE: Why don't you tie yourself up now, Henry.

HENRY: Who am I?

OUTLAW: Hard to say, huh?

HENRY: You mean how old am I?

OUTLAW: Start there, sure.

HENRY: Thirty.

OUTLAW: Go on.

HENRY: Not married. Live at the ranch.

ARCHIE: Lives at home.

OUTLAW: Big ranch?

HENRY: Pretty big.

OUTLAW: You ride?

HENRY: Ride. Good. Good rider, yeah. Rope. Shoot too.

OUTLAW: What.

HENRY: *Shoot* what?

OUTLAW: How's this for "talk," girl? This what you wanted to hear?

HENRY: I shot a Navy Colt before, but a Winchester's what's around most of the time. If you need somebody . . . if it's got a safe in it, I know Hercules powder and dynamite.

OUTLAW: Where'd you learn that?

ARCHIE: He didn't. He's lying. He reads *Police Gazette* in the barber shop.

HENRY: Shut up, Archie, or we'll gag you too.

OUTLAW: Well, you look strong enough all right.

HENRY: Would I be inside or outside? Lookout? Horse-holder?

OUTLAW: What are you like, cowboy?

HENRY: What do I like? Same as everybody. Money and a good time.

OUTLAW: No. Something you did once. Where you've been. How you are. How you'd . . . be.

HENRY: I don't understand.

ARCHIE: Something you did once, Henry. A story.

HENRY: Deaf Charley and Peep O'Day don't tell stories.

OUTLAW: They're dead.

ARCHIE: More outlaws, I guess.

HENRY: Outlaws, you bet. The Wild Bunch. O'Day was a horse-holder. *(Turning to the Outlaw)* Wasn't he?

ARCHIE: All the outlaws are dead, Henry.

HENRY *(Vicious)*: What do you know about it, Archie? Shut up!

LILY: Do you want a blanket, Archie? Something to drink? *(She comes over to Archie and moves him out of their way)*

ARCHIE: Why don't you go on. This isn't gonna be a very good time here. I know Henry when he gets like this and there's no stopping him. They won't hurt me. I hate this place.

LILY: Tom, stop this. Come home with me. Wherever you've been, it's been hard, I know, but I want you with me now. We've got some catching up to do.

OUTLAW *(Interrupting her)*: You gotta tell me *something*, cowboy.

HENRY: You know about Hole-in-the-Wall and I'm gonna tell you about egg hunts as a kid?

OUTLAW: You set traps for 'em? Trail 'em through the desert? Use your shotgun, what? I never been on a egg hunt.

ARCHIE: Tell him about breaking horses, tell him about threshing soybeans with a stick. Tell him about your life, Henry.

HENRY: I get thirsty. It's the same thing all the time.

ARCHIE: It has to last longer than that, Henry.

HENRY: Good story would be good company, I guess, at night. Hiding out. *(No response from the Outlaw)* Okay. I'll tell you about egg hunts and you tell me about Hole-in-the-Wall.

OUTLAW: Go.

HENRY *(Not enjoying this at all. It feels like school)*: The week before Easter, Mother would give us each a dozen eggs, each of us boys, marked so we'd know whose was whose. We'd hide 'em around the farm, this was back in Oklahoma. Then all week we'd look for—

OUTLAW: Hunt.

HENRY: Yeah, hunt. Hunt for each other's eggs and when we found some we'd hide 'em again in a harder place where only we knew so that at the end of the week on Easter morning, the boy with the most eggs won. Now it's your turn.

OUTLAW: Won what?

HENRY *(A sudden hostility)*: Just won. If you were smart, you buried your own eggs and ate the other ones you found.

ARCHIE: We knew you were doing that.

OUTLAW: You cheated at egg hunt?

HENRY: I won, didn't I? I wanted to win. *(Now brighter)* You can start with Flat Nose Currie. Did a horse really kick him in the face?

OUTLAW: Never knew the man. Before my time.

HENRY: Well, when *was* your time?

OUTLAW: I forgot.

HENRY: We made a deal!

OUTLAW: So maybe I'll cheat. You have a Christmas tree?

HENRY *(Disgusted)*: The man says he's an outlaw and then he asks me about our Christmas tree.

ARCHIE: He's crazy, Henry. It doesn't matter who he is. He doesn't have any gang to take you into. He's just crazy. Tell him about Christmas.

HENRY: You're Tom McCarty, aren't you?

OUTLAW: McCarty is dead. Tell me why you never have any money. Tell me how you done nuthin' for so long, Henry. Tell me why you're still living at home.

HENRY: It's none of your goddamn business!

OUTLAW: Tell me why you tied up your brother. Nobody I know *ever* tied up his brother. Why'd you do that? I mean, we got rules out here for this sort of thing, or used to. Is this how people do now? 'Cause if it is, I don't want any part of it. I'm goin' right back where I been and I'm stayin' put this time. *(Now as much to Lily as Henry)* I mean, you drop out of sight for a little while and look what we got for boys now. And you're drivin' a car and talkin' hard, girl.

HENRY: You tell me who you are!

OUTLAW *(Grinning)*: Kilpatrick.

HENRY: Dead.

OUTLAW: Sundance.

HENRY: Bolivia.

OUTLAW *(Laughing, mocking)*: Nope. Dead. I'm Billy the Kid. I'm Jesse James.

Henry pulls his gun, insisting on an answer.

OUTLAW: Okay cowboy. Now we all saw your gun. Now put it away.

Henry cocks the pistol.

ARCHIE: Please, mister . . . *(Then to Lily)* Or you tell. Tell Henry who he is.

OUTLAW *(Cooling down a little)*: I killed Tom McCarty. That help any?

HENRY *(Uncocks the pistol)*: How?

ARCHIE *(Thinks this is all ridiculous)*: Who is Tom McCarty?

HENRY: Tom McCarty taught Butch Cassidy to rob banks.

LILY: Handsome, funny.

HENRY: They got ten grand outta Telluride.

LILY: The best horse-handler in the business.

HENRY: Tom McCarty was smart!

LILY: Smelled like wild mint and wore a long leather coat, aspen gold.

HENRY: I don't believe you killed him!

LILY: I loved that coat. And a green scarf around his neck. Oh my.

HENRY: Who are you to kill Tom McCarty?

LILY: I figured somebody'd kill him for his money someday, he had so much of it. I should've married him.

ARCHIE: Did he want you to?

OUTLAW: He did.

LILY: Well why didn't he say something. I was crazy for him!

OUTLAW: He was scared.

LILY: You know what you have to do to forget a man like that? You have to buy an automobile, for God's sake.

HENRY *(Finding the Outlaw's satchel now)*: How do I know you killed him?

OUTLAW: You don't. But . . . I got his watch. *(Pitches it to Henry to make him drop the satchel)* Maybe I bought it. I got his spurs. Maybe he gave them to me. I got his satchel, there. Maybe I was his friend.

HENRY: This McCarty's?

LILY: Does it say Forget-me-not, LTK on the back?

HENRY: It does.

LILY: It's McCarty's. I gave it to him.

HENRY: How did you kill him? No. Tell us what happened to his money. She said he had a lot of money. What's in that suitcase?

OUTLAW: Whatever it is, it's mine.

ARCHIE: What a great idea, rob an old guy out in the wheat field.

LILY: There's no money in that case, Henry. It's old wanted pictures, newspaper articles, books about his friends, books with his name in them.

HENRY: He's no outlaw. Some whore sold him that watch. He's just some horse thief, some gone-crazy sheepherder. Just a copperhead, prissy-ass grandpa. He sneaked up on the smartest bank robber in the West and shot him in cold blood. A worm, unless I hear different.

ARCHIE: Shut up, Henry.

HENRY: You're gonna tell us how you killed Tom McCarty, *if* you killed Tom McCarty, and then we're gonna tie you up and turn you in. Get a hundred dollars! Outlaw Killer Killed.

OUTLAW: Look cowboy, relax. I apologize for playin' with you like this. I've just turned mean or something. Let's untie the kid here and—

HENRY *(A serious threat)*: You touch him and you're dead, mister.

OUTLAW *(Much more carefully)*: That is money in that case. You're absolutely right. I liked your eggs. I'll give you some.

HENRY *(Fairly contemptuous)*: I'm gonna take it *all,* after you tell me your "story."

OUTLAW: It's not much of a story. McCarty didn't want to hide, and didn't want to run. He asked me to do it.

HENRY: Shoot him?

OUTLAW: Bury him.

ARCHIE: After you shot him.

OUTLAW: I buried him alive. Just outside of Delta, Colorado.

HENRY *(Quietly, but firmly)*: I know who you are.

OUTLAW *(Bitterly)*: It's pretty exciting, isn't it?

HENRY *(His excitement building)*: Well, I think so. They're looking for you all over this country! Nobody knows what happened to you or where you are and you're sitting right here. What do you know about that! I'm taking you in!

OUTLAW: Come and get me then.

HENRY: You don't think I can.

OUTLAW: Listen, Henry, I've done this over and over for twenty years now. I know how it goes. Somebody wants to kill me so they pull a gun. They yell and scream or they sneak up from the back, it doesn't much matter. It never works. *I* live. They, you, end up dead. I swear it's the truth. It's only fair to tell you. Now, you tell me you heard what I said.

HENRY: Well I know what happened at Delta, Colorado. You were holding the horses behind the bank. You heard one shot and you ran. And you've been hiding ever since! Boy are the boys in town gonna be happy to see you at the end of a rope! Swing in the breeze, mister outlaw!

OUTLAW: I don't think I'd take too well to jail, Henry. Just shoot me. I'll get close enough so you don't miss and I'll put my gun in my hand so it looks fair and all.

HENRY: You never even went back to see they got buried, did you?

LILY: Stop this right now! Both of you!

OUTLAW *(Very firm)*: You know what to do here, Lily. Get out of the way and stand still!

HENRY: Bill and Fred, remember, Archie? Your brother Bill. His boy, Fred. You left their horses for 'em and you ran.

OUTLAW: They'd have done the same thing if it was me in there! That's just how it worked!

HENRY: They shot a man in the bank so they broke through the back door, but you weren't there. So they got on their horses and Freddie boy lit out toward Third Street on that big roan.

OUTLAW: Gelding. Suzy.

HENRY: You *don't* know what happened, do you? Well, how could you if you've been hiding ever since. This is some story, Archie. Some guy Simpson shot Freddie boy right through his left ear, loaded his gun, got where he had a better aim at Bill and took the back of his head clean off. Scalped him!

OUTLAW: You shut up! You read about me while you got your hair cut.

HENRY: The shot blew Bill right out of the saddle, but Fred's body kept riding around till somebody plugged the horse in the belly. Damn strong horse though. Made it all the way to the post office hitching post where it finally fell down in a big mess of blood, squashed Fred's body underneath, flat as flat. And where were you?

OUTLAW: Shut up! You just shut up!

HENRY: You were riding as fast as you could. Took West Gulch to that little island in the Gunnison River, picked up your fresh horse and disappeared. Left two mighty good fresh horses behind. Did I leave anything out?

OUTLAW: You . . . off hoping me or somebody like me would come save you from being a nobody all your life just by sticking a gun in your face.

HENRY: You're a coward! The smartest one of the bunch is nuthin' but a miserable coward!

ARCHIE: Stop it, Henry!

HENRY: I just told him a little story. See, Archie, you don't know all the stories. *(Making a lunge at the Outlaw)* Now, you're coming with me and—

OUTLAW: Don't touch me, cowboy!

Henry cocks his gun again, aiming squarely at the Outlaw's back.

HENRY: Coward! Coward!

OUTLAW *(Turns around)*: Why does it have to be you? Why couldn't it be somebody I—

HENRY: What are you waiting for, coward?

OUTLAW: You're asking me to kill you, boy.

HENRY: I'm daring you. You think you can say you're an outlaw and that makes you an outlaw? You ran. Real outlaws, real outlaws . . .

OUTLAW: It went wrong for me once in my life, Henry. It ain't gone right once for you. All you got in your life is my story to tell.

HENRY: And everybody's gonna know it was me that found you.

OUTLAW: Yeah, that's right. You got one shot. Turn me in and get your name in the paper.

HENRY: And my *picture* with you propped up dead on the ground beside me. Change my whole life.

LILY: He's warned you, Henry. This isn't a game to him! He'll kill you!

HENRY: Yes sir. I've been waitin' for this my whole life. All my miserable hot life!

ARCHIE: Sit down, Henry! He won't shoot you if you sit down!

HENRY: He don't have to fight back. He can just stand there if he wants, but I'm taking all that money. I'm taking you in!

OUTLAW: My brother dies so you can read about it in the barbershop!

ARCHIE: Run, Henry!

HENRY *(Taking a step toward the Outlaw)*: Nice and easy, now, pops. Throw your gun over there.

OUTLAW *(Standing still, his hand on his gun)*: I can't do that, cowboy.

HENRY: Then I'm coming after it. You draw and you're dead, mister.

OUTLAW: That's fair.

And instantly the Outlaw pulls his pistol, both men fire, and Henry falls dead. Lily screams.

ARCHIE: Henry!

OUTLAW *(Taking a step backward)*: He wasn't married, I hope.

ARCHIE: He was my brother!

OUTLAW: I'm sorry.

ARCHIE: You killed my brother!

OUTLAW: He did it himself, really. I'm sorry. You shouldn't draw if you can't shoot.

ARCHIE *(Straining against the ropes)*: Henry!

Lily walks over to the Outlaw.

LILY *(In a cold fury)*: Is this what you do now? Ride around daring people to kill you?

OUTLAW: It's not my fault he missed, girl. I stood still, didn't I?

LILY: You are disgusting.

OUTLAW: He didn't give me a chance, honey.

LILY: Give me the gun. Now your knife. Now . . . stay put. *(She walks over to Archie)*

OUTLAW: I'm fine. Just a little . . . stiff from riding.

Lily cuts the ropes tying Archie. Archie gets up quickly, runs to Henry and, crying, embraces him, as Lily turns to face the Outlaw.

LILY *(Hands the Outlaw's knife back to him)*: Want to start carving the notch now?

OUTLAW: It was a fair fight.

LILY: He never had a chance and you know it.

OUTLAW: I tried to tell him.

ARCHIE: I tried to tell him.

OUTLAW: Well, then. It was a fair fight.

ARCHIE *(Standing up, nearly screaming)*: Fair? You told him he would die! That's not *fair*. Fair is when both guys got a chance. Fair is when nobody knows how it will come out! You pulled him right in, didn't you. You dared him! If he could kill you, then he could be somebody.

OUTLAW: Henry wanted to kill an outlaw. Can't kill Indians anymore. Kill an outlaw instead. Everybody out here feels that way. Must be the water.

ARCHIE: What water? *(And he stoops to pick up the gun)* What's the matter with this country? This isn't what people are supposed to do! He's not supposed to tie me up and you're not supposed to . . . . He was my brother and he was no good, but now you've gone and killed him! How do you think that makes me feel!

OUTLAW: You have to believe me, Lily. I'm tired of killing these boys, but they won't leave me alone.

ARCHIE: Henry! Henry!

Lunging across the stage, Archie attacks the Outlaw in a fury of ineffective but desperate punches and kicks, which the Outlaw absorbs fairly passively.

OUTLAW: I'm sorry, boy. I said I was sorry. Jesus, kid, come on. *(Archie sinks to the ground)* It's okay. You're a baby. It's all right. It's all gonna be over in just a little bit.

ARCHIE: Why did you have to come here? Nobody asked you to come here.

OUTLAW: I came to see her.

ARCHIE *(Not listening to him)*: You didn't have to say anything about being an outlaw.

OUTLAW: I didn't! You did! She did! He did!

ARCHIE: You didn't have to pull that gun and ask for eggs. We'd have given you the eggs. But no! You sit around playing outlaw and my brother ends up dead. You could've lied about the money. If Henry didn't know you had money in that case, he'd have never told that Delta story and he'd still be here! Jesus God. Mother. What am I gonna tell Mother?

OUTLAW: You say this old outlaw wandered into your camp, hungry. He had a sack full of money and Henry wanted it. They fought. Henry died. Simple.

ARCHIE: Simple? Who's gonna believe an old outlaw came here. All the outlaws died.

OUTLAW: I wish.

ARCHIE: Just tell me your name. I have to have something to tell. Just sit down and tell me your name and then you and her can ride off.

OUTLAW: I'm Tom McCarty.

ARCHIE: That's who you said you killed.

OUTLAW: That's right.

ARCHIE: You killed yourself?

OUTLAW: I buried me alive. They killed Bill and Fred and I was the only one left. I gave it up. Disappeared.

LILY: So why didn't you come to me then?

OUTLAW: Because you're exactly where they thought I'd go. I couldn't put you in that kind of danger and you know it! I had to hide and I did. And then it got harder and harder to show back up, that's all.

ARCHIE: Is there money in that case?

OUTLAW: Forty, fifty thousand. Hard to spend that kind of money out here without attracting attention.

ARCHIE: So give it back.

OUTLAW: I don't know whose it is.

ARCHIE: You know what bank you got it from.

OUTLAW: Banks. Trains. It's a problem.

ARCHIE: What were you doing stealing it if you didn't really want it? What did you think you were going to do with it? You are one sorry outlaw, mister.

OUTLAW: I need a place to sleep, Lily.

LILY: How does prison sound?

ARCHIE: Give me the money. I'll give it to Dad, for Henry.

OUTLAW: It won't help. His son is dead. *(Now trying to be lighter)* But I gotta admit. "Henry's dead, here's forty thousand dollars," sounds a helluva lot better than just plain, "Henry's dead." *(They do not laugh)* I should've got it in the back. Gunned down on Main Street. But no. I was so smart. I got away.

ARCHIE: I don't want to hear it.

LILY *(To Archie)*: What are you going to do about Henry? His body.

ARCHIE: We'll bury him. There's three barrels. We'll put him in the barrels and bury him.

LILY: But your mother. Won't she want a funeral? What about the family? Your father won't want to see you without Henry, I bet.

ARCHIE: Well, he's not out here, is he, so I'm making the decision. You want me to watch him be dead till morning? Then what do I do? Carry him home in a sack? It's three days. He'd smell. I'd have to tie him on the horse. He'd fall off. I'd get off, tie him back up, ride on a little bit, he'd fall off again. Three days? No. We'll bury him. *(To the Outlaw)* But you're gonna dig this grave, "outlaw."

OUTLAW *(Fiercely)*: I never dug a grave in my life! *(Sees Lily's commanding look)* But I don't have to go just yet. I could help, I guess.

ARCHIE: You're not going to *help*. You're going to do it.

OUTLAW *(Still looking at Lily)*: That's what I said.

LILY: That's what I thought you said.

OUTLAW *(After a moment)*: Good. Ready. Good idea, kid. That's just what I'll do. Dig it as deep as you want, you just tell me. Yes sir. You got a shovel?

ARCHIE *(Fairly disgusted now)*: Around back there.

OUTLAW *(To Lily)*: You just watch and see, girl. Be the nicest grave you ever saw. Real comfortable. Be everything a man could want.

LILY: I'll make us some coffee.

OUTLAW: That's a good idea too. Everybody's just full of good ideas.

They stand there.

ARCHIE: I hate this place. Nobody acts right out here. *(And then aware that they are staring at him)* Shut up, Archie.

OUTLAW: That's the spirit. *(Wanting to get on with it)* Okay. One grave, comin' up.

And the Outlaw heads around the side of the cookshack and Lily starts up the steps into the cookshack and the lights come down.

End of Act One

ACT TWO

Lights come up as the Outlaw is shoveling the last dirt onto a low mound, which is Henry's grave. Archie sits back, quite disturbed but not saying anything. The Outlaw seems invigorated by his physical labor.

OUTLAW *(Resting on the shovel)*: There. All done. Rest in peace. *(To Archie)* Want a cross or anything? Marker? *(No response)* I could make one outta—

LILY: Tell him what you want, Archie. Do you want a marker?

ARCHIE: No. Just be in the way. The boys, coming back in the morning, still drunk, they'd trip over it. *(His anger building)* It's in the wrong place anyway. You dug the grave in the wrong place. This is right where we sit down to eat.

OUTLAW: Why didn't you say that before?

ARCHIE: I didn't want you to stop digging.

OUTLAW: I'll do another one if you want. Just getting used to the shovel, really. How about over there?

ARCHIE: I want a funeral.

LILY: You need a family and a preacher for a funeral. If you'd wanted a funeral, you should've taken him home.

OUTLAW *(Still so cooperative)*: I'll dig him back up.

ARCHIE *(To Lily)*: We're having a funeral. I'm the family. He's the preacher.

OUTLAW: I killed him. I can't preach over him too. Wouldn't be right.

ARCHIE: If we were doing what was right around here, you'd be locked up by now. You dug the grave and now you're gonna preach the funeral. And then you're gonna get the hell out of here and you're gonna take her with you.

OUTLAW: No sir.

LILY: You're preaching the funeral all right, but I'm not going with you when you're through.

OUTLAW: Yes you are too, girl. That's what I came for.

LILY: Why didn't you say that right off? We could be in my bed by now. Asleep, by now. We didn't need to see your Wild West Show.

OUTLAW: What did you think I wanted if I didn't want you?

LILY: I have my own life now, Tom. And if I had any thoughts about going with you, which I might have had, seeing you early on tonight, I've sure forgot 'em all now, after what you did. Now, you owe this boy a funeral and I'm staying just long enough to see that he gets it and then I'm getting in my car and going back to town and tell the sheriff you're out here, in case he's interested. You're dangerous. And, I might have been in love with you once, but now . . . I'm a good citizen.

OUTLAW: Well why did you come out here, then?

LILY: I didn't believe you were still alive.

OUTLAW *(Furious and hurt)*: And that's the only reason you came all the way out here? You were curious? You just had to know if the old desert rat died or not. Well I sure hope you're satisfied, girl. Contrary to popular opinion and in spite of everything I've tried, I am still alive. *(Quickly to Archie)* All right. What do I say?

ARCHIE: You're the preacher.

OUTLAW *(His anger taking another direction)*: We had a good time together, in case you forgot.

LILY: I remember.

OUTLAW: I'm the only man man enough for you, girl. I'm exactly what you need.

LILY: I need . . . a whole night's sleep and a hot bath and a month's vacation someplace green and a glass of gin, a couple more bartenders and running water, but I don't need you. And I don't know who does. You were mighty entertaining all those years ago, but we've got traveling comedians now and a circus once a year and I guess Pancho Villa could probably use a broken-down gunslinger, but other than that I just don't know. You even look better on the wall anymore.

OUTLAW: I took my time getting back here, I'll grant you that. But I've seen these new people. *(Looking directly at Archie)* There's nothing to 'em. All talk.

ARCHIE *(Has heard enough)*: We're having a goddamn funeral. Now will you get on with it! Preach!

LILY: Watch your language, Archie.

OUTLAW: I wish it was me there instead of him.

ARCHIE: That ain't what I had in mind.

OUTLAW: It's the truth.

ARCHIE: You start out, "Family and friends . . ."

OUTLAW *(Stalling)*: If he'd killed me, would you make him preach over me?

ARCHIE: Henry? He'd have drug your body into town to have its picture took by now.

OUTLAW: Well, if you're gonna take a picture, it's good to do it quick.

ARCHIE: Will you get on with this! I'm managin' to stay calm right now, but I'm not sure how long it's gonna last.

OUTLAW: If you think you might get really mad, I'll wait.

ARCHIE: So you can kill me too? Uh-uh. Preach or go.

OUTLAW *(Looking at Lily, hoping to see her change her mind as he preaches)*: I'll preach. *(To Lily)* You sing. *(She starts to hum)* Friends and family. Here lies Henry . . . *(He looks to Archie)* Middle name?

ARCHIE: Jackson.

OUTLAW: Tucker. Born?

ARCHIE: 1884, Thomas, Oklahoma.

OUTLAW: Moved to . . .

ARCHIE: Clovis when he was twelve. Lived there ever since.

OUTLAW: He just had a short time on this earth, but he spent it, well, to tell the truth, he pretty much wasted it.

ARCHIE *(Objecting)*: Hey!

OUTLAW: But it was his time. And if he wanted to waste it, well that was his business. His business was . . . *(He looks to Archie)* ranchin'? *(Archie nods yes)* And he was real good at the stuff you had to be a real sunuvabitch to do. Lie, cheat, steal.

ARCHIE: Go on. You're doing just fine.

OUTLAW: He was bored so he read outlaw books. And he hated himself, but he took it out on everybody else. Now he's dead. Leavin' behind a mother and father? *(Archie nods yes)* Some brothers and some other family, I guess and maybe some children, who knows? They might miss him, but I wouldn't know why. So, rest in peace, Henry Tucker. The rest of us sure will now that you're gone, so you might as well. You didn't have much love for this brother of yours, Archie, but he done more for you than you would have for him had I killed him instead of you and I want you to take note of that. *(Bitter, personal)* You didn't have to die, I tried to tell you that, but you didn't listen. Well, you were gonna die anyway, we all are, someday. But you were lucky. You had help. Unlike me. Yes sir, Henry Tucker, things are pretty bad when you can't count on somebody else to kill you. Dyin' just ain't something you should have to do for yourself.

ARCHIE: You're gettin' off the track here.

OUTLAW: Okay. Heaven and hell. I've got some bad news for you, Henry. But you might as well hear it right now, 'cause you're gonna be findin' it out for yourself pretty soon. I've been thinking about heaven and hell a lot here lately, like how they decide where to put you, and I think what it is, is that they put you in a big room forever with people exactly like you, how you were in life, I mean. And that's what makes it heaven or hell. Now you, you hated yourself, like I said, so it's gonna be hell. You'll be in with a whole bunch of ranch hands that never amounted to nuthin' and died mad.

ARCHIE: I got something to say. I didn't . . . we didn't get along, you and me, Henry, but you're my brother and I respect that. Rest in peace. *(Goes on, knowing they expect more from him)* Lotta times I thought I was ready to kill you, Henry, and I know you really did try to drown me at least twice, so no, I didn't care much for you, but I sure didn't like seein' you die. Tell you what, Henry, the story I'm gonna tell about how you died, it's gonna be some story when I get through with it. If you're ever listening, you're gonna be real proud. I think that's about all I can do for you now. *(To the Outlaw)* Now, finish up.

OUTLAW *(Wants this to be over)*: That's it. I didn't know him.

ARCHIE: We need something from the Bible.

LILY: "Man that is born of woman is of few days and full of trouble."

OUTLAW: God that's gloomy. Where'd you pick that up?

LILY: At my rancher's funeral. You've never read the Bible in your life. What do you know?

ARCHIE: "The Lord is my shepherd, I shall not want."

OUTLAW: Are we through now? I ain't prayin' to no sheepherder.

ARCHIE: "For yea, though I walk through the valley of the shadow of death I will fear no evil, for thou art with me. Thou preparest a table before me in the presence of mine enemies, my cup runneth over."

ARCHIE AND LILY: "Surely goodness and mercy shall follow me all the days of my life and I shall dwell in the house of the Lord forever."

OUTLAW: Dust to dust, an eye for a tooth.

LILY *(Not pleased with the Outlaw's offering)*: Say you feel bad. Say you're sorry.

OUTLAW: I *am* sorry. I don't know anything to say. I'm lonelier than I thought.

ARCHIE: Pray.

OUTLAW: I don't know how.

ARCHIE: Well, what do you want said at your funeral? Say that.

OUTLAW: What do I want said at my funeral? How 'bout, "Okay boys, reload!"

LILY: I don't believe this! You're not a bit sorry about this. This is just one more dumb boy that missed. What did I ever see in you? This is not a joke, here. This is a dead boy in the ground. Oh I wasted so much time waiting for you. Well no more! This is the end. I am free of you for good and praise the Lord for it.

OUTLAW: I am sorry. *(Louder)* I'm sorry, Henry. *(Genuine)* I really am sorry. I never stayed this long at a killing. *(Getting crazed)* I'm sorry. *(Reaching quickly into his pocket)* Okay. I'll show you, Henry Tucker. *(Swallowing the stuff he took from his pocket)* That's how sorry I am.

LILY: What was that?

OUTLAW: I sure am sorry. I'm also jealous. You got something I want, Henry, so I'm comin' after you. Archie figured out what to do with you and I trust him to figure out what to do with me. It's not in your honor, Henry, it's just that now that you're gone, it feels like family and a man should die at home. *(To Lily and Archie)* There! How's that for sorry! That was morphine. I've killed myself!

ARCHIE *(Contemptuous)*: Well, that really is sorry.

LILY: Anything for a little excitement, huh Tom?

ARCHIE: Yeah, how do we know it was morphine?

OUTLAW: You don't. Why don't you just wait and see. Sit down. Who is the sheriff now anyway?

LILY: Nobody you'd know. Kid from St. Louis. Don't worry about him. He thinks you're dead.

OUTLAW: I wasn't worried. What ever happened to Daisy?

LILY *(Lunging at him)*: Throw it up! You're going to throw it up!

He fights her as she's trying to get her finger down his throat.

LILY: Go ahead, bite me! Vomit! You can't do this!

ARCHIE: So this is an outlaw. This is how outlaws die.

OUTLAW *(Breaking away from Lily)*: Nobody knows how to die, boy.

LILY: How much did you take?

OUTLAW *(Pacing, raging)*: Nobody knows how to shoot anymore either! You'd think just one of these lousy cowboys could . . . *(Then like a drunken comrade)* See, Archie, the problem with hiding is there's nothing to do. *(Then back to Lily)* God I loved you, woman.

LILY: It's a little late for that, Tom.

OUTLAW: After I go here, Archie, shoot me. Just once. Don't overdo it. And turn me in. There's gotta still be a reward out somewhere. Buy yourself . . . something . . . Buick, something. *(Getting groggy now)*

LILY *(Pacing)*: How many times did I get asked to get married? Only once. And you heard about that and came chasing across the country to shoot him. Then did you ask me to marry you? Or come with you even? No! You take off and I don't see you for another ten years. That rancher was rich!

OUTLAW: You got rich on your own, girl.

LILY *(Angry)*: Yes I did.

OUTLAW: See? Say thank you.

ARCHIE: I'd leave the two of you alone, but I can't see sitting out in the wheat all night. I've got no place to go.

OUTLAW: I know how you feel. Same here.

LILY *(Beginning to believe it)*: Did you take enough to kill you? Goddamn you. You never even asked me to go to Bolivia with you. You just talked about it and then killed yourself!

The Outlaw slumps a little.

ARCHIE: Why didn't you take the morphine out in the desert? Big bravery this is. Take it where there's people to see you, cry over you. You make me sick!

OUTLAW *(Trying to defend himself)*: I went back to Hole-in-the-Wall and I didn't know anybody and there were . . . fences, everywhere, and I couldn't do it. And I'm dying in front of Lily because I want her to have my money. Not like she needs it, of course, but well . . . *(A silly, drugged smile on his face)* she's who I thought of first. It's time for it, that's all.

ARCHIE: I should've helped Henry shoot you. What kind of thing is this to do to her?

OUTLAW *(Enjoying the physical sensation the drug has produced)*: If you'll just shut up, this will all be over. How am I supposed to sleep with you yelling at me?

ARCHIE *(Irritated at the Outlaw's pleasure)*: Putting on quite a show, aren't you? Well, I don't feel a bit sorry for you. Go ahead. Go to sleep. Things getting dark yet?

OUTLAW: Hey, this is pretty nice, here. Just about perfect way to die, seems to me. It don't hurt . . . there's no mess to clean up. My heart's on this side, here. Put it right here.

ARCHIE *(Furious at the vanity)*: Keep your head clean for the picture?

OUTLAW *(To Lily, much more quiet)*: The doctor gave it to me when I broke my leg last year. He said, *(An uncomfortable laugh)* "You take this all at once, McCarty, it'll kill you, so go easy." I didn't take any of it. I thought I might get . . . the horse might fall on me sometime out where . . . *(Beginning to have trouble talking now)* where I couldn't get to . . . nobody around to help me and might not want to . . . couldn't just wait for it . . . or if you didn't want me . . . weren't around . . .

The Outlaw drifts off here for a moment, his speech getting very slurred. There is a sudden, awesome quiet and they both know he has really taken the morphine—something about the way his body looks leaning against the cookshack. Lily backs away and Archie seems hypnotized by the sight of him. Lily finally turns to Archie. There is no pleading, there is simply a decision to be made. Archie looks at her, then back at the Outlaw, and then to Henry's grave.

ARCHIE: Salt water will do it. If we can get it down him. *(Starting for the Outlaw)* Well go on! It's inside somewhere.

Lily rushes for the cookshack. Archie grabs the Outlaw and jerks him up.

ARCHIE: Get up you! Sit up!

OUTLAW *(Jolted awake)*: You don't have to squeeze. I'm not going anywhere.

ARCHIE: What am I doing?

OUTLAW: I was about to ask you that.

ARCHIE *(Yelling to Lily)*: He killed my brother. I can't save his life!

LILY *(Yelling back)*: Where's the water?

ARCHIE: Oh, hell, it's out here.

LILY *(Rushing out)*: Where?

ARCHIE: On the ground. All we had was in the barrels. Take too long to draw another bucket. Get some vinegar.

LILY: And salt? It'll kill him!

OUTLAW: Bring it on.

ARCHIE: Get it.

Lily goes back inside.

OUTLAW: Dark. Things are dark.

ARCHIE: It's night. Things are dark at night.

OUTLAW: My feet feel real heavy.

ARCHIE: Your boots are heavy. Your feet are in your boots. Your feet only feel heavy.

OUTLAW: That's what I said.

ARCHIE *(Yelling in to Lily)*: What are you doing in there? Come on!

LILY *(Coming out with the salt and a big unmarked can)*: It's dark in there. This is something sloshy, but I don't know what. Could be cherries or beans . . . . Got an opener?

OUTLAW: If I wanted my life saved, I picked the wrong crew.

ARCHIE: On the wall over the stove.

LILY: I looked already. You go.

ARCHIE *(Handing the Outlaw over to her)*: Jesus God! *(Rushing for the cookshack)*

LILY: You cold?

OUTLAW: Yeah. You know what happened to my coat?

LILY: I loved that coat.

OUTLAW: Dirty little Navaho took it. Stole it. Stole my coat. Little boy . . .

LILY *(To Archie)*: Hurry up in there!

ARCHIE *(Running out, having opened the can)*: Coming. Hold his head back. Come on, Tom. Open up now, drink this.

LILY: What is it?

The Outlaw swallows some, chokes immediately and throws it up.

LILY: Ah . . . tomatoes.

ARCHIE: Once more, Tom. You did just fine.

Archie forces more down the Outlaw's throat with the same result.

ARCHIE: I just had a bath, too.

OUTLAW: Taste . . . mouth . . . *(As he tries to reach in his pocket)* Get . . .

ARCHIE: I'll get it. What am I looking for?

OUTLAW: Mint.

ARCHIE *(Looking at Lily)*: Women really like this mint smell, huh? *(Finding some, putting it in the Outlaw's mouth)*

OUTLAW: I like it. *(Then he chokes again)*

ARCHIE: We have to walk around. Keep him moving. We can't let him sit anymore. *(Puts the Outlaw over his shoulder)* You're gonna talk, you.

You're gonna tell me your whole life story. Now, where were you born? Got any children? What color hair did your mother have?

OUTLAW: I'm all right. Just . . . late . . . tired . . .

ARCHIE *(Slaps him)*: You're dying. You're dead if you don't keep moving. Kick your leg. Here! *(Kicks it for him)* Kick. Kick.

Archie's feet get tangled in the Outlaw's feet and they both fall.

ARCHIE: Oh God. *(Trying to get a rise out of him)* They'll write about this. You killing yourself. How's that going to sound? Last Outlaw Kills Self.

OUTLAW: Bad. Sound bad . . . Lily . . .

LILY: Look at me, Tom.

OUTLAW: Pretty.

LILY: We can save you if you'll help us. You threw some up but there's still plenty left in you. You have to keep moving. Stay awake.

ARCHIE: Do you want us to save you? We have to know right now.

OUTLAW: I don't want to die. Don't let me die . . .

ARCHIE *(Again trying to force him to talk)*: Why not? Why shouldn't we let you die? You killed my brother and who knows who else? You've obviously been thinking about it. Yes or no? Die or not.

OUTLAW: Not. Not. Archie. Please. Lily . . .

ARCHIE *(Pulling Lily away from him)*: Prove it. Stand up. Stand up and we'll save you. Why do you want to live? You didn't a few minutes ago, and things haven't changed all that much.

OUTLAW *(Trying to talk)*: Pretty.

ARCHIE: Pretty! That's why you want to live? Because she's pretty?

OUTLAW *(Making it, standing up)*: Up. Live. *(And immediately, he falls back into Archie's arms)*

ARCHIE: She's a whole lot better than pretty. Walk. Walk.

LILY: Give me his other arm.

They shoulder the Outlaw between them.

ARCHIE *(After a moment)*: You cold?

LILY: Freezing.

ARCHIE: I don't know what I can do. I'd get you a coat but . . . he'd fall. *(She nods)* I know. Take his coat.

LILY: Good. Cold might pick him up some.

They struggle to take his jacket off as they continue to talk.

ARCHIE: That'd be good. We save him and you die of pneumonia.

LILY: You're cold too.

ARCHIE: Yep. Sure am. And so is Henry. That makes four of us. All cold. *(And he has awkward boyish awareness that now the two of them have to talk for what might be hours)*

LILY: Archie . . . I'm sorry about Henry.

ARCHIE *(Not wanting to talk abut it, starts to walk the Outlaw around again)*: Henry used to make Mother so mad. We'd be in church and Henry and some of his buddies would sneak up to the wagons parked out front. There'd be babies or little kids sleeping in the wagons and they'd switch the babies. People got home and found they had the right blanket with the wrong baby in it.

LILY: Is that how you got in your family in the first place?

ARCHIE *(Surprised that she guessed this)*: That's what Henry says. Dad too when he's mad at me. Which is always. I don't mind, really. You gotta have a mean streak like you gotta have a mule out here.

LILY: You don't have that mean streak, Archie.

ARCHIE *(Doesn't want to talk about that either)*: Dad wanted an orchard like we had back in Oklahoma. But the ground was so hard, we had to put dynamite in each hole to shake the dirt loose so the roots could take hold. Dad made me haul water on a sled for two years to keep those peach trees alive.

LILY: Did they make it?

ARCHIE: No. He's mostly raising cattle now. He's got this fool idea that the government's gonna need mules for the war, so he's just bought fifteen wild mares to start breedin' 'em.

LILY: There could be money in that.

ARCHIE: Hell, the war's gonna be over before the mules are old enough to sell.

LILY: You're old enough to leave home, Archie, find a place that suits you better. What are you waiting for?

ARCHIE: I can't leave, Lily, I was born here. Did Tom really shoot your husband?

LILY: We're all at the church. Saloon's even closed for the event. Roy Luther, tending bar, said he wouldn't believe I'd get married unless he saw it himself. Tom came in late. Sat at the back. Nobody saw him.

ARCHIE: But when the preacher said, "Anybody got any reason why I shouldn't marry these two," Tom stepped out in the aisle, said "Draw mister," and shot him.

LILY: Actually no, the rancher shot first, but Tom is quick, you know.

ARCHIE: I know.

LILY: He came by later. Said he rode three straight days to get there. Said they'd be after him so he had to go.

ARCHIE: Got on his horse and rode off.

LILY: Well, not right away, no. And the town, they didn't send a posse, after all. People knew the rancher was about to buy a herd of sheep and it got to be a joke. Roy Luther said I really did know how to take care of a sheepherder, all right. The town painted my house for me, to say thanks. *(A pause)* I thought Tom was dead. The man just disappears.

ARCHIE: But he wants people to know him.

LILY: Well, he doesn't want to be forgotten, that's true. But he doesn't want to be recognized and shot either.

ARCHIE: What he wants is you.

LILY *(Quickly)*: He wants it to be like it was. Every sheriff in—

The Outlaw stirs at the word "sheriff." He stands on his own, ready to fight, then breaks away from them, charging around.

OUTLAW: Sheriff! God, it's Hazen! I can smell him he's so close! *(Crouching as if in battle)* Reload!

LILY *(Sensing immediately what to do)*: There's no way out! There must be twenty!

OUTLAW *(Now creeping around as if behind rocks)*: Keep firing . . . one at a time . . . slip through. Take Teapot north. *(Now slumping as quickly as he awoke before)* Brakeman . . . shoulda killed the brakeman.

LILY *(Slapping him)*: Tom! Tom! *(But he doesn't recover)* That's how we have to do it! Who else is there? *(Then quickly, yelling at the Outlaw)* Jim Averill! It's Cattle Kate! We got a mess comin', honey!

OUTLAW *(Charging around again, firing his gun)*: The Regulators! Is it the Regulators?

ARCHIE *(Wanting to help)*: It's the Regulators!

OUTLAW: You're not taking me, Robert Connor. I got you, Bothwell!

The Outlaw grabs Archie as if to strangle him, then collapses and they both fall. Archie pulls the Outlaw up to sit on the ground in front of him, sits on the bench. Archie massages the Outlaw's face and neck, trying to think of some way to continue the conversation with Lily, as she is momentarily out of breath.

ARCHIE: So. Were you really a whore or not?

LILY *(Quite annoyed)*: What difference does it make? You wouldn't be helping me if I were?

ARCHIE: No, I just meant, well, you don't seem like, you know . . .

LILY: No, I don't know.

ARCHIE: If you were a whore, then . . .

LILY: You might be wrong about whores, huh? You might be in big trouble if you had the money?

ARCHIE *(Eager to change the subject)*: Tom! Hey Tom! *(Then to Lily)* Come on. All I know is Remember the Alamo.

LILY: Frank Canton!

OUTLAW *(Jerking up instantly)*: Kill Frank Canton! Come out here, Frank Canton!

ARCHIE *(Yelling)*: They got him, McCarty!

OUTLAW: Got who?

ARCHIE: I can't tell!

OUTLAW *(Losing consciousness)*: Nate? They got Nate?

ARCHIE *(Attempting to revive him)*: It was Nate all right!

OUTLAW *(Reviving)*: Light those fires, Brown. Burn 'em to kingdom come!

> *Then the Outlaw falls unconscious. Archie knows by now not to let him charge off by himself in these moments of being awake. As a result, Archie is dragged around the stage, as the Outlaw relives his past. Archie and Lily put him between them and begin to walk again.*

ARCHIE *(Trying to talk to Lily again, this time more carefully)*: Were you born out here?

LILY: I don't talk about my life. It sounds like one of those books.

ARCHIE: I got it. Your family came out here homesteading and they got wiped out in a drought and your mother died having a baby so your daddy left to join up with the Mexican army, leaving you in the house alone. Some preacher's wife took you in and raised you till they died in a fire at a barn raisin'. They left you everything they had, which was two oil lamps and a Bible, so you moved to the city and got . . . work.

LILY *(Has to laugh)*: Very good. You've been reading the books. *(Archie is pleased)* Your mother is . . . uh . . . a little fat lady who wears her hair in braids wrapped around her head and sits out on the stoop at night to wash her feet before she goes to bed.

ARCHIE: That's her all right. When I think about her, away from home like this, all I see is a big white apron. She pays me ten cents for every turkey nest I find. Turkeys hide their nests, you know.

LILY *(Distracted)*: No. I didn't know. *(Yelling again)* Hainer's gonna give himself up!

OUTLAW *(Charging out of his unconsciousness)*: Claverly, you lay one hand on me . . . I'll kill you. I'll give you all six of these and then I'll bash your . . . *(Then collapsing again)*

LILY *(Defeated, worried)*: Why did he do this? How are we supposed to go on? I can't do this all night. I don't know any more names. Why, Tom?

ARCHIE: But where did you get the money for the hotel?

LILY *(Suddenly depressed and bitter)*: It's none of your damn business.

ARCHIE: I know what you did! It was a big ranch. You sold it!

LILY: And everything on it! Kicked out the whores and turned the place into a hotel. That rancher was rich. I had money left. I built a school. I named it for the rancher. Least I could do, you know. *(Irritated again)* Don't you even know one sheriff's name? One deputy?

ARCHIE *(Stares at the Outlaw, then yells)*: Daniel Boone! *(The Outlaw slumps even more)* Sorry.

LILY: No. I'm sorry. Nobody knows those names anymore. Just as well, I guess. It wasn't as much fun as we said it was.

ARCHIE: I bet you didn't get too many proposals after what Tom did.

LILY *(Very hostile)*: Can't we talk about something else?

ARCHIE: Look. I know you're scared. But he'll make it. You'll see. His pulse is stronger already. Don't you think?

LILY: I don't know how to take it.

ARCHIE: You just count. You remember if you're counting faster than you did when you counted before.

LILY: I didn't count before.

ARCHIE *(Much too cheerful for Lily)*: So you'll count next time. I counted before. I think he just might make it.

LILY: And then what?

ARCHIE: And then what?

LILY: No, you don't say what I said. You say something new.

ARCHIE: I don't know what to say. I don't know what we're talking about.

LILY: So what *do* you know? Ever had a beer, Archie?

ARCHIE: No.

LILY: Ever seen a girl without any clothes on?

ARCHIE: Just my little sister.

LILY: It's not the same, you know.

ARCHIE: Yeah. It's different.

LILY: Real different. So what *have* you been doing?

ARCHIE: Don't make fun of me. You won't tell me anything, so I won't tell you anything either. And I know a lot of good stories. I could fill up this whole night telling you my life. How I learned to rope calves or the time Bill got his hand eat by a catfish. *(Gets tickled in spite of himself at this memory)* But I'm not telling! It's private! What do you care anyway?

LILY: I have everything all set and then he just drops in and tries to kill himself. And we're trying to save him! And all you know is stories. Well, you'll get a good one out of this, won't you?

ARCHIE: Do you want him to live or not, because if you don't then I'm a damn fool carrying him around all night. He killed my brother!

LILY: *That's* what we're talking about. He's a killer.

ARCHIE: I'll drop him on the ground right now if you say to.

LILY: You would not either.

ARCHIE: Go sit then. See what happens.

LILY: We should turn him in.

ARCHIE: Let's save his life first.

LILY: No. Now. While he's asleep. Let's put him in my car and take him into town and turn him in.

ARCHIE: He'd die on the trip. If you want him to live, we have to keep walking.

LILY: That car is the only reason we even stayed here two minutes, isn't it? He wouldn't ride in my car! Outlaws don't ride in cars, I guess. Well how's he going to get around anymore? What is he going to do if we save him?

ARCHIE: What will you do if we don't?

LILY: I'll do just fine! You give me one good reason for saving his life! It's over anyway and he knows it. That's why he pulled this stunt.

ARCHIE: You were his last chance, Lily. He had to take it.

LILY: Yours is the life worth saving here. If you leave right now, you can hop that early train. When the crew comes back tomorrow, I'll explain everything and you'll be on your own.

ARCHIE: I couldn't just disappear, Lily.

LILY: There's nothing for you here except winding up like Henry.

ARCHIE: I'm nothing like Henry and you know it.

LILY: Not now you aren't, but you wait. You'll get his work now that he's gone, won't you? It was that work that killed him. You'll dry up, Archie, just like he did.

ARCHIE: I'll get his share of the ranch, too, if I do his work.

LILY: Is that what you want, Archie? Twice as much desert to blow away. Your mother can get along without you. What are you so afraid of?

ARCHIE: Was that story true, about Delta, Colorado?

LILY: Yeah. Roy Luther told me the same thing. He ran away. Fast as he could.

ARCHIE: But why?

LILY: To get away, Archie. To live. So he could hide. It's not fair. I hate it.

ARCHIE: There's no way you can *hide* out here. I stand in the middle of our land and I think the only way out is straight up. I can see for fifty miles in any direction. I mean, if I could be in two places at once, I could ride a horse for a whole day and see myself. *(Lily doesn't understand)* I could see where I started from where I got to after riding all day. The only thing that ever really gets out of where we live is the train.

OUTLAW *(Sudden, unprovoked)*: Bill! Fred! *(Then falling back into Lily's arms)*

ARCHIE: Good! He woke up on his own that time!

LILY *(Almost tenderly)*: Whenever they were planning to rob a bank, Tom would always work a local ranch for a few months first. Get to know the town, you know. I always thought some of those ranchers missed his working their horses more than they missed their money in the bank. I guess he thought I'd bring him some beautiful horse to ride back tonight. I just . . . didn't think about it. I . . . forgot.

ARCHIE: What was it like when you . . . the old days, with him?

LILY: He'd blow in like the breath of God, horse sleek and black, and all you'd see was his flyin' coat and this big hat, and he'd make everybody else I'd ever met look real tired. And he knew you wanted him, and you did. Soon as you saw him you had to have him. That's still true. That's what happened to Henry.

ARCHIE: He'll make it. We'll pull him out of this. And then all you have to do is take that new picture he's got for you and burn it. Henry was an expert and Henry wouldn't have recognized him if Tom hadn't said Delta, Colorado, Bill and Fred.

LILY: He would never let me do that, Archie. You saw how proud he was of that new picture.

ARCHIE: So burn it.

LILY: But then what do I do with him? Drug his coffee when he gets mean?

ARCHIE: He loves you. He's old and he needs you.

LILY: But what about me? I'm not as old as he is. I'm not through yet!

ARCHIE: I don't blame him for wanting to look at you again.

LILY: He could've just asked me to send him a picture.

ARCHIE: No, I mean it. Your skin looks so soft.

LILY: And I have all the softest parts covered up. You should see *them*. *(She means this to sound irritated, so she is just as surprised as Archie when it comes out so seductively)*

ARCHIE: Now why did you say that?

LILY: Sounds good, huh?

ARCHIE: I just never heard it before, that's all.

LILY: You really are a virgin, huh? Saving yourself for some church girl could be a real mistake, Archie.

ARCHIE: Dad says not to worry about it. There's nothing to it.

LILY: Dad . . . is wrong.

ARCHIE *(After a moment)*: Well, if you want to tell me something I should know, you know, just one or two little things just to get me started . . .

OUTLAW *(Eyes opening, slowly gaining consciousness)*: Lily?

ARCHIE: He's alive!

LILY *(Smiling at Archie)*: Right here, Tom.

OUTLAW: Archie?

ARCHIE *(Really pleased)*: You bet.

OUTLAW: Henry?

ARCHIE: No Henry.

OUTLAW: Oh that's right. I'm sorry.

ARCHIE: We've been through that already.

LILY: Can you sit up?

ARCHIE *(Reaching in the Outlaw's pocket)*: Got something for you, old man. Nice piece of mint. Gonna cut that bad taste in your mouth. Here, open up. *(Taking some for himself)* Thanks. Don't mind if I do.

LILY: I never knew how he got that mint smell. I don't think it grows wild around here. He must have it planted somewhere.

ARCHIE: From what I feel in his pocket, he could have it planted in there. *(She laughs)* Tastes good. I see why he likes it.

OUTLAW: What happened?

LILY: You tried to kill yourself. You took the morphine.

ARCHIE: You threw some of it up. That's tomatoes there on your coat. And we walked the rest of it out of you.

OUTLAW: Why did you do that? It would be all over by now.

ARCHIE: You asked us to. You said don't let me die.

OUTLAW: Well, damn.

ARCHIE: We saved your life. You should say more than well, damn.

OUTLAW: You're some kid, Archie. You walked for me all night, and now you're gonna talk for me all day. What do you want me to say?

ARCHIE: Ask Lily to marry you.

OUTLAW: I can't. I don't have any money.

ARCHIE: You've got a suitcase full of money!

OUTLAW: No.

ARCHIE: There's forty-fifty thousand dollars in that case!

OUTLAW: I said no. Look for yourself.

Archie goes over and opens the satchel. He bends over it, looks through several layers and closes the satchel without saying anything, but he is shocked by what he sees.

OUTLAW: I'm so sleepy.

ARCHIE *(Very sympathetic)*: We wore you out, I guess. Kicked you, punched you, slapped you. Fought the Pinkertons with you all night. You took a real beating all right. *(To Lily)* Is it okay for him to sleep now?

LILY: I think so. I think it would be good. There's still a few hours left before morning.

ARCHIE: You were going to ask Lily to marry you.

OUTLAW: You saved my life. I owe you something. *(To Lily)* Lily, I've always loved you. I'm not much anymore. Will you have me? Will you marry me?

LILY *(A fairly serious look)*: What do you think, Archie? Should I marry this outlaw?

ARCHIE *(Beaming)*: It was my idea!

LILY: I think you're right. Yes, Tom, I'll marry you. But it better be tomorrow or I don't ever want to see you again.

OUTLAW: I can't live in town.

LILY: I have a farm. There's a house. There are horses.

OUTLAW: Good horses?

LILY: Not yet.

ARCHIE: That's your part. You got work to do when you wake up.

OUTLAW: Farm. *(And he drifts off into what looks like normal sleep)*

LILY: We should sleep too. I feel terrible.

ARCHIE: I feel great! I never saved anybody's life before. The way I feel, I could thresh this whole field myself before they get back.

LILY *(Enjoying his thrill)*: I bet you could, Archie.

ARCHIE: We did it! We saved his life! We really did it! The fight was Henry's fault anyway, mostly. He got to telling that story and things just got all out of hand. Tom tried to tell Henry not to come after him. Why, as far as Tom's concerned, it was just about self-defense, don't you think?

LILY: I'm not thinking about it.

ARCHIE: Saving somebody's life! That's got to be the best feeling in the whole world.

LILY: It's in the top three anyway.

ARCHIE: Did you see, Tom even knew my name when he woke up. He'll have you, that farm, those horses. He'll have a whole new life. And you, you'll have him. You sure he's all right here?

LILY: He's out till morning, I'm sure. How old are you, Archie?

ARCHIE: Seventeen.

LILY *(Standing up)*: That's old enough. I need a favor.

ARCHIE: Well you just name it! I done all I could for both of them and they neither one deserved it probably. So you just tell me what it is and I'll do it.

LILY: I want you to take me in the cookshack or wherever your bed is, someplace warm where—

ARCHIE: God, yes. You must be exhausted.

LILY: —we can lie down. I want you to take off all these hotel clothes I've got on and I want you to make love with me. And if you'd like to dance first, that's all right. Or if you want to have a drink of whiskey, that's fine too. The only thing you can't do is say no. Don't say anything.

ARCHIE: You don't have to thank me, if that's what you're trying to do. I couldn't just let him die here.

LILY *(Very firm, and very fast)*: I said you couldn't say anything. You must learn to shut up, Archie, and you must never . . . ever . . . assume that you know why anybody is doing anything.

ARCHIE *(Gets the message)*: I said I would do whatever you wanted and I meant that.

LILY *(Now much more personal)*: I don't know what's going to happen in the morning. He could wake up mean and kill us both. Or he could take off for Bolivia or just disappear for another ten years. Then again, he might take you up on your offer and marry me. So, this is just a little waiting time before we know what *is* going to happen. It's free clear time. We might as well be all alone in the whole world. And whatever happens in the morning, I won't be seeing you very often, and you are the first person I have genuinely liked in a long time. And if you start threshing wheat, I'll end up helping you, and it'll kill me. This way, unless I've forgotten what to do, which is possible, because it's been ten years I've spent waiting for that man, we're both going to feel a lot better. Now, take my head in your hands and kiss me.

Her speech has affected a considerable change in Archie. He seems taller, more poised.

ARCHIE *(After the kiss)*: Dancing, or drinking first . . . would just waste our time, don't you think?

LILY: You're going to do just fine.

ARCHIE: You are the most beautiful woman I have ever seen.

LILY: You're catching on real fast, Archie. I knew you would.

ARCHIE: I even have one of Mother's quilts.

LILY: Sh-h-h.

> *And Lily smiles and a single light remains on the sleeping Outlaw as Archie and Lily step into the cookshack. There is a change in the lighting as we go from night to dawn. Then morning light comes up as Archie and Lily walk out of the cookshack, Archie carrying a coffeepot, Lily a skillet and some eggs. Lily has a quilt around her shoulders.*

ARCHIE: I guess it would be an engineer. The railroad . . . I don't know, it's important to me. I could sit there all day, swap stories with the fireman, check my pressure gauge, watch the sky cloud up, look out back at where we've been, see our smoke . . . . Chief engineer on the Overland Flyer. What a job. *(Pauses)* Or the war could need me, I guess.

> *They sit down near the fire.*

LILY: The war would've had you already if they'd elected that Teddy Roosevelt.

ARCHIE: My dad says President Wilson is just plain yellow. Wouldn't last two weeks as sheriff of Clovis.

LILY: I'd like to see New York.

ARCHIE: Me too. Know what they've got there? Crowds. *(She laughs)* I want to bump into things, people, cars . . . I don't even know what things. I don't know what I'm talking about. Do you believe there's airplanes?

LILY *(Laughs)*: Oh, Archie. This is going to make you so mad. I've seen one!

ARCHIE: You have not! You saw a picture of one. I've seen a picture of one. I want to see one fly over my head. Would you ride in one?

LILY: Three years ago, I took the train to St. Louis. It's as far east as I've been. That Teddy Roosevelt was up in an airplane with somebody called the Wright Brothers Flying Team. We were all down there watching him. He was waving to us. We were waving at him. He got so excited waving he almost fell out of the plane! Oh, it was the best day. People were standing around saying things like takeoff and air pocket. *(Her excitement is unlike anything we've seen from her to this point)*

ARCHIE: Why didn't you tell me this before?

LILY: It's the only story I know. I was saving it for you.

ARCHIE: It's the best story I ever heard.

LILY: There are plenty more out there. All you have to do is get on the train.

ARCHIE *(Defensively)*: Things happen here. Things are changing here too. I want to be here when it happens. People like me have to stay here and make it happen.

LILY: When it happens here, Archie, it will be secondhand. But I'm not going to say any more about it. You know what I think. Now, tell me how your brother got his hand eaten by the catfish.

ARCHIE: No, you tell me what else you saw in St. Louis.

Before Lily can answer, the Outlaw stirs and we see that he is awake. Lily and Archie exchange pleased looks.

ARCHIE *(Much too bright)*: Good morning!

OUTLAW: Hold it right there!

The Outlaw is seriously disoriented, and at the sound of Archie's voice, he springs up, then dives back down beside the cookshack and holds the gun on them. Archie protects Lily by moving in front of her.

ARCHIE: Easy, buddy. It's just us.

OUTLAW: Buddy?

LILY: It's all right, Tom.

OUTLAW *(Very grumpy, stands up)*: The hell it is!

ARCHIE: How do you feel?

OUTLAW: Bad.

LILY: We've got the coffee all ready.

ARCHIE: How about some eggs?

OUTLAW *(He grabs his satchel)*: I gotta get out of here.

LILY: We can have some coffee first. And I'm hungry.

OUTLAW: Good-bye, Lily. Boy.

ARCHIE: Now, you wait a minute. We walked you around for hours, just the two of us, and it was cold out here and you're heavy, mister. We saved your life last night.

OUTLAW: Yeah, and if I don't get going, that threshing crew will come back and you'll get another chance to save my life. You may not care if your brother is dead, but your crew boss is gonna care that he's a man short today. I already said good-bye. That's all you're gonna get! *(Turns to go)*

ARCHIE: You're on foot, remember? *(A pause)* Only way out of here's in that car of hers. *(Then having a little fun)* If you act nice, though, she might let you drive.

LILY: How many eggs, Tom?

OUTLAW: Just two.

LILY: And bacon?

OUTLAW: I'd rather have peaches. Are there any peaches?

LILY *(Getting up, starting for the cookshack)*: I'll look. Archie?

ARCHIE: I'm not hungry.

OUTLAW: You are too. You should have some eggs. You like peaches?

ARCHIE *(Setting the frying pan on the fire)*: Okay. Same as him.

Lily goes into the cookshack as the Outlaw sits down.

ARCHIE: They won't be back before noon. Probably not till six. It's Sunday. Can't miss church. *(The Outlaw nods)* Do you remember what you said last night?

OUTLAW: I didn't say a thing.

ARCHIE: You asked Lily to marry you. She said yes.

OUTLAW: Out of my head, I guess.

ARCHIE *(Angry now)*: And you asked me to look in your case, there.

This disturbs the Outlaw.

OUTLAW *(Firm, hostile)*: Nobody looks in my case.

Lily comes out with the can of peaches and some bowls, which she hands to Archie.

LILY *(Starting to cook the eggs)*: Now, it won't be but just a minute.

OUTLAW *(Brightly)*: So, got away again, did I?

LILY: You had help.

OUTLAW: I guess I should thank you.

ARCHIE *(Angry)*: I wondered when you'd get around to that.

OUTLAW: You didn't have to do it, so I don't have to thank you. You think you always know the right thing to do, boy, well you don't. Maybe I was ready for it. Maybe if you knew about anything besides egg hunts, you'd have let me die. I mean, what do you know about anything, Archie?

ARCHIE: It was Henry told you about the egg hunts. And Henry's dead. I know about *that*.

LILY *(Insisting that they both calm down)*: We'll just eat out of the skillet, here.

She hands them each a fork and we have a moment of peace.

OUTLAW *(As they begin to eat)*: I love eggs. Thing I don't understand is how something so good can come from a chicken. A chicken!

ARCHIE *(Matter-of-fact)*: I like fried chicken.

OUTLAW: Me too. With biscuits and gravy.

LILY: There are chickens on the farm.

ARCHIE: Her farm. Remember about her farm? Where you're going to live with her?

OUTLAW: Can't stand 'em. Make me nervous. Dirty animals. Shouldn't even be called animals.

ARCHIE: They're not. They're birds.

OUTLAW: They're ugly. They can't even fly.

ARCHIE: They lay eggs for you. They die to make your fried chicken.

OUTLAW: I couldn't live with chickens and that's the end of it.

ARCHIE: Cattle?

OUTLAW: Cattle are dumb.

ARCHIE: Crops?

OUTLAW: Work.

LILY: Just horses then. The horses on the farm are—

OUTLAW: Have to be young to work horses.

LILY: There are young people for hire.

OUTLAW: I don't like young people either. Jumpy. I don't like any of it. I only like eggs.

LILY: No chickens. I promise.

OUTLAW: No. No nuthin'. No marriage. No farm. No nuthin'.

And there is a terrible pause, while everybody understands what has just been said.

ARCHIE: You are so dumb. Nobody cares about outlaws anymore. You should've killed me, instead of Henry. He was your last real admirer and you shot him.

LILY *(Trying to be calm)*: How are we going to wash these dishes?

ARCHIE *(Bitter, hostile)*: Leave 'em. They'll figure it out! A new grave and dirty dishes. Sombody came in here, killed Henry and ate breakfast.

OUTLAW: They're gonna think you killed him! How about that! After we leave, there's gonna be one gun with one shot fired and one dead man with one bullet in him . . . and you. Dammit all, you're gonna get the credit for my good shot.

ARCHIE: You killed my brother and I saved your life!

OUTLAW: And I wouldn't tell anybody if I were you.

ARCHIE *(Defensive)*: They'll understand. It was the exact right thing to do.

OUTLAW: It's as wrong as it can be, boy. It's one of your new ideas and it's nothin' but trouble. You wait and see.

ARCHIE: That's ridiculous.

OUTLAW: If you had an inch of guts you'd kill me back, and that's what they're all gonna say, the crew, your dad, all of 'em! Aren't they. I can hear 'em now. "So what'd you do, Archie?" "You did what, Archie?" That's exactly what they'll say. Isn't it!

ARCHIE: I don't know what they'll say.

OUTLAW: You do too. It's exactly what they'll say!

ARCHIE: What if it is? That doesn't make it right. It only means they're as backward as you and Henry.

OUTLAW: No, boy. You should've shot me. You have to kill 'em while you got the chance, or else you'll just have to fight 'em again some other day.

ARCHIE: Well I don't believe that.

OUTLAW: Well I'm glad I'm not gonna be there for the future then. This ain't something Jesse James made up, boy. This is how things are . . . here.

ARCHIE *(Very strong)*: Were . . . here.

OUTLAW *(Stronger still)*: Are! Everywhere!

ARCHIE: No! Not anymore. Not everywhere! No! Just out here in this damn scrub country. We're so far away from everything, everybody acts like there's no rules at all and anybody can just do whatever they like—well they can't. Or if they can, I don't have to sit here and watch them, not anymore. I've got my own ideas about how people should live and this ain't it. No sir.

OUTLAW: I shot the wrong boy all right. You're scared.

ARCHIE *(Rejecting both ideas out of hand, suddenly seems very alert, self-possessed, proud)*: I am not. I've got a better idea. *(Picks up the Outlaw's satchel)*

OUTLAW: That's mine.

ARCHIE *(Triumphant, taking charge)*: I'm going to burn them!

OUTLAW: You will not! You put that down! They're all I've got!

ARCHIE: She's all you've got but you don't know it. Once they're gone, you'll have a chance of finding that out.

OUTLAW *(Pulls his gun)*: You give them to me!

Archie pulls a wanted poster out of the satchel and crumples it up.

ARCHIE: You'll have to kill me for them. I don't think you will. Wouldn't be fair. Actually I like that about you. That and the mint. *(Throwing the poster in the fire)*

OUTLAW *(Archie is right, puts the gun away)*: It won't make any difference. They'll still know who I am.

ARCHIE: Good then. I have your permission.

Archie upends the satchel, dumping all the newspaper articles, wanted posters and other bits of evidence of the Outlaw's exploits on the fire.

ARCHIE: *(Very formal)*: All the outlaws are dead. McCarty was an outlaw. McCarty must be dead.

LILY: And the only picture we have of him is twenty years old, so who is this old-timer we got here?

ARCHIE *(Now much more personal)*: You can't just keep riding around. She loves you. You can forget everything that's happened and start all over.

OUTLAW: If I forget everything that's happened, then what do I have that she would want, boy?

ARCHIE: How should I know? But she said she would marry you so there must be something.

OUTLAW *(To Lily)*: Look, I was pretty groggy last night. I don't remember any of this.

LILY: That's what I said all right.

OUTLAW: Boy I sure don't know why.

ARCHIE: Maybe she likes your talk. *(Pauses a moment)* Come on. Do you ever know why anybody does anything?

LILY: I also said it better be today or I never want to see you again.

And there is another pause, but this one is much more pleasant. This one has some acceptance in it.

OUTLAW *(Looking at Lily, but talking to Archie)*: Go ahead. Burn the satchel too, why don't you?

ARCHIE *(Holding it out to him)*: That'd be wasteful. Nice case.

OUTLAW *(Looks at Lily, then at Archie)*: Keep it.

ARCHIE *(Dusting it off, looking at it)*: Thanks. I will. I'm gonna need something like this. *(To Lily)* Do me a favor.

LILY: I owe you one.

ARCHIE: Write to my mother. It's Olivia Tucker, Clovis. Tell her to take care of herself. Tell her—

LILY: —you did what you could. You'll write when you can.

ARCHIE: Yeah. Thanks.

OUTLAW: Running away, huh, Archie? They'll know you did it for sure now. Gonna go east? Where they do things civilized?

ARCHIE: I don't know where I'm going. I'm just getting on the train. There's just got to be some town that makes some sense.

OUTLAW: Go east. You'll fit right in.

ARCHIE: Prissy little boy like me.

OUTLAW: Exactly.

And Archie heads for the cookshack to gather up his things.

ARCHIE *(As he steps up into the cookshack)*: He needs a bath.

OUTLAW: The hell I do!

LILY: I'll see that he gets it. *(As Archie is inside the cookshack, she and the Outlaw try to talk again)* It was the car, wasn't it. If I had come on a horse, none of this would have happened. You just didn't want to ride away in an automobile.

OUTLAW: Just seemed awful fancy, that's all.

LILY: That didn't used to be a problem for you.

OUTLAW: I liked a fancy girl, all right. I sure did.

LILY: Well, then . . .

OUTLAW: I'm gonna need a new coat. Long, gold color.

LILY: I think we can handle that.

And he stands there a moment, just looking at her.

OUTLAW: Now just how, exactly, are you gonna "see" that I get my bath?

LILY: Oh I'll draw the water, hand you the brush, get myself a beer, pull up a chair and watch. You remember.

OUTLAW: Yeah, it's all comin' back to me now.

LILY: But we'll have to call you something else in town. Tom McCarty is dead.

OUTLAW: It won't work. Roy Luther will know it's me.

LILY: He'll call you whatever you want. He'll call you Clara Mae if you buy him a beer.

OUTLAW: I could be Doc. How about Doc. I was courtin' a Doc's daughter so they called me Doc. It's a joke.

LILY: Doc is good.

OUTLAW: Doc it is.

And now Archie comes out of the cookshack carrying his things, one of which must be his mother's quilt all rolled up.

LILY *(Walking over to him, kissing him)*: Good-bye, Archie.

ARCHIE: I'll send you picture postcards, so don't sell the hotel or move or anything.

LILY: Send me one from France.

ARCHIE: From the war if I get there.

LILY: From France. From New York. From France.

ARCHIE *(As the Outlaw takes her arm)*: You bet I will. Good-bye, Lily.

OUTLAW: Come on, girl. *(Practically dragging her now)* A war is just what you need, runt.

ARCHIE: The name's Archie.

OUTLAW: That's a runt name, for sure. Come *on*, girl. *(Walks offstage)*

LILY *(Backing away toward the Outlaw)*: Goodness and mercy.

ARCHIE: Huh?

LILY *(A blessing)*: . . . follow you all the days of your life.

ARCHIE *(Affectionately)*: Oh yeah. What do you think the chances of that are?

LILY: I don't know. Fair.

ARCHIE: Good-bye, Lily.

LILY *(As she turns to join the Outlaw)*: Let's get out of here. They could be back anytime. It's almost noon.

Archie watches her go, then walks up to Henry's grave and takes a look around the camp area. Finally, he seems ready to go.

ARCHIE: Jesus God in heaven, it's Archie Tucker from Clovis, New· Mexico. And I know you can see me, so you must've seen everything that went on down here tonight and listen, I want to know . . . *(Very flip and irritated)* Was this all your idea? *(Pauses)* Because if it was . . . go work on somebody else for a while. I've got things to do. *(Starts to walk off, then stops when he hears Lily's voice)*

LILY'S VOICE: Well, what are you waiting for? Get in. The handle's right there on the door.

OUTLAW'S VOICE: Just getting the feel of her, that's all. Real smooth, isn't she.

LILY'S VOICE: Real shiny too. Wait till it's light. You'll see.

And as we hear the car doors slam, Archie has something else to say to God.

ARCHIE: Well, okay. I do appreciate what you did for me with that coyote back on the road there, so I'm grateful. Thank you. I mean, I do want to stay in touch.

Archie pauses, knowing he won't be in touch as often as he has been in the past, but excited about what lies ahead for him. We hear the car's engine start, then drive off.

ARCHIE: Tell you what. First time I get up in one of those airplanes. You keep your eye on ol' Archie Tucker. I'll . . . *(Raises his hand in a fond salute and smiles)* wave to you.

The lights, which by now are down to a single light on Archie's face, black out, as the sound of a train whistle and the faint strains of some World War I song end the play.

End of Play

TRAVELER
IN THE
DARK

ABOUT THE PLAY

Traveler in the Dark was first staged at the American Repertory Theatre in Cambridge, Massachusetts, under the direction of Tom Moore, in February 1984. The West Coast premiere took place at the Mark Taper Forum the next year, in a production directed by Gordon Davidson.

CHARACTERS

STEPHEN, a pale twelve-year-old boy, the son of Glory and Sam. He is a smart boy who speaks quietly and hasn't watched much television or played with many other children. He has an alert, questioning manner, a fierce respect for his father, and a more childlike love for his mother.

SAM, a world-famous surgeon. He is a brilliant loner, a man who has found his problems not quite worthy of his skills in solving them. He can seem preoccupied, impatient and condescending. But he can also be counted on to handle any situation. His sense of humor is what makes you put up with his infuriating personal security.

GLORY, a lovely woman, who takes her responsibilities as a wife and mother quite seriously. She speaks quickly and laughs easily. She is blessed with a rare grace, an elegance of spirit, and nobody understands how on earth she has stayed married to Sam for all these years.

EVERETT, a country preacher, Sam's father. He is a one-time fire-breathing evangelist who now spends his time burying the same people he worked so hard to save. Everett has gotten old, but Sam, in particular, has not noticed this. He is a great favorite with the ladies, has a wizard's command of the language, and a direct, personal relationship to God and the heavenly hosts.

ACT ONE

The play takes place in the overgrown garden of a country preacher's house.
There are stone animals, including one large goose, stone benches, a crumbling
stone wall and a small pond. Various objects are imbedded in the wall—toys,
mainly, but also such household objects as cups and saucers. It is not important
that these objects be seen by the audience. In fact, the less impressive this
garden appears, the better. It is Sam's connection to the garden that is
important, not ours.

    Sam comes out the back door onto the porch, then walks down the steps and
into the garden. He smiles and nods, happy to see it again. As he walks
through the leaves, he kicks a hidden toy, bends over, picks it up and recognizes
it as an old toy car of his. He brushes the leaves out of it, then races it up his
arm. Then he puts the car back in the wall and walks to the other side of the
garden, where he discovers a geode. He picks it up, looks at the upstairs
window of the house, then puts the geode back where it was. Now, Sam sees
that a section of the wall is completely gone, and with it, apparently, the stone
goose. He begins to lift the rocks back into place. Glory opens the back door
and calls out.

GLORY: Sam?

SAM: I'm out here. Come. Look.

GLORY: Don't tell me now. Let me guess. *(She looks around)* It's the backyard.

SAM: It's Mother's garden.

GLORY: I'm sorry. *(She walks into the garden)*

SAM: There are all kinds of stone animals, rabbits and things down there,
somewhere, and watch where you step. One of those piles of leaves is a
pond. *(Now he sees the stone goose buried under a pile of rocks)* Wait a
minute. *(He lifts the goose up and puts her in her rightful place on the wall)*
There she is. Mother.

GLORY: *(Shakes her head)*: Sam . . .

SAM: This place is a mess. Dad never did like this garden. He said Mother
should save her knees for church.

GLORY: Sam, I'm worried about Stephen. He doesn't understand.

SAM *(Going to the old tool chest near the porch)*: What's there to understand?
Mavis is dead.

GLORY: Sam, she was more than your head nurse. Mavis carried a puzzle for
Stephen in every purse she owned. She was his friend. He doesn't believe
it.

SAM *(As he sweeps the top of the wall with a whisk broom)*: He will. He'll be fine.

Nobody ever died on him before, that's all. He'll get the hang of it, you'll see.

GLORY: He's upstairs right now going through all your old books.

SAM: That's all right, too. They can't hurt him now. Here, hold this a minute. *(He hands her a stone rabbit, while he cleans out the space in the wall where it belongs)*

GLORY: Stephen needs you to explain this to him, Sam. I try to get him to talk about it, but he won't. You've got to tell him something that will make him feel better.

SAM: Like what?

GLORY: If I knew like what, I'd tell him myself.

SAM: What did you say to make *you* feel better?

GLORY: I don't feel better.

SAM: See what I mean?

GLORY *(Irritated with him)*: But I want to feel better, and so does Stephen.

SAM: There isn't anything to say. Mavis waited too long to have herself checked. I did the operation. She died. Stephen knows all of that already.

GLORY: But he doesn't know what it means.

SAM: It doesn't mean anything. It's just . . . bad luck. *(He takes the stone rabbit from her and replaces it in the wall)*

SAM: There. Doesn't that look better?

GLORY *(Giving up for now)*: I called your dad. He had another funeral to preach this morning. He'll be here as soon as he can.

SAM: There's no reason for him to come home. We can just meet him at the church.

GLORY: He wants to see you, Sam, and the funeral's not till two o'clock.

Sam resumes his work on the wall.

SAM: Is everybody coming back here or what after the funeral? I know Mavis didn't have any family left here.

GLORY: We're all going to Josie Barnett's.

SAM: Josie Barnett is a joke.

GLORY: Mavis loved her.

SAM: Mavis loved Dad.

GLORY: You don't want them all coming here, do you?

SAM: God, no.

GLORY: Well, then . . .

SAM: Is Josie Barnett . . . going to . . . try to . . . sing . . . at the funeral? *(She doesn't answer, so he knows the answer must be yes)* Christ.

GLORY: Sam.

SAM: It's just an awful lot to pay for a free meal. *(Still she doesn't answer)* Couldn't we just go to a restaurant?

GLORY: I don't believe you. Can't you let up on these people for one day? One day? Mavis was one of these people, you know, and your dad is one of these people, and I am one of these people. *(She pauses)* And so are you.

SAM: Okay, okay.

STEPHEN *(Calling from inside the house)*: Dad?

SAM: Out here, Stephen.

GLORY *(To Sam)*: Will you try? Will you try to get him to talk about it?

SAM: If he wants to talk, I'll listen. *(Pause)* If that's what you mean.

GLORY: You know what I mean.

By now, Stephen is walking up to them, carrying a stack of old nursery rhymes and fairy tales.

STEPHEN: What a great house! Why didn't we ever come here before?

SAM: It's just easier for Grandpa to visit us, Stephen.

STEPHEN: This garden is terrific! Did you put all these things in the wall?

SAM: No, Stephen, Mother did. *(Smiling at Glory)* It was her way of teaching me not to leave my toys outside.

STEPHEN: I found a whole room of books, Dad, way at the top of the house. Like a forest of books growing up out of the floor. Just books and a rocking chair. I've never seen a room like that.

SAM: Those were Mother's books, Stephen.

STEPHEN: The ones I saw were all kids' books. *(Pause)* But where did you sit? Is it your rocking chair or hers?

SAM: Hers.

STEPHEN: They're strange books, Dad. I didn't see a single one I'd ever seen before.

SAM: I know. Your books . . . make sense.

GLORY: I'm sure Grandpa would let you take some of them home if you wanted to.

SAM: Stephen's way too old for those books, aren't you?

GLORY: This is a beautiful *Mother Goose*. I can just see her holding you on her lap and reading this to you. *(And she reads)*

Humpty Dumpty sat on a wall.
Humpty Dumpty had a great fall.
All the King's horses and all the King's men,
Couldn't put Humpty together again.

STEPHEN: I don't get it.

SAM *(Laughs)*: Good boy.

GLORY *(Carefully)*: Stephen, it just means, there are some things that once they happen they can't be fixed.

STEPHEN: But how did he get on the wall in the first place? Eggs can't climb.

SAM *(Breaking the bad news)*: His . . . mother . . . laid him there.

GLORY: Sam.

STEPHEN: Then how did he fall? Eggs can't walk either.

SAM: She told him he was a man. See? She dressed him up in a little man's suit. He didn't know he could fall. He didn't know he could break. He didn't know he was an egg.

STEPHEN: So what happened to him? Did he run all over the sidewalk and people slipped on him or did he dry up in the sun or what?

Sam tests a big stone and finds it loose.

SAM: Something like that.

GLORY *(Not pleased with Sam's answer)*: I'm sure somebody cleaned it up, Stephen.

STEPHEN: But who?

GLORY: Who do you think? *(Pause)* Mom.

SAM: No. I think Mom fell off the wall the day before.

Glory is irritated with Sam, but she does her best not to show it. Sam puts the big stone where it belongs, as Glory turns her attention to Stephen.

GLORY: Now Stephen, the funeral is at two o'clock. But Grandpa's coming home first, and then we'll all go to the church together. He was sorry he couldn't be here to meet us when we got here, but he had another funeral to preach this morning.

STEPHEN: Okay.

GLORY: We'll have to be very careful what we say to Grandpa. Mavis called him every Friday night, you know, told him everything that had gone on at the hospital all week. He loved Mavis more than any of us did, I think. *(Pause)* I know . . . he was disappointed when your dad fell in love with me instead of Mavis. There's nothing he likes better in this world than Mavis and your dad.

STEPHEN: Liked.

GLORY: What?

STEPHEN: Liked better. Nothing he liked better than Mavis and Dad.

GLORY: You don't stop liking people just because they die, Stephen.

SAM: Sometimes you like them better. Harry Truman, for example.

Glory picks up another book and starts to look through it.

STEPHEN: Can we go fishing while we're here? Mavis told me that's what you do in the country. You fish till you're hungry, eat till you're sleepy, then sleep till it's time to wake up and go fishing.

GLORY: I don't know why not.

SAM: We're not going to be here that long, Stephen.

GLORY: Do you want us to tell you what's going to happen at the funeral?

STEPHEN: Am I going to sit by myself?

GLORY: No, you'll sit with us.

STEPHEN: Then no. If I need to stand up or anything, you can just grab me.

Sam gives Glory a "let-him-alone" look, and Glory returns his look, as if to say "this is what I was talking about."

SAM: Stephen, is there anything you want to ask me about any of this?

STEPHEN: Do I have to say anything at the funeral?

SAM: No. And you don't have to listen, either.

Glory doesn't think this is helping Stephen a bit. She tries to interest him in the book she has.

GLORY: Now here's one I like, "The Princess and The Frog." See, Stephen? The princess kisses the frog and he turns into a prince.

Sam makes some move that indicates he has understood her irritation.

STEPHEN: You've got the frog colored in, Dad, but you made him all brown.

SAM: That's what color frogs are, Stephen.

STEPHEN: Now how could a frog turn into a prince?

GLORY: It was magic, Stephen. Magic always works.

SAM *(A direct communication to Glory)*: Magic had nothing to do with it. The frog *believed* that the beauty could turn him into a prince. One kiss from her and he would be handsome, and play tennis, and mix martinis, and tell jokes at parties, just like all her other boyfriends. *(Pause)* But years later, the prince started to turn, slowly at first, but finally and irreversibly, back into the frog he always was.

STEPHEN: It doesn't say that in this book.

SAM *(Scraping the dirt off some of the toys that have fallen out of the wall)*: It doesn't have to. You are born a frog and that is it. It's not so bad, but it is *it*. Frogs should know better, but they don't.

STEPHEN: Then they're not as smart as they think they are.

SAM: Smart isn't magic, Stephen. It's just smart.

GLORY: That is not how the story ends.

SAM *(Quite intense)*: It is how the story ends. The princess got old and the frog croaked. *(As Glory stares at him)* Get another book, Stephen.

STEPHEN *(Getting what he thinks Sam means)*: Go away, Stephen.

SAM: No. Come back. But no more fairy tales. There *are* some good books up there. *Call of the Wild. Lord of the Flies.* Read about Donner Pass.

Stephen jumps down off the wall and goes into the house. There is a moment of silence.

GLORY *(After Stephen has gone)*: Is that your idea of help?

SAM: What?

GLORY: You, the frog, married me, the princess, and Humpty Dumpty was a hit-and-run.

SAM: He's old enough to know what happens.

GLORY: Nobody's old enough to know what you think happens.

SAM: I refuse to lie to him. He could live a long time *hoping* it will all work out.

GLORY: He could live a long time *having* it all work out, unless you convince him it's impossible and he doesn't even try.

SAM: What do you want me to say?

GLORY: Life is good.

SAM: When?

GLORY: All the time!

SAM: Like today, for example.

GLORY: No, not like today. People don't die every day.

SAM: Oh Glory, I'm afraid they do.

GLORY: Not people you know.

SAM: Oh, I see. It doesn't count if we don't know them.

GLORY: It doesn't hurt if we don't know them.

SAM: It doesn't matter, you mean.

GLORY: No, I don't mean that.

SAM: What *do* you mean?

GLORY: You tell him the wrong things.

SAM: I tell him the truth.

GLORY: And he believes you!

SAM: Well, I can't help that.

GLORY: He's a child!

SAM: I want a divorce.

GLORY: I want this day to be over.

SAM *(After a moment)*: I do want a divorce. I want to leave here in the morning and take Stephen with me.

GLORY: You can go for the weekend, Sam, but Stephen has school on Monday.

SAM: Since we're having one funeral anyway, we might as well have the other one and be done with it. When we all wake up, this will *all* be over.

GLORY: What is the matter with you?

Stephen opens the porch door, but they don't hear him. He starts to come down the steps, but then realizes what this conversation is about. He goes back up the steps, climbs quietly over the railing and sits, out of sight, behind a tree.

SAM: I just never stopped to think about it, I guess. It doesn't make sense, this marriage. It never has. Ask your mother.

GLORY: It works well enough, Sam. It calms you down, and it keeps me from getting too comfortable. And no, we don't always agree on things . . .

SAM: We don't ever agree on things.

GLORY: But it's good for Stephen to hear both sides.

SAM: No. It confuses him. I'll tell Dad tonight, and in the morning I'll go over and tell your mother and then I'll get Stephen and go. I'll send you as much money as you need and you can have everything we own. All the houses, all the cars, everything.

GLORY: That's ridiculous.

SAM: Okay. I'll keep the cars.

There is a long silence.

GLORY *(Finally)*: You're serious!

SAM: Always have been. *(Then oddly cheerful)* I thought you knew that.

GLORY: You're upset.

SAM: True.

GLORY: I mean you're upset about Mavis. You don't think you can work without Mavis. Well, leaving me isn't going to bring Mavis back to you.

SAM: Mavis has nothing to do with this.

GLORY: Nice work, doctor. Quick and clean. You find the tumor and you cut it out. You don't even need your fancy table or your hotshot team for this surgery, do you? You're so good, you can do it in the backyard.

SAM: Wherever.

GLORY: Look. Let's just get through the funeral, okay? And then if you still feel this way we'll talk about it when we get home.

SAM: I don't want to talk about it. I want to quit. I want to go somewhere else. I want to start over.

GLORY: Life doesn't start over. It starts, it goes on for a while, then it stops.

SAM: God that's gloomy.

GLORY: I sound like you!

SAM: No you don't. I would never say *that*. Mavis didn't have to die. There *was* a time she could have done something about it. This is that time for Stephen and me.

GLORY: You can't leave me.

SAM: You'll be okay. Move back here if you want. I know your mother has room out there.

GLORY: Of course I'll be okay. I'm talking about you. Do you have any idea what it takes to live your life?

SAM: I can probably figure it out.

GLORY: I know you can't take care of Stephen.

SAM: Stephen is old enough to take care of himself.

GLORY: Stephen would end up taking care of you. And you're important, so somebody should do all the things that allow you to work, but it shouldn't be Stephen.

SAM: We'll share it. I'll help him. He'll help me.

GLORY: I think we better wait till we get home to talk about this.

SAM: I think we're talking about it already.

GLORY: The answer is no.

SAM: Yes, well, it wasn't really a question, Glory.

GLORY: I'm going inside.

SAM: I'm not.

GLORY: Fine.

SAM (*Staring at the goose*):
> There once was a woman called Nothing-At-All
> Who rejoiced in a dwelling exceedingly small.
> A man stretched his mouth to its utmost extent
> And down in a gulp both house and woman went.

Stephen appears from behind the tree. He is holding a framed photo and another fairy-tale book.

STEPHEN (*Pointing to the photo*): Is this you, Dad?

SAM (*Startled by his presence*): Stephen!

STEPHEN: Is this you in this picture?

SAM (*Staring at the photo*): Yes.

STEPHEN: Who is this with you?

SAM: That's Mother . . . and that's . . . Mavis.

STEPHEN: And it's Halloween I hope.

SAM: Yes.

STEPHEN: What were you? I can't tell.

SAM: Elves.

STEPHEN: Did Mavis tell you I lost her cat?

SAM: I gave her that cat.

STEPHEN: I know. I'm sorry, Dad.

SAM: When was this?

STEPHEN: Last Saturday. After the movies we went back to her apartment, and I asked Mavis if I could let Peaches out, only Mavis didn't hear me because she went in the bedroom to rest a little bit. But Peaches kept crying and scratching at the back door. So I opened it and she got away. When Mavis woke up, we looked and looked, but we couldn't find her anywhere. (*Pause*) I guess Mavis didn't tell you because she didn't want you to be mad at me.

SAM: It's all right, Stephen. Cats just . . . go like that.

STEPHEN: Maybe Peaches knew something was wrong.

SAM: Maybe she did. (*Pause*) Stephen, your mother and I were just talking—

STEPHEN (*Quickly*): I guess your birthday's going to be pretty lonely this year.

SAM (*Pause*): Yes. I guess it will be.

STEPHEN: I wouldn't like it if I had the same birthday as somebody. I mean, I know there are plenty of people born on the same day as me, but—

SAM: People used to ask Mavis where she met me, you know, and she'd say, "Oh, at the hospital. In the nursery." And then she'd say, "I hadn't been alive two hours when in came Sam Carter screaming at me already." (*Pause*) That's a picture I'd like to see, all right. Dad and Mavis's dad staring through the glass window looking at the two of us side by side in our little beds. One howling boy for the preacher, and one rosy-faced dumpling for the custodian at the church.

STEPHEN: Mavis wasn't fat, Dad.

SAM: No. But I did have the idea that she put on her uniform in the morning, and then stepped on an air pump to puff herself up for the day.

STEPHEN: I'm not going to like Saturday much either.

SAM: She loved you so much, Stephen. You were the only little boy she had. You were so good to her, you gave her so much.

STEPHEN: All we ever talked about was you, Dad.

SAM: Yeah, well, she just loved to talk, Stephen. And I didn't leave her time to learn anything else. *(Pause)* It never occurred to me that she would die, Stephen. It just didn't seem like something she'd do. I'm sorry I didn't warn you, I should have known it, my mother died, didn't she? I guess I just forgot.

STEPHEN: Yeah.

SAM: Well . . .

STEPHEN: Why do people read these books?

SAM: What?

STEPHEN: I know you told me not to read any more, but I was taking it back upstairs and I didn't get this one either.

SAM: Which one?

STEPHEN: I think Sleeping Beauty's father was a fool.

SAM: All right. But don't just say he was a fool. Prove it to me. Build your case.

STEPHEN: He gives a party for his daughter and he invites twelve of the thirteen fairies in the land. Twelve good fairies he invites. He does not invite the thirteenth fairy.

SAM: Because she's a bad fairy, that's right.

STEPHEN: But the bad fairy comes anyway, and now she acts even worse because she wasn't invited. "I have a gift for the little princess," she says. "When she is eighteen, she will prick her finger on a spinning wheel and die."

SAM: That's how it goes, all right.

STEPHEN: It's ridiculous. If you know you have a thirteenth fairy living in your country, and you know what she can do, then how, exactly, can you forget to invite her to a party?

SAM: Well . . .

STEPHEN: How did anybody that dumb get to be king?

SAM: He wasn't dumb. He just forgot.

STEPHEN: He forgets there's a bad fairy living there and look what happens. Everybody sleeps for a hundred years, till he wakes up with his kingdom turned into a jungle and some prince upstairs kissing his daughter.

SAM *(Strangely affected by this story)*: He forgot because he didn't want to remember! He didn't want her to come to the party! The *last* person you want at that party is that thirteenth fairy. So you just hope she doesn't show up because you know if she does show up, there isn't a damn thing you can do about it.

STEPHEN *(Reacting to his father's anger)*: It's just a story, Dad.

SAM: Yeah, I know. That's why I never let you read them.

STEPHEN: But you read them.

SAM *(Disclaiming all responsibility)*: Mother read them to me. *(Almost a confession)* And then, when I learned how, yes, I would read them to her. *(Pause)* Every day when I came home from school, here she'd be, with a glass of milk for me and a pile of things she'd found in the ground that day, like dragons' teeth, witches' fingers and fallen stars. *(Then remembering so clearly)* I would sit, there, where you are, and she would work. And we would sing. Her favorite Mother Goose was page twenty. *(He sings as Stephen is looking for it)*

> We're all in the dumps
> For diamonds are trumps,
> The kittens have gone to St. Paul's.
> The babies are bit,
> The moon's in a fit
> And the houses are built without walls.

STEPHEN: The houses are built without walls?

SAM: Yes.

STEPHEN: How could they stand up?

SAM *(Suddenly very distant)*: She died before I could ask her that, Stephen.

STEPHEN: What was she like?

SAM: She was the gingerbread lady. Curly red hair and shiny round eyes and a big checked apron. Fat, pink fingers, a sweet vanilla smell, and all the time in the world. Sing to you, dance with you, write your name on the top of a cake.

STEPHEN: Did she die all of a sudden like Mavis?

SAM: Mother was sick for a long time, Stephen, but sick or not, everybody dies all of a sudden.

STEPHEN: I guess that was pretty hard, too, huh?

SAM: I was awful. I took it, well, like it happened to me instead of to her. I wouldn't eat. I broke things. But now, well, if she hadn't died, I'd be the biggest momma's boy you ever saw.

Everett enters from the side of the house. He walks with some difficulty, but he's keeping his spirits up with an extraordinary act of will.

EVERETT: Samuel!

SAM: Hello, Dad.

They embrace, but it is difficult for them.

SAM *(A bit awkward)*: I'm sorry I couldn't save her.

EVERETT *(Pulling away)*: You did your best, didn't you?

SAM: Yes.

EVERETT: Well, that's all anybody expects, Sam. *(Shifting his attention to Stephen)* Hello, Stephen. Remember me?

STEPHEN: It's only been a year, Grandpa.

Stephen gives him a small hug.

EVERETT: Where's your mother?

STEPHEN: Inside. Want me to go get her?

EVERETT: I'm glad she's here.

SAM: You knew she would come, Dad. *(He helps Everett)* Here. Sit down.

EVERETT: I'm fine. I'm fine. Are you all right?

SAM: I'm fine.

EVERETT: You look tired, Sam.

SAM: I'm not tired, Dad. I'm just grown up.

EVERETT: I miss seeing you, son.

SAM: I'm sorry, Dad. They keep me pretty busy these days.

EVERETT: Oh I know. Mavis told me. *(His fatherly pride showing)* She said you could do things nobody else even thought of. She said there were dead people standing in line at the water fountain because of you. She sent me all the clippings. I liked that one about the governor. That was a good picture of you. *(No response from Sam)* Oh how she loved you, son. "Well," she'd say, "we had another miracle today."

Another long silence.

SAM: How was your other funeral? Who was it?

EVERETT *(Glad to have something else to talk about)*: Connie Richards. I told her to come see you when she first got sick, but she wouldn't hear of it. She said you were too famous. You were too far away. *(Sam does not answer)* She felt the same way about God. But I guess she figured she didn't have to get on the bus to go see Him.

Everett reaches down to pat Sam, but he moves away, and Everett goes over to pat Stephen. He just needs to pat somebody, and Stephen is too polite to resist.

STEPHEN: Where did you tell them she went, at the funeral?

SAM: Stephen, Grandpa's sermons are his business. He says what he has to say.

EVERETT: I told them she went to heaven.

STEPHEN: Why did you have to say that?

EVERETT *(Ignoring Sam's silencing look)*: Because that's where she went.

STEPHEN *(Doesn't believe this for a minute)*: And that's where she is right now, singing and flying around? It sounds like fairy tales to me.

EVERETT: Oh no, God's heard enough of her singing already. He'll have her light the candles or something.

STEPHEN (*A conspiratorial look at Sam*): They have candles in heaven? Isn't it too windy for candles?

EVERETT: If God wants a candle to stay lit, it stays lit. What they don't have in heaven is matches. But then, angels don't need matches. They just put their pointer finger up to it, like so, and poof, it's lit.

STEPHEN (*Much simpler, actually childlike*): How do they do that?

EVERETT (*Sounding more like the wizard he is*): It's because they're pure spirit now, Stephen. The life in them is like sparks, like fireworks. Oh, they could really light up the sky if they felt like it, but they don't want to show off, you know. They don't want people dying down here just to get in on the fun. But now, shooting stars . . .

STEPHEN: Meteors, you mean.

EVERETT: Right. That's somebody new up there. Somebody hasn't quite figured out how to control themselves. (*Suddenly flinging his arms out wide*) Pow!

STEPHEN: Great!

SAM (*Quietly, but firmly*): Stephen, go find your mother. Tell her Grandpa's here.

Stephen leaves.

SAM (*After a moment*): That's enough, Dad.

EVERETT: Don't be mad at me, boy. I can't help talking about angels. I just know so *many* of them, now.

SAM (*Being careful not to get angry*): I don't want you telling Stephen there's a heaven and a hell, because if you do, I'll have to tell him who it is who assigns the rooms.

EVERETT: You do want him on the right waiting list, don't you?

SAM: I don't want him thinking about it at all. (*Then more calm*) Let's just say, if there is a hell, if Stephen does go to hell, I'd like for it to be a surprise.

EVERETT: No grandson of mine is going to hell.

SAM: No grandson of anybody's is going to hell. There is no hell. There is no heaven. Life is summer camp and death is lights out. It's all just over, Dad. Time's up. The end. You lose.

EVERETT: Is that what you tell their families at the hospital?

SAM: What is there to say?

EVERETT: There's comfort.

SAM: There's all your friends waiting for you? There's your Heavenly Father with His arms open wide? No, no. I've been straight with them all along, so I'm not about to get to the end and lie. I do what I can and then we both just quit.

EVERETT: Mavis would never quit.

SAM: Mavis quit before I did. I briefed the team, I opened her up, but what did I find? Her bags were packed. She was checking out. She was going, as you say, home. No, I keep them out of God's hands as long as possible, so you just keep your sermons to yourself.

EVERETT *(Carefully)*: Was Mavis in any pain?

SAM: No.

EVERETT: Did she . . . know it was happening?

SAM: No.

EVERETT: So she couldn't give you any . . . message for me.

SAM: No. *(Then trying to concentrate on something else)* But she just bought a new car. I know she'd want you to have it. It has power steering and everything. We drove it down here for you. That's it . . . *(Motioning in that direction)* out in the driveway.

EVERETT: I appreciate the thought, son, but I don't think I could . . . *(Pause)* No. You were right to bring it.

SAM: Glory packed up all her clothes and put them in the trunk. We thought there might be people around here who could use them. Everything else, furniture and everything, was rented. Except her TV, and I took that in for the nurses' lounge. So, it's all done, I think.

EVERETT: That part's done, anyway. *(He notices the picture Stephen brought out before)* Anything I have—of hers, you know—you can have it if you want it. I'd like to keep her letters, but after I die, they'll be yours too, of course, like everything else I have. Do you want this picture?

SAM: Stephen found it.

EVERETT: I always liked this one. *(Hoping Sam will say no)* You don't want it, do you?

SAM: No.

EVERETT: Yes, I guess you have plenty of pictures of the two of you. They're probably all up and down the halls at the hospital.

SAM: Can we talk about something else?

EVERETT: I'm sorry, son. Just all those years of her hanging around you, I think of her as part of the family. Probably thought she'd *be* part of the family someday.

SAM: She loved you, Dad, not me.

EVERETT: Oh, she loved you, all right. If it hadn't been for you, she'd be right here, working at County General.

SAM: She was too good for your little hospital.

EVERETT: But not good enough for you.

SAM: We don't have to have this argument anymore, Dad. Mavis is not yours and she's not mine. She's dead.

Stephen enters with a book of illustrated Bible stories.

STEPHEN: Hey, I like this one about the whale. What does it mean? This guy, Jonah, gets swallowed by a whale and then the whale throws him up.

EVERETT: It means you can't run away from God, Stephen.

SAM *(Annoyed that Everett is talking religion again)*: No, Stephen, it means you shouldn't go to sea in too small a boat.

Glory comes out, wearing an apron and drying her hands on a dish towel.

GLORY: Hello, Everett.

They embrace.

EVERETT: Glory Butler, you are still the prettiest girl in ten counties.

GLORY: Are you doing all right, Everett?

EVERETT: Yes I am, thank you.

GLORY *(Remembering how distant this man can be)*: I hope you don't have this too often, two funerals in one day.

EVERETT *(Making an effort to talk to her)*: Your mother was at the one this morning.

GLORY: How'd she look?

EVERETT: Rich.

GLORY: She does like to show it off, doesn't she?

EVERETT: All she could talk about were her two new fillies—both jumpers, she said. And she's got a new exercise boy. He was . . . there with her today.

GLORY *(A knowing smile)*: Was he all dressed up, or was he just driving the car?

EVERETT *(Confirming her worst fears)*: All dressed up.

GLORY: She's so funny. When Daddy died, she walked me up to the casket, held my hand and said, "Glory, I'm never going to be lonely again."

Glory laughs and Everett smiles.

EVERETT: I told her you were coming down for Mavis's funeral, but she said she wouldn't bother you here. *(A pause)* Our house always was a little plain for her.

GLORY: I made us some sandwiches. They're on the counter if you want one.

EVERETT: I should eat something I guess. Don't you want one, Sam?

No response from Sam.

GLORY: We'll be there in a minute. *(Pause)* I straightened up your kitchen a little. I hope you don't mind.

EVERETT: No. Just so you put it back the way it was before you leave.

GLORY: Everett, I was just trying to help. I'm sorry.

EVERETT *(Walking toward Stephen)*: I know Stephen's hungry, aren't you?

STEPHEN: Grandpa?

EVERETT: What, son?

STEPHEN: If the people in heaven are all spirit, if they don't have any flesh anymore, how does God know who's who?

EVERETT *(Putting his arm around Stephen, and walking him out of the garden)*:

Spirit's how God tells us apart anyway, Stephen. When we get to heaven, why as far as He's concerned, we haven't changed a bit.

Glory is left alone with Sam. Sam has a pair of snippers from the tool chest and is cutting the weeds that have grown up around the wall.

GLORY: I'm beginning to see the garden now, Sam.

SAM: I don't know why I'm doing this. He'll just let it go again.

GLORY: Did you and Mavis play out here when you were kids?

SAM *(Putting the snippers down)*: Maybe I've done enough.

GLORY: Where did your mother find these animals?

SAM: I don't know.

GLORY *(As she picks one up)*: Was she strong enough to carry them? They're very heavy.

SAM: Please. *(Taking it away from her)* Just leave them alone, okay?

GLORY: He won't let me touch anything in the house, and you won't let me touch anything out here. It's just me, I guess, I mean, your mother was . . . allowed to work here, wasn't she? Or maybe it's a museum, or a shrine.

SAM: What's the matter with *you*?

GLORY *(Has to laugh)*: What's the matter with me.

SAM: Did you call your mother?

GLORY: I did, in fact. I told her you were leaving in the morning and taking Stephen with you.

SAM: And what did she say?

GLORY: She said she would see you at the funeral and tell you good-bye.

SAM: So we'll have something to talk about anyway.

GLORY: She said it was another woman. She said you and Mavis were . . .

SAM: . . . having an affair? No.

GLORY: Someone else, then. Do you want to leave me for another woman?

SAM: I don't want another woman. I want you to be the woman I want.

GLORY: Can I have a straight answer please.

SAM: We've both had affairs. Haven't we.

GLORY: Well, that's it, I guess.

SAM: It what?

GLORY: The truth.

SAM: That is not the truth. That is just a fact. The truth is what the facts mean.

GLORY: I am so tired of your mind. You would've been so much better off without it.

SAM: I would have been nothing without it! With the exception of a mother who died and left me with the preacher, my mind is all I ever had. *(He stops)* Except Stephen.

GLORY *(She shakes her head)*: And your mother and Mavis and me.

SAM: Yes.

GLORY: Did you forget us for a moment?

SAM: No, I didn't forget you. But it *is* getting easier. There's only one of you left.

GLORY: What a lovely thing to say. What a great time we're having here. Such a good reason to come home and such a spirit of love and understanding. Just relax, Glory. This will all blow over in just a little while. He's always like this, but he's not always so much like this.

SAM: I'm not always like this.

GLORY: No. When you're sick, it's worse. When you're tired, it's worse. But the rest of the time you are exactly like this. You just don't notice it, because this is how you always are. Like I said.

SAM: Then why have you stayed with me.

GLORY: I don't know, it's not over yet. Something like that.

SAM: It is over.

GLORY *(Picking up the Sleeping Beauty book)*: No, this is just the part where I sleep for a hundred years. Then the prince comes and I wake up.

SAM: Jesus Christ.

GLORY: I'm still here for two reasons. One is that you need me. And I have no idea why you need me but you do. I can feel it. I see it all the time. I don't understand at all, but I have no doubt whatsoever.

SAM: And what is the other reason?

GLORY: The other reason is my business. And I'm not about to tell you when you're threatening to leave me.

SAM: Well, I know it can't be that you're having a good time. You should've married that baseball player.

GLORY: If I had married Jerry Pine, I would've spent half my life at Yankee Stadium, wishing he wouldn't chew tobacco, and hoping he won't spit on national TV. *(A pause)* Maybe I would have a better time without you. I could laugh and travel and give away Mother's money, but you . . .well . . . . This is not a job that just anybody could do, you know, putting up with you.

SAM: So this is your chance. I'm offering you a way out.

GLORY: I want a way in, Sam.

SAM: There isn't any way in. There never was. You never had a chance. I married you to spite my father. *(Pause)* There. Can you hate me now? Can I leave now?

GLORY: I know you loved me.

SAM: Do you?

GLORY: I know you love me now.

He turns to go.

GLORY: Where are you going?

SAM *(After a moment)*: I have to find Stephen before Dad turns him into a Christian.

GLORY: Let them alone. You can't change your father and you can't protect Stephen from the entire world. It's one thing to take away the television and give him *Scientific American* instead of *Mother Goose,* but Everett is his grandfather. Let them talk. Stephen can see what there is and decide for himself.

Before Sam can answer, Everett comes back outside alone.

EVERETT: Maybe you two been gone so long you forgot this, but we have a thing out here called respect for the dead.

GLORY: What?

EVERETT: And Glory, if you're going to your mother's, I wish you'd go on and go so we could have our funeral in peace.

GLORY: Everett, I don't know what you're—

EVERETT: Don't you realize what you're doing to that little boy?

GLORY: What did he tell you, Everett?

EVERETT: That he's leaving tomorrow with Sam and you're moving in with your mother. Is that right?

GLORY: He hears everything we say, Sam, I've told you that over and over again. Jesus Christ.

SAM: Why shouldn't he know? I'm just sorry I didn't tell him before he heard it through the wall, like that. He wasn't surprised, I'm sure. Divorce is not exactly unknown in the world. Now that he knows the truth, he'll feel better.

GLORY *(To Everett)*: What did you say?

EVERETT: I didn't know what to say. I said, "Maybe Mom is just lonesome for the country. She'll get tired of it soon enough and be right back home, quick as quick." *(Very strong, as Sam shakes his head)* I said that to make him feel better. I wanted him to feel better.

SAM: And he believed you?

EVERETT: I *saw* him feel a little better, yes.

GLORY: Thank you, Everett. You did the right thing.

SAM: Cover it up, that's right. Put a little Band-Aid on it. It worked with me, didn't it? I have spent my life straightening out the lies people have told him. No, Stephen, there is no Santa Claus. No, Stephen, when you die, you do not go to heaven. No, Stephen, people won't like you better because you're smart, they'll be afraid of you because you're smart. No, Stephen, love is not forever, and God is not good. And tomorrow is not another day. Tomorrow is this day all over again.

EVERETT: Well, wasn't he lucky to have you around.

GLORY: I'd better go find him.

EVERETT: I think that's a good idea.

Glory goes into the house and Everett and Sam are left alone.

SAM: I don't want to hear what you have to say about this, Dad. You don't know what you're talking about, and you're not going to change my mind.

EVERETT: That's as good a confession as I ever heard.

SAM: You never liked Glory in the first place. You should be happy I'm leaving her.

EVERETT: She's a good girl, and she's been a good mother to Stephen. Whatever is the matter between Glory and you . . . is probably you.

SAM: I see.

EVERETT: But it's your boy who'll end up paying for this, Sam.

SAM: Doesn't seem fair, does it? Well, I'm sorry, Stephen, that's just how God is. Suffer the little children to come unto me, for theirs is the wages of sin.

EVERETT: When somebody dies it makes everything hard, Sam, but what we all do is try not to make anything worse.

SAM: When somebody dies, you try to make it make a difference, make it mean something.

EVERETT: Sam, I never thought this marriage would work, you know that. But we're having a funeral today. Can't you take one day of your life to think about Mavis? God knows, you took everything else she had for your own use, but now you're even taking her funeral. *(Pause)* I'm sure she's happy for you to have it, that's just how she was, but it makes me mad, Sam. You make too much noise, son. You always did. Relax. Grieve.

SAM: No. This marriage was never right, and I want it straight now.

EVERETT: After the funeral, just leave Stephen with me for a few days, and you and Glory go down to Green River, work this thing out.

SAM: I don't want to work it out. What could we work it out to? Back to where it was at the beginning? In the beginning was the word, and the word was *pretend*.

EVERETT: I saw that beginning, same as you, and there wasn't any pretend about it. You were hopeless. You drooled around here for years until Glory called you with that math problem. Here was poor Mavis practically polishing your shoes to get your attention. But no, all you wanted was the pretty little rich girl, swimming in her own private lake out there. But how was she ever going to notice the preacher's kid? So you took up cross-country, didn't you? And pretty soon, you could run the ten miles out to her farm, and still have the breath to stand there and smile.

SAM: Why don't you say what you mean. Divorce is a sin.

EVERETT: Sam, your mother used to say your marriage was like your favorite shirt. You could wear it day after day, and you could try to keep it clean, but sooner or later it was going to have to go in the wash. But as soon as it was clean, you could press it fresh, and put it back on, looking good as new.

SAM: I don't have a favorite shirt. And I don't need advice from you.

EVERETT: What does she say? Does she say "Whatever you want, Sam"?

SAM: She will. Glory will do what Stephen wants. Stephen wants to be with me.

EVERETT: Stephen will be ready to go home tomorrow morning. Glory may not have all the answers to his questions, like you do, but she's *home* when he gets there.

SAM: That's not enough.

EVERETT: If you leave her, you'll lose him.

SAM: Stephen is mine. He always has been.

EVERETT: And you're supposed to be so smart. *(No response)* Maybe you ought to make a list of the things you don't know, just for your own protection, see. *(A pause)* Put this at the top.

SAM: This . . . what?

EVERETT: Boys and their mothers.

SAM: Whatever you say, Dad.

EVERETT: This is . . . a subject I took a few lessons in myself, Sam.

Glory comes out onto the porch carrying a cup of coffee for Everett.

GLORY: Sam? Don't you want a sandwich? We should leave in twenty minutes.

SAM: No thanks. I don't want to spoil my dinner.

Stephen runs past her and down the steps.

GLORY: Don't get dirty now, Stephen. Watch where you sit.

Stephen is carrying a Bible he has found inside. Glory follows him into the garden.

STEPHEN: Dad, I found your Bible!

SAM *(Alarmed)*: Glory, where—

STEPHEN *(Still very excited)*: I thought it was Grandpa's, but it's yours!

GLORY *(To Sam)*: In your old bedroom, I think.

STEPHEN *(Showing it to him)*: See? It says Samuel Carter.

SAM: The church gives them away, Stephen.

STEPHEN: No, look, Dad! On the next page, it says—

SAM *(To Everett)*: Did you give this to him?

Everett shakes his head no.

STEPHEN: See, it's right here. It says August 27, 1949, Jesus came into my heart.

SAM: Well—

STEPHEN: Only you've got it spelled H-E-R-A-T. Jesus came into your heart before you could even spell it!

Glory hands the coffee to Everett.

SAM: I didn't have any choice, Stephen. Night after night you sit there in the revival and every head is bowed and every eye is closed, and Dad is down there at the altar calling "Oh sinner, come home." And people all around you are saying "Bless me Jesus, save me Lord."

And the first night eight people go down and the second night twenty people go down, and the third night everybody in the whole third grade goes down, and those are the big kids, so I'm impressed. And you look up at Dad and he's looking straight at you, saying "God see my boy, see my own dear child, speak to him, Lord," and I heard it, all right. I couldn't go home if I didn't.

So before I could stop myself, I walked down the aisle, shaking and crying, saying "Here I am, Daddy." I knelt down at the altar, and he put his hand on my head and said "Praise the Lord," and I was saved. And he . . . was relieved. What kind of a preacher are you if you can't save your own child?

EVERETT: I didn't save you. He did.

SAM: Then after the service, we all waited for him in the front pew where he gave us all brand-new Bibles and had us turn to the front page and write down August 27, 1949—

SAM AND STEPHEN: —Jesus came into my heart.

STEPHEN: Did you read this?

EVERETT: He read it straight through before school even started that year.

SAM: I was too young to read, Dad. I just looked at the pictures, Stephen.

EVERETT: He knew hundreds of verses by heart. I'd be reading a verse in a sermon, and I'd look down at him in the front row, and he'd be mouthing the words right along with me.

SAM: Take it easy, Dad.

EVERETT: But I was so proud of you, son!

SAM: I know, but—

EVERETT: Stephen, we had Junior Church one Sunday a month, you know, where only the kids would come, and your dad started preaching there when he was only nine years old. By the time he was twelve, people all over the state had heard about him.

STEPHEN: You never told me you were a preacher, Dad.

EVERETT: That summer, at the revival, I announced in the newspaper that your dad was going to preach the sermon one night, and so many people came that there wasn't enough room for them all in the tent, so we had to open up the sides so people could sit on the grass and see him. He talked about Abraham that night. Abraham and Isaac.

STEPHEN *(Finding the picture in the Bible)*: Here's Abraham right here. *(Walking toward Sam)* But he's killing his little boy.

SAM: That's him all right. God says to Abraham, "If you really love me, you will sacrifice your son. You will build a fire, tie him to the top of it, slit his throat, say a prayer, and burn him up."

STEPHEN: Why?

EVERETT: The Lord was testing Abraham, Stephen.

SAM: The Lord was bored, Stephen. He was just looking for something to do.

EVERETT: Oh no. God had big plans for Abraham. And He had to make sure Abraham was the right man for the job.

STEPHEN: Is this God, here, in the clouds?

SAM: There's a much better picture of Him on page fifty-eight. That's Him in the burning bush.

STEPHEN: And He isn't burned up?

EVERETT: He *is* the fire.

STEPHEN: He is?

EVERETT: God really knows how to get your attention, all right.

SAM: He's lonely, Stephen. He sits and waits for somebody to notice Him, and then, when they don't, or when they don't notice Him enough, well, He plays His little tricks, He gives His little tests.

EVERETT: He has His reasons for His tests.

SAM: That's what you said when Mother died. God is testing us, son. God has His reasons, only we can't know what they are.

EVERETT: God didn't kill her.

SAM: He just let her die. He took her back. He was only kidding. She wasn't mine. She was His.

GLORY: Stephen, why don't you take the Bible inside. We don't want it to get—

SAM: She died when I was about your age, Stephen. About a month after my preaching triumph. But we didn't call it dying, did we, Dad? We just said God was missing her something awful and she went on back where she belonged, didn't we?

EVERETT: Yes, we did. And I don't know how He got along without her for as long as He did.

STEPHEN: I don't understand. Could God have saved Granny if He wanted to?

EVERETT: Yes, Stephen.

STEPHEN: Then why didn't He?

EVERETT: We do not understand everything that happens, but if we believe He loves us, we don't need to understand. Understanding is His work, not ours.

SAM: That's right. He sets it up, we live through it, and He writes it down. What we think of as life, Stephen, is just God gathering material for another book.

STEPHEN: Was God missing Mavis too?

SAM: Stephen—

EVERETT *(Quickly)*: I don't know, Stephen. But I do know He has His mysterious ways of working things out. Your daddy is a doctor today because his mother died when he was so young.

SAM: Jesus Christ.

EVERETT: They worked puzzles on her bed right up to the day she died. I'd come in to check on her, and she'd be asleep, but your dad would be reading *Mother Goose* to her like she could hear every word. He worked real hard but he couldn't save her. He was just a boy.

SAM: Jesus God.

EVERETT: But now, every time he goes into that operating room, God gives him another chance. How many people are alive today because of him! Hundreds! Thousands maybe. Praise be to the power and the wisdom of the Almighty God.

SAM: You are a hopeless old fool!

GLORY: Sam, you apologize to your father!

SAM: God is not in control.

GLORY: Please, Sam, remember what we're doing here.

SAM: I will not have Stephen walk into that funeral believing God has some reason for this! *(He turns to Stephen)* He's lying to you, Stephen. He lied to me and now he's lying to you and I won't have it! God had nothing to do with Mavis dying. It just happened. It was a goddamn rotten thing to happen, but God didn't do it. No. God is not in control and hasn't been in control for some time. *(He pauses and shifts into the master storyteller he can be)* He lost it . . . over Job. God made a bet with the Devil and lost it all.

Glory shakes her head and wanders off a bit. Sam relaxes a little, now that he has won.

SAM: The Devil said, "Sure Job loves you. Why shouldn't he? He's the richest man on earth. But you take all that away, and he won't pray to you then, no sir."

Well, God just had to find out. So in one afternoon, He killed all his sheep, all his camels, all his oxes and his asses and his daughters and his sons. And Job still prayed. So the next afternoon, God set a fire that burned up his house and everything in it, turned all his friends against him, sat Job down in the ashes and gave him leprosy.

And even then, Job prayed. Job suffered more than any man had ever suffered. As much, in fact, as God had ever suffered. And when God realized that Job could suffer just as well as He could, everything changed. For God saw that He had sinned, but Job loved Him still. And in that moment, God found God, and it was man.

And ever since that time, God has been up there believing in us with all His heart, believing we can do whatever we want, and wondering why, exactly, we do what we do. We must have our reasons, but He can't, for the life of Him, figure out what they are.

So He watches, but He can't help us. So He weeps. All God can do now is cry. The oceans, Stephen, are the tears God has cried since Job.

GLORY *(Coming back)*: We need to go, Sam.

SAM *(Continuing)*: God is not in control. We are. There is no heaven, there is no hell. There is this life, created, in your case, by your mother and me. Life on earth, which we can make better through careful thought and hard work. But *we* make the progress, and *we* make the mistakes. Not God. God has nothing to do with this, so there is no point in believing in Him. He's just another fairy-tale king, as far as I'm concerned. If you want to believe, believe in yourself. In your power, in your mind, in your life. This life. Because that's all there is.

Everett looks at his watch, then straightens his tie.

GLORY *(Coming quickly to be near Stephen)*: That's all your father thinks there is, Stephen. But he really doesn't know. Other people . . . *(Her anger is making it hard for her to talk)* find other things. Other people believe other things. And it makes them feel . . . different. Better.

SAM: Well, what can I say after that.

EVERETT *(Standing up)*: Maybe you can tell me what to say at this funeral.

SAM: No thanks.

EVERETT: I'll say it was an accident, how's that? I'll say it was a stupid mistake that somebody made. And we won't pray, of course, but we will sing. Something like "Moon River," you know, whatever we feel like. It doesn't matter what we do, does it, Sam? It doesn't mean a thing.

SAM: I don't know, Dad. It's your show.

EVERETT: This is no show!

SAM: It is a show and you know it.

EVERETT: Well I'll tell you one thing, boy. My show works.

SAM: Oh, you think so, do you?

EVERETT: Yes I do. My show works. It works so well that you—yes, even you—have come home to see it. Haven't you?

SAM *(Brushing off his pants)*: We need to take two cars.

GLORY: No we don't.

SAM: I'm not going to the supper. I don't want anybody coming up to me with coleslaw on their plate. I don't have anything to say about it.

GLORY: Stephen, go with your father, then, and I'll take Grandpa.

STEPHEN: Am I going with Dad forever, or just to the funeral?

SAM: I want you to do both those things, Stephen. I want you with me. Some new town, some other place. I'm sorry I didn't tell you myself, but I wanted to—

GLORY: Stephen, do you remember what I told you inside?

STEPHEN: Yes.

GLORY: All right, then.

EVERETT: Let's go, Glory.

GLORY: I'm ready. *(To Sam)* You *are* coming.

SAM: Yes. We're coming.

After Everett and Glory have left, Sam puts on his suit jacket.

SAM: What did she tell you inside?

STEPHEN: She said I shouldn't worry about it. She said you were just upset. She said everything would be all right.

SAM: Did she say how it would get that way?

STEPHEN: No.

SAM: She just believes it will.

STEPHEN: That's what she said.

SAM: Funny, huh?

STEPHEN: I don't know.

SAM *(Straightening Stephen's hair)*: Well, we can talk about it some more tonight. You're a real smart boy, and you'll just think your way through it. Just like any other problem. And you'll make your decision.

STEPHEN: Do I look all right?

SAM: You look good.

STEPHEN: So do you.

SAM: Thanks. Okay. *(Looking at Stephen)* Do we have a handkerchief?

STEPHEN *(Pats his pocket)*: Mom gave me some Kleenex.

SAM: Okay, then. Here we go. *(Then quietly)* God help us.

They walk offstage.

End of Act One

ACT
TWO

The lights come up, but they are not bright. It is sometime after midnight. Sam wanders into the garden and looks up at the house. There is only one light on, in that little room at the top of the house. Sam whistles the little tune he sang for Stephen in the first act and the light goes out. He sits down on the wall. Stephen opens the back door and walks out. Stephen is wearing his pajamas and a big sweater.

SAM *(As Stephen sits beside him)*: Hello, Stephen.

STEPHEN: I waited up for you.

SAM: Yeah. I saw. What time did you get home?

STEPHEN: I don't know. Eight-thirty, something like that.

SAM: Is everybody asleep?

STEPHEN: I don't know. They probably think I'm asleep and I'm not, so I probably think they're asleep and they're not. Grandpa was pretty tired. He might be asleep.

SAM: Did you see Granny Butler at the supper?

STEPHEN: She told me I needed a haircut.

SAM: What do *you* think?

STEPHEN: I told her she smelled like bug candles.

SAM: And what did she say to that?

STEPHEN: She said she liked it. She said it kept the bugs away.

SAM: So. What time did you get home? *(Then remembering)* Oh, I'm sorry. You already told me that. Let's see. Did you talk to anybody else?

STEPHEN: Not really. This one lady asked me if I ever met Mavis. I said yes and she asked me if I wanted a coke. *(Pause)* But *everybody* was talking to Grandpa, like Mavis was almost his daughter or something.

SAM: She was, in a way. *(Pause)* You know what he did for her? *(Then realizing what he is about to tell)* If I tell you this, you've got to promise me not to let him know you know. I mean, you can't ask him for it.

STEPHEN: What is it?

SAM: Well, Mavis's father was the custodian at the church, and her mother worked late, so when she was little, Mavis was always hanging around the church after school. And Dad didn't want her to feel she was any less than me, you know, so . . . *(An odd pause)* Dad sent off for the books, and learned some magic tricks for Mavis. Not big tricks, but . . . making a salt shaker disappear, things like that. And it was their secret, but I found out, of course. Mavis told me. So I went right in and asked him to do it for me, but he said, "What are you talking about? I can't do any magic tricks." But I badgered him for a solid week until one night at supper, he gave in, picked up the salt shaker and said, "Watch close now."

STEPHEN: Terrific!

SAM: No. Not so terrific. I watched too close, I guess. I saw how it worked and ran around the table to his jacket pocket, reached in and pulled out the salt shaker. I said, "Don't put it in your pocket, Dad. Make it disappear."

STEPHEN: You spoiled it.

SAM: Yes. *(Pause)* Well. What were you reading upstairs?

STEPHEN: Donner Pass.

SAM *(Laughs a little)*: Oh yes. The Family Picnic.

STEPHEN: Come on, Dad. Did they really eat each other? Got caught in a blizzard and ate each other?

SAM: That's all they had, Stephen. They had to eat.

STEPHEN: But they died anyway, the Donner Pass people. They ate each other up and it didn't save them.

SAM: They did what they thought they had to do. They didn't know it wouldn't save them. *(Pause)* But the whole trip was like that. Day after day, they'd left things behind, thrown out beds and chests and tools and toys . . . to make the wagons lighter, so they could travel faster . . . so they could get to Donner Pass.

STEPHEN: If they threw everything out, what did they think they would live on once they got there?

SAM: They thought it was enough just to get there. They thought they were smart enough to figure it out, whatever it was, up the road. It's a pretty standard American idea. All you need is your brain. Then if all you have is your brain, well . . . you can eat it.

STEPHEN: Can we go there sometime? I bet there's a marker, isn't there? Donner Pass Memorial Park or something.

SAM: Sure, Stephen. *(As if reading it)* In memory of the families who died by the side of the road, because the things that would have saved them were too heavy to carry such a long way.

STEPHEN: Didn't anybody tell them what could happen?

SAM: Yeah, probably. But they didn't listen. Other people get caught in blizzards and have to eat their families, not me. I'm smart.

STEPHEN: Not smart enough, huh.

SAM: Nobody is smart *enough*.

STEPHEN: Somebody out there might be. Some spaceman.

SAM: I don't think so, Stephen.

STEPHEN *(A bit disappointed)*: Why not?

SAM: See that cloud? Straight across the sky, there?

STEPHEN: Yeah.

SAM: It's not a cloud. It's us. It's the Milky Way. You can't see it in the city, but out here, you can. *(Pause)* The earth spins around the sun, while the sun spins around the center of the Milky Way, while the Milky Way chases Andromeda going like a billion miles an hour. *We're* the spacemen, Stephen.

STEPHEN *(After a moment)*: Is there a center of everything?

SAM: The Big Bang Theory says there *was* one, but it blew up.

STEPHEN: Grandpa would say God did it, God lit the fuse.

SAM: Yes. He would.

STEPHEN: Did He? *(Sam doesn't answer)* Is there a God, Dad?

SAM *(Taking Stephen in his arms)*: When I am out here, on this wall, in this garden, looking up at the sky, I think, yes, there is something out there. I actually want there to be something out there. I want there to be a God, and I don't want it to be me.

STEPHEN: Are you feeling better, Dad?

SAM: I'm sorry about all this, Stephen. But once we get going . . . . First thing in the morning, we'll put all our things in Mavis's car and take off. Dad doesn't want it he said. So we might as well take it, don't you think, like she left us a getaway car. When we stop for the night, you can call your mother if you want, and just see if she can guess where we are.

STEPHEN: I don't want to move, Dad.

SAM: You want to stay with your mother, you mean.

STEPHEN: I don't want you to leave us.

SAM: We'll go someplace wonderful. Northern California, maybe, with the ocean out the front door, and the redwoods out the back. And we could get a horse if you want. I always wanted a horse.

STEPHEN: I can't leave, Dad. Mom needs me. She doesn't have anybody.

SAM: Stephen, your mother has more friends than the Red Cross.

STEPHEN *(Getting up off the wall now)*: It's not the same thing. She needs *me*.

SAM: No, you're right. That's true. She does. I need you too, but . . . she said it first, huh?

STEPHEN: Don't you love Mom anymore?

SAM: I guess not.

STEPHEN: What did she do?

SAM: Nothing.

STEPHEN: Did you love her when you married her?

SAM: Yes.

STEPHEN: Did she change?

SAM: No.

STEPHEN: Did you change?

SAM: No, not really.

STEPHEN: So what happened to it?

SAM: Stephen, there will be days when it doesn't matter that you're smart. When it won't help. When your extraordinary mind is of no use whatsoever. When all it will do is tell you how bad things are.

STEPHEN: But you told me to think about it.

SAM: Yes, but . . . *(Struggling here)* You can't think about this the way you would any other problem. You can't just add up the numbers and read the result, because it doesn't work that way. It's like you wanted to open a bottle of beer, but all you had to use was your calculator. It wouldn't work. You need to use something else.

STEPHEN: I would sell the calculator and buy a bottle opener. *(No response from Sam)* I would go next door and borrow a bottle opener.

SAM: I would call upstairs and ask your mother where she hid the bottle opener.

STEPHEN: She didn't hide it. You just didn't look. You never look. You're out of the house for eight hours and you act like we've taken all the stuff out of the cabinets and hidden it away like a treasure hunt. *(Imitating Sam's call)* Glory, where's the peanut butter?

SAM *(Defending himself)*: I just got home. I'm tired. I don't want to go looking. I want the peanut butter.

STEPHEN *(Very angry)*: It's in the basement. It's in a box marked Dad's Old Shoes.

SAM: What does she do? Hold little indoctrination sessions with you?

STEPHEN: I don't want to move, Dad.

SAM: We don't even have to stay in this country, you know. We could go to South America and become river rats. Or how about Africa. Spend the whole day outside.

STEPHEN: So what would I do? Wait outside the hut all day for you to come home?

SAM: You'd go to school.

STEPHEN: I already go to school. And I already sit and wait for you to come home and I already don't like it. I wouldn't like it any better in Africa.

SAM: I'll come home.

STEPHEN: No you won't.

SAM: We'll go fishing.

STEPHEN: No we won't, Dad.

SAM: I love you, Stephen.

STEPHEN: If you could stop loving Mom, you could stop loving me.

SAM: No, Stephen. Your children are not the same as your wife or your husband.

STEPHEN: Your children are an accident.

SAM: Stephen!

STEPHEN: You didn't want any children at all. I wouldn't even be here if it weren't for Mom.

SAM: Did she tell you that?

STEPHEN: No, but it's true, isn't it. Isn't it!

SAM: Yes. But I didn't know I would get you. If I had known it was you, I'd have wanted you. *(No response from Stephen)* I know I've been gone too much and never taken any time off, but I want to change all that. I want to be with you now.

STEPHEN: You don't want to do anything but work and you can't even do that right. What kind of doctor are you if you can't save your own nurse?

Suddenly the back-porch light comes on and Everett steps out.

EVERETT: Stephen? Are you out there?

SAM *(More quiet, but more intense)*: Stephen, I didn't kill Mavis. You don't understand.

EVERETT *(Calling again)*: Stephen!

STEPHEN *(To Sam)*: What's there to understand? She's dead.

EVERETT *(To Glory, who is in the kitchen)*: They're outside, Glory.

SAM: Stephen, medicine doesn't always work.

STEPHEN: Then it might as well be magic, Dad.

SAM: Stephen, people die all the time. People have to die sometime.

Everett walks out into the garden.

STEPHEN *(Louder than necessary)*: And it's no big deal, huh.

EVERETT *(Hearing him)*: There you are. We thought we lost you.

SAM *(Sees his father, but keeps talking)*: It's sad, Stephen, but no, it's not any big deal.

STEPHEN *(Standing up)*: Well, if it's not any big deal when people die, then it's not any big deal when they live, or where they live, so I'm living with Mom.

Everett sits down, making Sam even more uncomfortable.

SAM: Stephen, I tried to save her—

STEPHEN *(Jumping up now)*: I'm living with Mom.

SAM: Ask him! He'll tell you. I did everything—

STEPHEN *(Screaming)*: I'm living with Mom.

SAM: Are you listening to me?

STEPHEN: Don't call us! Don't come see us!

SAM: Stephen!

STEPHEN *(Moving toward the house)*: Don't come get your things!

SAM: What do you want me to say?

STEPHEN: Buy new things!

Stephen runs out of the garden and up the steps into the house. Sam just stands there a minute, then turns to Everett, who is still sitting by the wall.

SAM: If you're looking for Stephen, he went inside.

EVERETT *(After a moment)*: That's good. It's cold out here.

SAM *(Very controlled)*: Then why don't *you* go inside.

EVERETT: And do what?

SAM: And talk to somebody else! *(No response from Everett)* God, for example.

EVERETT: I *did* talk to God.

SAM: I'm sure you did.

EVERETT: He told me to come out here and sit with you, and He'd get back to me in the morning.

SAM: Did He tell you what to say to me?

EVERETT: No. God's not much good on detail.

SAM: But you have some ideas, I guess.

EVERETT: Are you mad at God or me?

SAM: I'm not sure. I get you confused.

EVERETT: What did I do?

SAM: You let Mother's garden go to hell.

EVERETT: Sam, I'm an old man.

SAM: You didn't deserve her.

EVERETT: Of course I didn't. She was a gift. Like Glory is a gift. Like Stephen is a gift.

SAM: She was nothing to you. Nothing at all. You never paid any attention to her. You spent all your time tending the flock.

EVERETT: I did love your mother, Sam.

SAM: You loved God more.

EVERETT: Of course I did. And she knew I loved God more. She knew I loved *you* more.

SAM: You didn't love me, you loved Mavis. Yes! You even loved Mavis more than Mother. First God, then Mavis, then the ladies in the choir, then the congregation, then the shut-ins, then the sick, then the starving Chinese and the heathen, wherever they are, then me, then Mother.

EVERETT: I'm sorry if it seemed that way.

SAM: It *was* that way!

EVERETT: All right. It *was* that way. She was last on my list. All right. But there was a power in me, like there's a power in you, and I couldn't let anything get in its way.

SAM: Why couldn't you let anything get in its way? What good did it do? I mean, it didn't work, Dad.

EVERETT: I was called to it, Sam. Same as you. And you know your Glory understands what your work means to you. Your mother was exactly that way for me. Of course, I never saved lives the way *you* do, but I *was*—

SAM: We can't save lives. God couldn't save Mother. Medicine couldn't save Mavis. Lives are lost from the start. All you do is promise them another one, and all I do is make this one last longer. But it's *our* victory, not theirs. My work saves *my* life. Or used to. Oh boy. Day after day I've been real proud of myself 'cause I won one more round. Right? Wrong. Death wins. Death always wins.

EVERETT: Not in my book.

SAM: No, not in your book. But I don't believe in your book. I don't, in fact, believe in anything. It has taken me my whole life, Dad, but I have finally arrived. I am free of faith. Glory be. Praise the Lord.

EVERETT *(Almost laughing)*: Oh, He's really after you this time, isn't He?

SAM: And He has to shake me to make me listen, doesn't He?

EVERETT: Well, I probably believed that in the old days, but God's not as physical as He used to be.

SAM: That is *not* what you "probably believed" in the old days. That is *exactly* what you said from the pulpit the Sunday after Mother died. You pointed to me, sitting there on the front row of the choir, where everybody in the whole congregation could see me, and you told them the story. "There was my little boy, Samuel, sitting on his dear mother's bed, and he didn't know she was dead, he was just sitting there, reading as loud as he could, as fast as he could, but he was shaking like a young tree in a driving rain. And I walked in and saw that she was dead and put my hands on his shoulders and made him stop shaking and made him stop reading and listen. And I said, 'Son, your mother has gone to her reward.' And he heard me."

Now by this time, they're all crying, the whole church is crying, but you weren't through, were you? You walked over to me and pulled me up out of my seat in the choir and grabbed my hand and held it to your heart and you said to your congregation, "That's what God has to do, sometimes. He has to shake us to make us listen."

EVERETT *(Quite shaken himself)*: I didn't mean to talk about it, Sam. Not that Sunday, anyway. I just lost my place in my sermon, somehow. And everything got all blurry, all of a sudden, and all I knew was, I had to keep talking and . . . that was the best I could do, son.

SAM: Yeah, well, do you want to know what God said to me? What I heard when I quit shaking?

EVERETT: Sam, Sam . . .

SAM: I heard God say, and He was almost laughing when He said it—God said, "Sam, Sam, how could you have been so dumb."

EVERETT: I don't know what to say to you, son.

SAM: I don't want you to say anything to me. I want you to leave me alone.

EVERETT: Where am I supposed to go, Sam? This is my house.

SAM: This is Mother's house. Yours is the one with the steeple on the top.

EVERETT: No. That's God's house.

SAM: Then where do you live, Daddy? I mean, when you go home, who opens the door?

EVERETT: Oh, son. *(Pause)* You do.

SAM *(Very cold)*: Well I'm awful sorry about that, Dad, but you don't get the boy you want, you get the boy you get.

EVERETT: This hurts me too much now, Sam. You're the only one who . . . . Look, maybe you shouldn't come down here anymore. I'm happy here.

My whole life is peaceful here. And I can still pray for you and keep up with you, but well, I'll just see you in the newspapers from now on, okay? Maybe you'll send Stephen to visit me now and then, but I won't come there, and you don't come here, all right?

Sam is suddenly still, and there is a long silence.

SAM: Will Stephen forgive me?

Everett takes a long time here.

EVERETT *(Quietly)*: I don't know. Do you forgive me?
SAM *(Much more quiet)*: I don't know.
EVERETT: Well then, it's hard to say. Some of these things are inherited, I think.

Glory comes out of the house.

GLORY: Everett? Sam? What are you two doing out here?
EVERETT: Oh, you know. Reminiscing.
GLORY: Look Sam. Look what I found. I thought you gave me all your letter sweaters, but you didn't. You kept one for yourself, didn't you.
EVERETT: He couldn't get in the sports banquet without it.
GLORY: I remember that banquet. You were the only member of the cross-country team.
EVERETT: I remember they served cauliflower. Bless your mother's heart, you were the only athlete who ate it.
GLORY: Everett, you need to put on something warmer if you're going to stay out here.
EVERETT *(Standing)*: Did Stephen go to bed?
GLORY: I made him some warm milk.
EVERETT: I didn't think I had any milk.
GLORY: I made a glass for you, too.
EVERETT: I'll go sit with him, then.
GLORY: Don't you like milk?
EVERETT: I don't know. I'll see. *(He goes into the house)*
GLORY *(Turning to Sam)*: Come on, Sam. Put this sweater on.

Sam takes the sweater finally, and puts it on as he talks.

SAM: I liked that run before school every morning. Out of the house . . . down the street . . . . Everybody asleep but me and the milkman. I got to feeling real useful, you know, like I was supposed to check out the town before everybody got up. Mile after mile, so far, so good, I'd think. No fires, no stray dogs, and no lights on, so nobody's sick. We did okay. We made it through another night.
GLORY: You were right not to come to the supper, Sam.
SAM: Did they wonder where I was?

GLORY: They're used to your being gone, I think.

SAM: Like you.

GLORY: No. I'm not used to it. But I don't take it personally anymore.

SAM: Like they do.

GLORY: Maybe they do. I don't know.

SAM: They think . . . that I think . . . that I'm better than they are.

GLORY: You do!

SAM: I know. They're right.

GLORY: And that's why you don't go. You can't stand for them to be right.

SAM: That's right.

GLORY *(After a moment)*: Well . . . you missed some great stories about Mavis.

SAM: I'm sure I did.

GLORY: Your dad told one about you and Mavis, and Timmy somebody—he didn't remember the name—coming back from church camp down at Green River. And you were speeding down the road in that old Volkswagen of hers. And suddenly you saw a policeman coming up behind you and you realized not only were you all three drunk, but you didn't have your driver's license, and you knew you'd never get into medical school with that on your record, so Mavis said, "I'll drive." And you said, "What?" And she said, "Change places with me. I'll drive." And you said, "Mavis, we're going seventy miles an hour." And she said, "Move over."

SAM *(Realizing she doesn't know the end of the story)*: Is that all he told of it?

GLORY: Is there more?

SAM: We climbed over each other and she got behind the wheel. I told her to slow down, but she told me to shut up. When the police car pulled up beside us, she rolled down the window and yelled to the officer that the accelerator was stuck, and he took one look at the car, and believed her. He made some motions with his hands like she should downshift or kick the accelerator, which she did, then she hit the brake, smiled at him, pulled off the road, got out of the car, and threw up.

GLORY: So she wasn't drunk anymore.

SAM: Right.

GLORY: Smart.

SAM *(With great, unprotected joy)*: Yeah. Mavis was as smart as they come.

Pause.

GLORY: Sam, I've been thinking about all of this.

SAM: Yes. It's that kind of night, isn't it.

GLORY: I think you're right. I think I'll go to Mother's for a while. A month maybe. You take Stephen and go, Sam. Back to the city or on a trip, whatever you think is best. I don't want to fight with you now. I'd just like a month to think.

SAM: I see.

GLORY: I didn't bring the right clothes to suit Mother, but she'll take me shopping, I guess. And she's giving a big party next week. People I haven't seen in years. Maybe some of them will have learned something in the meantime.

SAM: Don't count on it.

GLORY: My riding clothes are still out there, so that's good. I'll be able to check out this exercise boy of hers.

SAM: Uh-huh.

GLORY: And I thought maybe Everett might need me. We can go through Mavis's clothes, and I'll help him sort her letters and look at the pictures with him and hear the rest of the stories again. *(Pause)* I'm all packed.

SAM: Glory . . .

GLORY: I just came out here to—

SAM: Will you not leave . . . just yet? Will you sit with me awhile?

GLORY: I will.

SAM *(This is hard for him at first)*: When you went to the supper, I drove over to Mavis's house. Where they lived when we were kids, I mean. I don't even know who lives there now. I just parked out front for a while. I always liked that house. Those lilac bushes are still there, remember?

GLORY: Sure I do. All over the place.

SAM: And for one moment, I was sixteen and I had it all to do over again. And I could forget your hair, and forget your mouth and your smell, and love Mavis. Marry her. Somebody exactly like me. Somebody who believed in hard work, who couldn't wait to be an adult. Somebody who never read "Sleeping Beauty" and never said a prayer except, "God let me stay awake long enough to get everything finished."

GLORY: You were two of a kind all right.

SAM: And in the next moment, the moment after I was sixteen and could forget your hair, I was sixteen and I wanted your hair in my mouth, in my eyes, all over me. I wanted to catch you swimming naked in your pond. I knew you did it. You told me you did it.

GLORY *(Confessing)*: Of course I did. I wanted you to catch me.

SAM: I never had a chance. I hopped over to that pond like every frog in every fairy tale my mother ever read me, and you kissed me, and I believed. I remember that kiss, I can still taste the butterscotch sucker I took out of your mouth to have that kiss, and I'm still dizzy and hot all of a sudden, and I remember loving you. *(Pause)* And I guess that kiss . . . was the last I ever saw of Mavis.

GLORY: Bless her heart, she worshiped you. I knew it, everybody knew it.

SAM: So, once I was in love with you, she had to go to nursing school, didn't she? But she never married, just in case you got hit by a truck or something. *(Glory laughs but knows it's true)* Right. Nursing school was her last chance to get my attention, but it didn't work. I didn't look at her in high school and I haven't looked at her since. Why should I look? I knew she'd be there.

GLORY: Sam . . .

SAM: Mavis was two feet away from me, across the table from me, her whole life, and what did she get from this life with me? Nothing. Invitations to dinner from you. Tennis on Saturday with you. The four of us at the movies, me sound asleep and Mavis holding the popcorn between you and Stephen. Nothing.

GLORY: Mavis got as much from you as you would let her have. That's all she wanted. You're a genius. People make exceptions. They settle.

SAM: You have done more than settle. You have bet your lives on me. It was worse for Mavis, but it's the same for all of you. None of you had any right to count on me, but you did, and I let you, and now, instead of saving any of you—

GLORY: Is that what you think you're doing in our lives, saving us?

SAM: I want to help you.

GLORY: We're all right down here. We think our little thoughts and we have our silly troubles and we fight our losing battles as bravely as we can. The last thing we need is for you to come in and solve our problems for us. Our problems, Sam, are how we fill up our days.

SAM: It's easier for you in the winter, I guess. Your days are shorter.

GLORY *(A flash of anger)*: I don't need you to save me! *(Then recovering)* I just need you to . . . be on my side whenever you can. *(When he doesn't respond, she continues)* See me . . . hear me . . . give me some room, and save me some time. That's all. *(Still no response from Sam)* I've already got a God, Sam. And I see Him all the time, everywhere I go. And He may seem limited and primitive to you, but the dances are fun and the songs are sweet, and every day is a holy day.

SAM: So what is your God doing tonight?

GLORY: I don't know. Maybe He's just . . . watering the grass.

SAM: Okay. I can't save you. But neither do I have the right to destroy you all.

GLORY: I am not destroyed! I'm mad at you because you're acting like this, but I am not destroyed. And if you think you destroyed Mavis . . . if you're out here feeling sorry for Mavis . . . Mavis had you all day, Sam. Mavis had the best of you! I never had the conversations she had with you. I never sweated with you for twelve hours to work one of your miracles. We—you and I—never held our breath till the dead man sat up, Sam. *(And he doesn't respond)* No, Sam. Don't feel sorry for Mavis. And don't be mad at me. I have been—Stephen and I have been— happy, all these years, to have what was left over when Mavis finished with you.

SAM: So you're happy she's gone.

GLORY *(Horrified)*: How can you say that?

SAM: You sounded jealous, that's all.

GLORY: I was jealous. You loved her. But that doesn't—

SAM: No, Glory. I didn't love her. I had every opportunity to, but I didn't.

GLORY: Well . . . I loved her. And I think she loved me. And right now, I'm feeling real lost without her.

SAM: She was jealous of you.

GLORY: What on earth for?

SAM: You've got it all.

GLORY: I've got you, you mean.

SAM: You're a great-looking woman and Stephen adores you, and you float through everything like you're on a . . . like you were born wearing a life jacket. *(Pause)* Mavis had to work hard for everything she ever had, while you . . . well, you . . . just enjoy yourself.

GLORY: Listen, Sam. It's not as easy as it looks.

SAM: Yeah, well, you've had a lot of practice.

GLORY *(In a rage)*: I did not agree to sit here and take the blame for this. It's not my fault! *(She starts for the house)*

SAM: I didn't love her, I used her. And then . . . when she really needed me . . . . She was counting on me to see it, Glory, only I wasn't looking. And I wasn't looking because I didn't want to see it. Other people die, Glory—not me, not my family, not my friend!

GLORY: None of us were looking, Sam. Three weeks ago, I knew she looked awful. I told her to get a haircut.

SAM: It's the thirteenth fairy, see. You don't invite her to the party because you don't want her to come, but she comes anyway, because she lives there, just like you do. But you forgot, didn't you?

GLORY: Sam . . .

SAM: I forgot Mavis was alive and she died.

GLORY: You were trying to save her!

SAM: I was showing off! I could fix it. I could pull her through. I could make it disappear. She could have lived for months. A year maybe, but no, I have to go in and save her.

GLORY: Even if it was a mistake . . .

SAM: I believed I could save her.

GLORY: Well you couldn't.

SAM: So now I just turn around and believe I couldn't?

GLORY: Yes!

SAM: No! It was the belief that was the problem in the first place! I believed in everything. I even believed in you—or love, I guess. Didn't I? Yes. And in God, and fairy tales, and medicine and the power of my own mind and none of it works!

GLORY: Sam . . . please . . .

SAM: But I want to believe! Stephen wants to believe! He does! I see it! After everything I've told him, he still wants to believe. But how can I let him believe when I know what happens, when there is no good reason for what happens, when there is no reason to believe.

GLORY *(Trying another tack)*: Sam, you've got this all mixed up. You married me because I'm good for you, and you operated on Mavis because you were the best one to do it, because she wanted you to do it, because you wanted to do it.

SAM: No! *(In his own private hell now)* I believed, once again, I believed I might be able to do something and . . . *(Very distant, suddenly)* Mavis believed I could save her and all the faith in the world wouldn't save her. Won't save any of us. Won't do a thing except make fools of us. Give us tests we cannot pass. Bring us to our knees, but not in prayer—in absolute submission to accident, to the arbitrary assignment of unbearable pain, and the everyday occurrence of meaningless death. Only then can we believe . . . that dreams, like deadly whirlpools, drown us in their frenzy . . . that love blazes across a black sky like a comet but never returns . . . and that time, like a desert wind, blows while I sleep, and erases the path I walked to here, and erases the path that leads on.

Sam's anger has been so raw and so violent that he now simply stands, but we are certain he will not speak for quite a while.

GLORY *(Without looking up)*: Oh, Sam . . . . Oh, sweet baby . . . *(Now standing up, but not looking at Sam)* I went in to see her, you know Tuesday morning, and she'd already had her shot, so she was pretty dopey, but she said, well, she said a lot of things. "Well," she said, "it looks like Sam's gonna get his hands on me after all."

She looks to Sam for a response but there is none. As Glory continues, Sam walks slowly downstage and sits on a rock and buries his head in his hands.

GLORY: Anyway, then she said, "Glory . . . Sam might not be able to fix this, you know. I might not be there for him, this time, when he needs me . . . I might not be as helpful as I have been. I'll be asleep, see, that's my excuse. Anyway, if I don't make it . . . I want him to know what I loved . . . why I loved him. It was only one thing he did, really. We were ten years old, and Everett had this magic trick and Sam knew how it worked, and he showed me how it worked. He knew it wasn't magic, and he knew it didn't always work, and he wasn't afraid to know. Tell him that's why I loved him. He wasn't afraid to know." Then she said, "I've caught it from him, I guess. I'm not afraid either."

As Glory and Sam remain seated, spent, on the ground, the back door opens and Stephen comes out.

STEPHEN: Mom?
GLORY: You need to be in bed, honey.

STEPHEN: Are you going to sleep out here?

GLORY: I don't know.

STEPHEN: Want me to get you a blanket?

GLORY: No thanks, sweetie. I'm going to stand up, just . . . any minute now.

STEPHEN: What's the matter with Dad?

GLORY: It's just late, honey. He's real tired.

STEPHEN: Why doesn't he say anything?

GLORY: He just needs to be quiet now, Stephen.

STEPHEN *(Walking toward Sam)*: Dad?

GLORY: Come over here if you want to. Keep me warm.

Stephen comes to sit down with Glory and they hug.

STEPHEN: Maybe we should eat again.

GLORY: Anything sound good to you?

STEPHEN: No.

GLORY: Did you and Grandpa have a nice talk?

STEPHEN: He was going to teach me how to play Chinese checkers, but, well . . . he lost his marbles.

GLORY *(Laughing)*: Did you say that or did he?

STEPHEN: I did. He said . . . he couldn't find them. But I thought . . . you could use a joke.

GLORY: Boy, is that the truth. I'd give you a dollar for it . . .

STEPHEN: . . . if you had a dollar.

GLORY: You got it.

STEPHEN: I'll put it on your bill.

GLORY: Done.

STEPHEN: Maybe he's asleep.

GLORY: Who?

STEPHEN: Dad.

GLORY: He might be asleep. But I wouldn't say anything you don't want him to hear.

STEPHEN *(Picking up the geode)*: What's this?

GLORY: I don't know. A rock.

STEPHEN: It's round. Rocks aren't round.

GLORY: I don't know, Stephen. Ask your father.

STEPHEN: You ask him.

GLORY: You're the one who wants to know.

STEPHEN: Maybe it goes in the wall.

Stephen gets up and walks around the garden looking for a place the geode might go. At one point he gets close to Sam, but Glory motions for Stephen to go around him.

STEPHEN: A rock this big ought to be heavier. *(Glory doesn't know how to answer him, so she just smiles and watches)* How did it get so round?

GLORY: I don't know, Stephen.

Everett comes out of the house and takes a couple of steps. He is very reluctant to interrupt this, whatever it is.

EVERETT: I'll say good night, I guess.

GLORY: Good night, Everett.

EVERETT: You can come inside now, if you want. I'm going to bed . . . and there's chairs in here.

GLORY: We're all right, Everett.

EVERETT: Well, then . . .

He looks at Sam, then at Glory, who shakes her head and motions for Everett not to say anything.

STEPHEN: Grandpa, do you know what this rock is?

EVERETT: No, Stephen.

STEPHEN: I found it out here in the garden.

EVERETT: I found a whole drawer full of them upstairs. I brought that one out here to look at one day.

STEPHEN: But whose are they? Where did they come from?

EVERETT: They're Mary's.

STEPHEN: Who's Mary?

EVERETT: Your grandmother. Sam's mother.

GLORY: I saw those dancing pictures upstairs, Everett. If she danced as great as she looked, she was a real catch.

EVERETT *(Pleased to be invited to come talk)*: She sure was. And nobody could understand why she married the preacher except she was having a better time than anybody else and she had to find some way to pay for it.

GLORY: She sounds like me.

EVERETT: If she were alive today, she'd bake you a batch of chocolate chips and eat them every one while they were still hot. Then she'd send you the wax paper she baked them on and write you a note, telling you to let her know the minute you went off your diet.

STEPHEN: And she liked these rocks?

EVERETT: Well, I don't know. I guess so. I didn't even know she had them till she died. I was looking for a list she made, who she wanted to have her piano, things like that, and I found them. I found a lot of things. I found the world she lived in, a world I knew very little about. I know she loved me, but I don't know why. She must have loved those rocks, but I don't know what they are. *(Now he looks at Sam)* I guess you can be a real big part of somebody else's world without ever understanding the first thing about it. Somebody can give you their life and you'll never know why. Never know what they wanted from you, or if they ever got it. Then when they die, well, knowing so little about these people makes it real hard to lose them. *(Pause)* I kept meaning to ask Sam about those rocks. I know she'd want him to have them.

SAM *(Finally)*: It's not a rock. It's a geode.

STEPHEN *(Running down to him)*: You mean with the crystals inside?

SAM: Yes.

STEPHEN: Well, let's open it up and see it! Where's the hammer?

SAM *(Sudden alarm)*: No! *(Then more quietly)* Once you crack them . . . . She didn't like to crack them.

STEPHEN: Then how do you know what's in there?

SAM: You don't. She said . . . it was better for it to be safe than for you to know what it was, exactly.

STEPHEN: Dad?

SAM: I'm here, Stephen. *(He sits, but still holds the geode)* I thought I could save Mavis. *(To Stephen)* I thought I could protect you. I can't do any of those things. I don't know what I *can* do. I don't know what to say. I have nothing for you.

STEPHEN *(Pointing to the geode)*: I'll take that.

SAM: The geode?

STEPHEN: Yeah.

SAM: It's not mine.

EVERETT: Yes it is.

SAM: It's nothing.

STEPHEN: It's okay. I like it.

SAM: I like it too. When Mother died I gathered them up and put them in that drawer. Yes, you can have it. It's . . . your mystery now.

STEPHEN *(Taking the geode)*: Thanks.

There is silence all around.

STEPHEN: Dad?

SAM: Yes.

STEPHEN: Where did she go, Dad?

SAM: Where did Mavis go?

STEPHEN: Yes.

And there is more silence.

SAM: I don't know, Stephen.

STEPHEN: I saw her in the coffin, but it wasn't her.

GLORY *(Gently)*: It was her, Stephen.

STEPHEN: I mean, she wasn't there anymore.

SAM: No.

STEPHEN *(Carefully)*: Did you see it go, Dad?

SAM: What?

STEPHEN *(Still very careful)*: In the operating room? Did you cut her open and it got out?

And Sam doesn't answer for a moment. His heart is broken, his anger turned to grief and longing. Glory, Everett and Stephen are silent and perfectly still.

SAM: Yes. *(Pause)* I cut her open and it got out. I was standing there over her and . . .

STEPHEN *(Quietly)*: What was it like? *(Now very slowly)* Could you feel it or see it or hear it? Was it cold or white or like air maybe or what?

And Sam stands there a moment, searching for the answer, searching for the memory, trying to see it again. Finally, he shakes his head. The words are coming, but he has no idea what they are.

SAM: It was . . . *(And suddenly, the words come from him the way "it" came from Mavis in that moment)* It was forgiveness.

Sam stands there quietly a moment, as a kind of peace seems to come over him, and then over Everett, and then Glory. Stephen, however, doesn't quite understand.

STEPHEN *(Finally)*: For what, Dad?

SAM: I don't know, Stephen. For whatever I did. For all those years.

STEPHEN: Did she forgive me for losing her cat?

SAM *(Not directly to Stephen, and not quickly)*: Yes, Stephen.

EVERETT *(Quietly)*: I wondered what happened to that cat. Every week, on the phone, I had to say hello to that damn cat.

STEPHEN *(To Everett)*: I didn't mean to lose Peaches, she just—

GLORY *(Interrupting him, to soothe him)*: It's all right, Stephen. I owed Mavis money.

SAM: You? What for?

GLORY *(A bit embarrassed as the story begins)*: I had my eyes done. Last March when I told you I came to see Mother, I flew to Chicago and had my eyes done. I didn't want you to know it, so I borrowed the money from Mavis.

SAM: And I never noticed it.

GLORY: No.

SAM *(Inspecting her eyes now)*: Nice work. *(Then inspecting more carefully)* Great work.

GLORY: She said we had to preserve your illusions.

SAM: I like it.

GLORY: That's good. It was a lot of money.

EVERETT: It was four thousand dollars.

SAM: I didn't know Mavis had any money.

EVERETT: It was my money.

GLORY: I didn't know that.

EVERETT: I didn't know it was for you.

SAM *(To Everett)*: I'll pay you back.

EVERETT: Good.

GLORY: Thank you anyway, Everett.

EVERETT *(After a moment)*: I owe you an apology, Glory.

GLORY: What on earth?

EVERETT: I told Mavis your marriage wouldn't last. That your mother was stingy with her money and your looks wouldn't last forever. I told her if she'd just wait, she could have Sam all to herself.

STEPHEN: Why did you do that?

EVERETT: It was . . . an old dream of mine.

SAM: You were wrong.

EVERETT: I know.

GLORY: Well, not completely. Mother *is* cheap.

EVERETT: I'm sorry, Glory.

GLORY: It's all right, Everett. You didn't know.

SAM *(After a moment)*: I'm the one who needs to apologize to you, Glory.

GLORY: It's all right, Sam.

SAM: I only wanted to leave because—

GLORY: You don't have to tell me that, Sam.

SAM: I don't know why I wanted to leave you. I can't leave you. But maybe I didn't want to hurt you like I . . . maybe I was afraid I would lose you, too.

GLORY: Sam, it's been a sad, sad day. We're all so lonely for her, we've all . . . said things.

SAM: Yeah, I know, but I said mine on purpose.

GLORY: You were mad.

SAM: That doesn't make it right. I need you. I love you.

GLORY: I know, Sam. I tried to tell you that this afternoon.

SAM: I guess I wasn't listening.

GLORY *(Carefully)*: No, I didn't think you were.

SAM *(Takes his time before he begins)*: Glory, if you could . . . hold on a little longer, I want to be a better man.

GLORY: I can do that, Sam. *(He shakes his head, first out of relief, and then in confusion)* You don't understand, do you. *(He shakes his head no)* I'd explain it to you if I could, or maybe you'll explain it to me in a week or so, or maybe we'll just love each other anyway and never know.

SAM: Please . . . forgive me.

And Glory extends her arms to Sam, and they embrace. And when they break the embrace he sees his father.

SAM: And Dad . . . I'm sorry, Dad.

EVERETT: I'm all right, son.

SAM: No, Dad. I want you to know that I—

EVERETT: I said it's all right, son.

SAM: I love you, Dad.

EVERETT: Yes. I know.

STEPHEN *(After a moment)*: I'm cold. Is anybody else cold? It's cold out here.

And Sam knows they are all waiting for him to speak, to say whether he is finished here.

SAM: Well, maybe . . . we could . . . go in the house. I didn't think I wanted to go in the house, but now—

EVERETT: I haven't changed a thing, Sam.

SAM: Yes, well, *(Smiling at Everett and himself)* that's what I was afraid of.

Glory squeezes his hand or laughs a little at him, and Everett shakes his head, but they are all still waiting for Sam to make the next move.

SAM: Dad, if it's all right with Stephen and Glory, we'd like to stay here a few days, if it isn't too much trouble.

STEPHEN: Hey! Great!

EVERETT: What do you mean? You *have* to stay here. You haven't finished cleaning up this garden. And Stephen hasn't read all my books and I know I can't eat all that food we brought home from the supper.

GLORY *(Gathering up something she has brought outside)*: You can't eat all that food because Josie Barnett can't cook. I thought people in the country could cook.

EVERETT *(Now moving toward the house)*: What Josie Barnett can't do is sing. None of these girls can sing a lick. I keep praying I'll go deaf, but then . . . *(Looking to heaven, but aware that he's making a joke)* I ask Him for so much.

Stephen follows Everett's eyes to the heavens and finds the stars.

STEPHEN *(As though they were in the middle of a conversation about stars)*: But Dad, what holds the stars up there? Why don't they fall?

And there is a pause, while Sam doesn't explain it.

EVERETT: Sam, what was that other verse, do you remember, that other verse of "Twinkle, Twinkle."

GLORY: I didn't know there was another verse.

EVERETT: Well, maybe it wasn't a real verse, but Sam's mother sure said it all the time.

SAM: No, it was a real verse. I remember reading it. I just don't remember . . .

EVERETT *(Getting it now)*:
    As your bright and tiny spark

SAM *(Remembering)*: Yes, yes. *(Then repeating)*
    Guides the traveler in the dark
    Though I know not what you are
    Twinkle, twinkle little star.
    (He continues to look at the stars)

EVERETT: Right. That's it, exactly.

End of Play